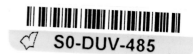

Under the Arctic Sun

Gwich'in, Caribou, and the Arctic National Wildlife Refuge

Text and Photographs by Ken Madsen

Foreword by Norma Kassi

EarthTales Press

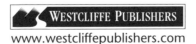

Westcliffe Publishers

www.westcliffepublishers.com

International Standard Book Number: 1-56579-466-4

Editor: Martha Ripley Gray
Assistant Editor: Elizabeth Train
Managing Editor: Jenna Samelson Browning
Production Manager: Craig Keyzer

Published by: Westcliffe Publishers, Inc.
EarthTales Press
P.O. Box 1261, Englewood, CO 80150
www.westcliffepublishers.com

Printed in the USA by Versa Press, Inc.

Library of Congress Cataloging-in-Publication Data:
Madsen, Ken, 1950-
Under the Arctic sun : Gwich'in, caribou, and the Arctic National Wildlife Refuge / text and photographs by Ken Madsen ; with a foreword by Norma Kassi.
p. c.m.
ISBN 1-56579-466-4
1. Caribou—Alaska—Arctic National Wildlife Refuge—Anecdotes. 2. Wildlife conservation—Alaska—Arctic National Wildlife Refuge. 3. Arctic National Wildlife Refuge (Alaska) 4. Madsen, Ken, 1950- I. Title.

QL737.U55 M2723 2002
333.95'9658'09798—dc21

2002072391

For more information about other fine books and calendars from Westcliffe Publishers, please contact your local bookstore, call us at 1-800-523-3692, write for our free color catalog, or visit us on the Web at **www.westcliffepublishers.com**.

Dedication

This book is dedicated to the Gwich'in of Alaska and Canada. Their struggle to protect the calving grounds has been an inspiration. Also to Malkolm and Yudii—and the other children who will live in the world that we leave them. Finally to the "elders," people such as the late Johnny Charlie and my mother, Katy Madsen—without their sacrifices, our world would have fewer pristine places left to protect.

Acknowledgments

The ongoing struggle to protect the Arctic National Wildlife Refuge has been a monumental effort. Thanks to all of the people who have taken the time to demonstrate that they care about the Arctic National Wildlife Refuge. Listing all of the people who have been involved would fill an entire book. Special thanks to Wendy Boothroyd, Glen Davis, Norma Kassi, Matthew Lien, Peter Mather, and Sandra Newman for their special help during our small part of the campaign.

The following individuals have helped directly with the Caribou Commons Project or have inspired me in my work (and play); Irene Alexakos, Elaine Alexie, Walt Audi, Larry Bagnell, Jeff Barrie, Chantal Batt, Luci Beach, Boots Boothroyd, Jill Boothroyd, Jim Boothroyd, Margot Boothroyd, Sa Boothroyd, Jay Burr, Tom Campion, Sara Callaghan Chapell, Albert Charlie, Bruce Charlie, Christine Cleghorn, Larry Duguay, Erik DuMont, Calvin Elanik, Frank Elanik, Inga Eliot, Derek Endress, Linda Enticknap, Peter Enticknap, Emily Ferry, Alex Frid, Marvin Frost, Paul Gatien, Faith Gimmill, Clayton Gordon, Bobbie Jo Greenland, Louise Hardy, Stephen Hazell, Eric Holle, Linda Hoffman, Vicky Hoover, John Hummel, Monte Hummel, Sarah James, Jen Johnson, Sue Johnson, Hal Jordan, Mary Kassi, Caroline Kay, Andy Keller, Lennie Kohm, Adam Kolton, Louis LaRose, Dan Lavery, Tim Leach, Min Lee, Thea Levkovitz, Joe Linklater, Sharon MacCoubrey, Joyce Majiski, Bob Madsen, Carol Madsen, Kirsten Madsen, Mary Madsen, Polly Madsen, Athan Manuel, Paul Mason, Elizabeth May, Colleen McCrory, Devon McDiarmid, Colin McDowell, Jocelyn McDowell, Alix McKee, Bill Meadows, Debbie Miller, Pam Miller, Deb Moore, Richard Mostyn, Gladys Netro, Hannah Netro, Dirk Nickisch, Stanley Njootli, Mary-Ellen Oman, Jim Owens, Eric Patterson, Juri Peepre, Evon Peter, Lorraine Peter, Steve Philp, Danette Readman, Dan Ritzman, Don Ross, Don Russell, Jody Schick, Jen Schmidt, Ken Searcy, Rachel Shephard, Cindy Shogan, Sam Skinner, Jonathon Solomon, Tyler Sutton, Joe Tetlichi, Cora Theile, Elma Theile, Shiela Tooze, Doug Urquhart, Eric Wald, Karen Walker, Tom Walker, Dr. Edgar Wayburn, Darcy Weavers, Kate Williams, George Wuerthner.

And to John Theile, who died too young. He had a special place in his heart for the Indiana Dunes and for the Arctic National Wildlife Refuge.

The following groups continue to be critical in the effort to protect the Arctic Refuge: Gwich'in Steering Committee, Alaska Coalition, Alaska Wilderness League, National Audubon Society, Canadian Parks and Wilderness Society–Yukon Chapter, Caribou Commons Project, Defenders of Wildlife, Natural Resources Defense Council, Eyak Preservation Council, Northern Alaska Environmental Center, National Wildlife Federation, Sierra Club, Sierra Club of Canada, The Wilderness Society, Trustees for Alaska, World Wildlife Fund, World Wildlife Fund–Canada, Yukon Conservation Society.

Grizzly bear, coastal plain, Arctic National Wildlife Refuge.

CONTENTS

Foreword 6
Preface 8
Map 11
The Calving Grounds 12
Political Winds in Washington, D.C. 29
A Visit to Old Crow 31
A Vegetarian in Eugene 39
Prudhoe Bay: "No Impact" on Wildlife 41
A Gwich'in in Oil City 49
Caribou Pass 56
Radio Key Largo 67
Hiking Through a Nursery 71
The Buffalo Commons 84
The Firth River: Just as it Should Be 95
A Caribou Calf in London 103
Under the Arctic Sun 116
Worlds Apart 128
Gordon in L.A. 135
Gordon, Alaska 142
A Clash of Cultures 154
Return to Old Crow 160
Afterword: The Fight to Protect the Arctic Refuge 171
Postscript 187
What You Can Do 189

FOREWORD

I grew up near the Arctic community of Old Crow in the northern Yukon. I spent most of my childhood in Old Crow Flats and at Crow Point on the Porcupine River. The land was my best teacher—it was there that I learned the traditional values that have guided my life. People say that Old Crow is a "remote" village, but for us it is our home—a secure place in an unsettled world. The caribou are the foundation of that security. The first milk that I drank was rich and nutritious, because my mother was able to eat caribou meat and other natural foods from the land. Caribou meat was my first solid food. Our elders do not exaggerate when they say that caribou blood flows in our veins.

For thousands of years, our people have lived in peace with the Porcupine caribou herd and the land. We had food on the table and warm skin clothing. We thought that we were safe. We were the last of the indigenous cultures to be affected by Western industrial culture. Then the oil companies discovered oil under the sacred calving grounds of the caribou.

In 1988, our elders called the Gwich'in Nation together for a historic gathering in Arctic Village. They told us that multinational oil companies wanted to drill for oil on the coastal plain of the Arctic National Wildlife Refuge, which is the birthing grounds for the caribou. They told us that the Gwich'in were no longer safe. They told us that we needed to spread the message about the importance of the caribou to our way of life. I was one of six people chosen to carry our story to the outside world.

The struggle to protect the calving grounds of the Porcupine caribou herd has taken me, and the Gwich'in, down many strange paths. In the past 15 years I have traveled hundreds of thousands of miles and spoken to tens of thousands of people. Protecting the calving grounds of the caribou is critical to the Gwich'in, but I have come to realize that the Arctic National Wildlife Refuge means much more than that. We know that our increasing use of oil threatens the future of all living things on the planet. Climate change and industrial pollution will not just affect my children and grandchildren, it will also affect future generations across the world. Aboriginal people offer the world an alternative to a culture of consumption.

The Arctic Refuge is a symbol of something much bigger than the future of the caribou and the Gwich'in. It is a line in the sand that we dare not cross. We have to have the courage to leave whatever oil might be under the calving grounds where it is. I hope that when people hear the story of my people, the caribou, the migratory birds, and the polar bears, they will be deeply affected. If people care enough, anything is possible. We can protect the Arctic National Wildlife Refuge and start to build on a healthy future for us all.

Ken Madsen has devoted the past five years of his life to spreading the message about the need to protect the Arctic Refuge. I have traveled with Ken to meeting halls in Nebraska and South Dakota. We have stood together on the windswept shores of the Porcupine River, outside the British Petroleum Annual General Meeting in London, and on the stage at the Canadian Embassy in Washington, D.C. We've spoken to audiences in dozens of cities from Old Crow to Minneapolis to Sioux Falls to Key Largo.

Ken's 100-day trip from the calving grounds of the Porcupine caribou herd to Old Crow was a remarkable adventure. That 1,000-mile trek, however, was just the start of his journey. He is one of few who have walked across the Arctic Refuge and spent time with us in our villages. We are grateful that he has joined us as we fight for the protection of the sacred calving grounds.

When you read this book, I hope you will understand what it means to us when a baby caribou struggles to its feet and begins to nurse. What it means when we see migratory birds such as tundra swans and loons flying overhead on their way to the coastal plain. What it means when bowhead and beluga whales swim through clean Arctic waters toward their own calving areas.

I hope you will reserve a place in your own heart for the Arctic Refuge. Please join us in our journey to protect the calving grounds—the sacred place where life begins.

Nanh gwaltsaii k'iighe" nakhwa nan k'anaatl̀h. Juudik gwanchii. Mussi cho. (Through our Creator we are able to take care of our lands. Thank you.)

—Norma Kassi

Norma Kassi is one of six Gwich'in people chosen by members of her Arctic community to represent their interests in the "outside world." Since 1988, she has shared her story of the vital bond between her people and the Porcupine caribou herd with audiences across the globe. Norma, who also serves as co-chair of the Gwich'in Steering Committee, was awarded the 2002 Goldman Prize for her efforts to protect the natural and human environment of the Arctic National Wildlife Refuge.

PREFACE

I don't know how I ended up traveling across America giving public presentations about the Arctic National Wildlife Refuge. When I was younger, public speaking scared me spitless. I broke out in a cold sweat the first time I sat down for a radio interview. My face and chest turned blotchy red, and it suddenly seemed that there was no connection between my tongue and my brain.

I don't know how I ended up writing books. I was a mediocre English student. I enjoyed reading Shakespeare or Robert Frost about as much as my first hangover. I never learned the difference between a participle and a parsnip, although I knew I didn't like either.

My chief asset in my conservation work is stubbornness. Why else would I stick with the ridiculous projects that I come up with? It all started with the Tatshenshini Wilderness Quest. A few friends and I paddled all of the rivers that would have been threatened by a giant copper mine slated for the heart of an intact wilderness near Glacier Bay National Park. The culmination of the Quest was Turnback Canyon, a wild stretch of rapids on the Alsek River that had only been kayaked a handful of times before. After we survived that, I hit the road with a slideshow. My slides were marginal and the music tinny. I was too naive to know any better and too pigheaded to pack up and go home.

When I was young I was so stubborn that I turned pouting into an art form. When I was three years old, my family took me on a camping trip to a remote part of Kings Canyon National Park in California's Sierra Nevada Mountains. When I found out that I was expected to eat something other than Cheerios with applesauce, I stuck my lower lip out and went on a hunger strike. My mother told me that she wasn't a short-order cook, and if I didn't like camp food I could starve. After several days, she caved in. She couldn't stand seeing my "little stomach shrinking" and listening to me cry myself to sleep. She traveled out to the nearest store that sold Cheerios, and I learned a valuable lesson. Don't give up, no matter what the odds.

Somewhere in my formative years I learned to value wildlife. Maybe it started with Chippy, an orphaned brewer's blackbird that walked out from behind a tree one day and adopted my brother Bob. My mother concocted a revolting recipe of dog food, scrambled eggs, and crushed calcium pills that Chippy gobbled with delight. I was ecstatic when she let me feed him. When I waved a tweezerful of food above his head he'd flutter his wings and open his beak wide. His squawks became strangled croaks as the dog food funneled down his throat. When Chippy learned to fly, we let him go.

Raising Chippy made me an important kid on the block, but that status evaporated when he fluttered away to join a wild flock. I waited impatiently for another bird to show up. Finally, I couldn't wait any longer. I knew where there was a sparrow's nest near my third-grade classroom. My friend Teddy and I rode our bikes to the school. The mother sparrow fluttered away as I climbed the tree. There were four chicks in the nest, each with bulging blue eyes and featherless pink skin. I plucked one out and handed it down to Teddy who was waiting with a shoe box.

When my mother asked how I got the bird, I lied and told her that it had fallen out of its nest. Unfortunately for my credibility, the bird was too young and feeble to wriggle to the edge of a nest and fall out. My mother stared at me reproachfully and explained why baby birds are better off with their own parents. I rode back to school to put it back in the nest. For weeks my brother mercilessly reminded me that mother birds will abandon their nest if it reeks of human scent. I felt awful, imagining the baby bird and its three nest-mates slowly starving to death. Like most kids, however, I had a short memory. Soon I was back playing baseball, catching lizards, and tormenting my sister, all with a clear conscience.

I didn't think about Chippy and the sparrows again until Glen Davis and I flew to the coastal plain of the Arctic National Wildlife Refuge at the start of the Caribou Commons Project. Glen is a friend from Toronto who is also a generous financial supporter of my conservation projects. I first heard the term "Caribou Commons" spoken by a Gwich'in elder, Sarah James. She was referring to the importance of caring for the entire range of

Arctic fox pups, coastal plain, Arctic National Wildlife Refuge

the Porcupine caribou herd—although the herd's calving grounds on the coastal plain were her people's top priority.

The Caribou Commons Project was my most ambitious idea yet. I would travel a thousand miles by foot, kayak, and canoe, photographing everything in sight and visiting the aboriginal people who lived along the way. At various points in the journey, I'd meet up with a group of musicians who would record the sounds of the land and compose music. After returning home, we'd create a concert event and a multimedia slideshow. Then we'd set off across the continent with our Gwich'in friends to convince people that the Arctic National Wildlife Refuge should be protected.

Our Arctic travels were not yet 24 hours old when Glen and I discovered an abandoned caribou calf near our campsite on the Jago River. It was a shock. Living was supposed to be simple out in the wilderness. I wasn't prepared to deal with life's contradictions.

Like many people, I am well schooled in not probing below the surface of the way I live my life. When I throw a log in the wood stove, I don't see the greenhouse gases thickening in the atmosphere. When I eat a tomato from Mexico, I don't see a mist of DDT spraying from a nozzle and wonder why fewer migratory birds return north each spring. When I fill up my aging car with gas, I don't see the *Exxon Valdez* or oil derricks on the Arctic tundra.

When the caribou calf in the Arctic Refuge stared at me with its unblinking brown eyes, however, I couldn't dodge my responsibility. I had come to the coastal plain to help in the campaign to prevent oil development in the critical habitat where the caribou return each year to give birth. This calf, however, was in danger precisely because I'd come. The memory is still painful, like a deeply buried sliver that grates against nerve endings whenever pressure is applied.

Despite the pain, I hope I don't forget the calf as easily as I forgot Chippy and the baby sparrow when I was a kid.

—Ken Madsen

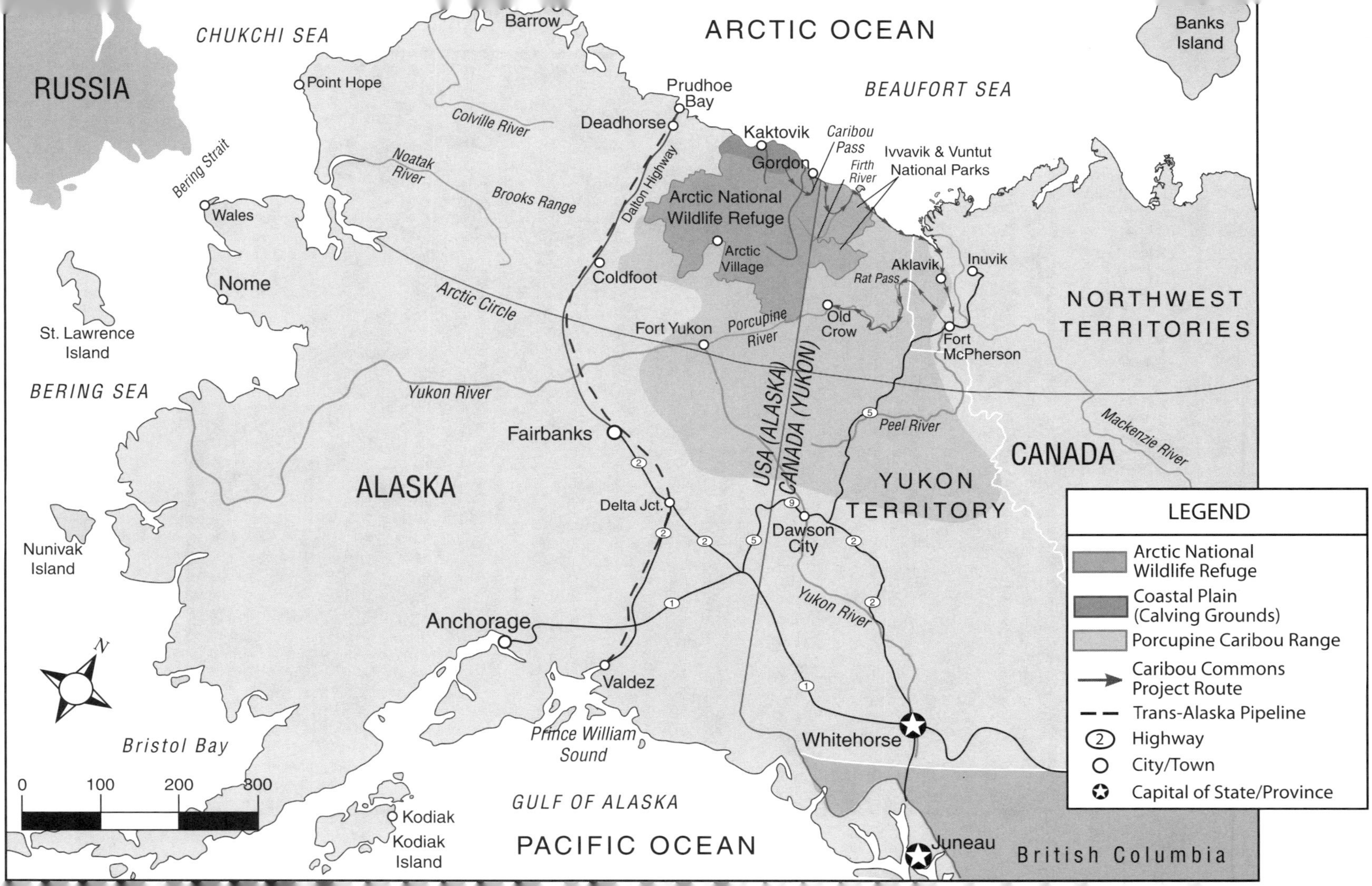
ARCTIC OCEAN
CHUKCHI SEA
BEAUFORT SEA
RUSSIA
Banks Island
Barrow
Point Hope
Prudhoe Bay
Deadhorse
Kaktovik
Gordon
Caribou Pass
Firth River
Ivvavik & Vuntut National Parks
Colville River
Noatak River
Brooks Range
Dalton Highway
Bering Strait
Wales
Arctic National Wildlife Refuge
Arctic Village
Coldfoot
Nome
Arctic Circle
Aklavik
Inuvik
Rat Pass
Old Crow
Fort Yukon
Porcupine River
Fort McPherson
NORTHWEST TERRITORIES
St. Lawrence Island
BERING SEA
Yukon River
USA (ALASKA)
CANADA (YUKON)
Peel River
Mackenzie River
CANADA
Fairbanks
ALASKA
YUKON TERRITORY
Delta Jct.
Dawson City
Nunivak Island
Anchorage
Yukon River
Valdez
Whitehorse
Prince William Sound
Bristol Bay
GULF OF ALASKA
Kodiak
Kodiak Island
PACIFIC OCEAN
Juneau
British Columbia
0
100
200
300
N
LEGEND
Arctic National Wildlife Refuge
Coastal Plain (Calving Grounds)
Porcupine Caribou Range
Caribou Commons Project Route
Trans-Alaska Pipeline
Highway
City/Town
Capital of State/Province

THE CALVING GROUNDS

"We aren't the only ones heading north," says Don Ross, his voice scratching through the headphones like a fingernail across a blackboard.

Don is wearing a patched, grease-splotched blue jumpsuit and a black baseball cap that says SPAM. Except for the hat, he looks as if he just flew his bush plane out of the pages of a World War I Nevil Shute novel. He's pointing out the window at a dozen red-throated loons with outstretched necks and wings flapping like mad. Evolution designed loons for water. In the air they look like flying submarines. If their wings stopped churning they'd plummet like feathered stones. Still, they're better off than Don, Glen Davis, and I in our single-engine, single-prop, flying coffin. How often do you hear about loon crashes?

"How long have you been a bush pilot?" I ask casually.

"Since I flew spotter planes in Vietnam," says Don.

I relax a little. Surely Arctic flying can't be as dangerous as dodging Viet Cong antiaircraft fire. And Don has been flying up here for decades. He used to work for the U.S. Fish & Wildlife Service as assistant manager of the Arctic National Wildlife Refuge. He couldn't handle the bureaucracy, though, so he turned back to flying.

Our destination is a gravel bar beside the Jago River about 25 miles south of the Arctic coast. It's early in the northern spring, only May 30, and this is Don's first trip of the year to the coastal plain. He isn't sure if the tundra will be clear of snow, but he's hoping that the gravel bar he uses as an airstrip will be dry enough to land on. We're hopeful that the Porcupine caribou herd will be on hand to greet us, even though the migration schedule of the caribou is never a certainty.

We gain altitude and latitude, and the forest thins out at the feet of giant, tumbled talus slopes. Before long we leave the last tree behind. We fly into a snow squall, and all I can see is the belly of the cloud. I hope Don knows where he's going. The cloud spits us out into a monochrome world of rock and glaciers. We slip through a pass at the Continental Divide and fly down a sheer-walled valley. There is a river below us and rock and ice beside each wing. After a while the vertical world of the Brooks Range falls behind, and the flatlands where the caribou calve open out in front of us.

"You're in luck," says Don. "The coastal plain is clear of snow."

Tawny grasslands flow out from the foothills of the Brooks Range, like melted butter, like a flashback to the Great Plains before Lewis and Clark arrived with blazing guns, trailing a future of barbed wire and industrial agriculture. There are no interstate highways here, no power lines, no hog farms or cattle. No buffalo, but there are caribou.

"There's the strip," says Don, "but there's a group of caribou on it. I better run them off."

He drops the nose and swoops low over the caribou, who are grazing peacefully beside the Jago. He guns the Cessna as if he's flashing back to Vietnam and bursts of flak are exploding around us. He banks so steeply that the wing points straight down toward the caribou. My face mashes against the window. The caribou stampede in panic. One bowls over her calf and bounds away. The plane straightens, drops low, and buzzes like an angry hornet over the gravel bar. The last caribou races onto the tundra. We bank once more, skim over the willows, and lurch to a stop on the gravel.

Don climbs out of the plane and holds the door open. I unfold myself from the cramped back seat and step outside, gulping deep breaths of Arctic air. A white-crowned sparrow ruffles its feathers on a willow branch and belts out its breeding song. Don circles to the other side and lets Glen out. Glen is a well-known "funder" from Toronto who gives generous financial support to many conservation projects. He is an unusual man, at least as far as I can tell in my limited experience with the rich and infamous. Glen doesn't simply open his checkbook and retire gracefully to the plush comfort of his boardroom. He experiences the many joys of the wilderness at close range, getting wet, dirty, sunburned, and thoroughly chewed by mosquitoes in the process.

Don tosses our gear down to us, and soon there is a small mountain on the gravel bar. Glen sees no point in traveling light. His duffel bags bulge with Gore-Tex rain suits, several tents, minus-forty-degree sleeping bags, down jackets, long underwear, boots, gloves, tuques, bowls, mugs, sun hats, string, gum, lip-glop, sunscreen, Band-Aids, and enough books to stock a mobile lending library. He could set up an Arctic Refuge convenience store. Unfortunately, since I'm bringing two cameras, a heavy tripod, six lenses, and 100 rolls of film, I'm not in a position to complain about excess baggage.

"What is this thing?" asks Don, nudging a limp pile of camouflage fabric with his foot.

"It's a hunter who starved on the gravel bar waiting for you to pick him up," says Glen.

"It's a portable blind," I say, "for photographing caribou without disturbing them."

"It worked great up in Prudhoe Bay," says Glen. "He scared everything for miles around."

"Want some hot chocolate before you take off?" I rummage through the mountain. "I think there's a stove here somewhere."

"Thanks, but I guess I should head back home before the clouds sock in." He climbs back in the cockpit, revs up the engine, and blasts off toward Fort Yukon.

The roar of the Cessna becomes a waspish drone, then a mosquito buzz. It is lost behind the murmur of the river and the wind rustling the willow branches. We're alone, the only people in 30,000 square miles of wilderness. The nearest human is in Kaktovik, an Inupiat (Eskimo) village on Barter Island, a 35-mile hike north (including 10 miles of rotting sea ice). We're smack in the middle of nowhere, according to the woman who sold me cinnamon buns at a bakery in Fairbanks. I disagreed. I told her that Washington, D.C., or Los Angeles is the middle of nowhere. I told her that the Arctic Refuge is the middle of somewhere. She wasn't convinced.

It was 80 degrees and the air was hazy with forest-fire smoke when we left Fairbanks at noon. Up here the air has the bite of February. Cirrus clouds float above us like wisps of eiderdown. Stratocumulus clouds squat over the Brooks Range, towering masses with dark skirts that brush the foothills with showers. A wedge of bright mist hovers over the sea ice beyond the northern horizon.

Glen and I haul our gear toward a flat camping area near the river. As I drop my first load I'm distracted by movement on the tundra: two dozen female caribou with a couple of babies. Two dozen *cows* and *calves*. I don't know which biologist thought that it was an honor to name wild caribou (and moose and elk) after dull-witted cattle. These wild creatures have a glint in their eyes and a spring in their stride that haven't been seen in "white-faced prairie maggots" since before they were domesticated and bred to be wider than they are tall.

These caribou have been drifting toward the calving grounds since April. Biologists call this the "spring migration," although their journey isn't triggered by blooming cherry blossoms. Blizzards lash the northern Yukon and Alaska throughout April and May, and temperatures can drop to minus 40. Despite the weather, something—perhaps the lengthening of daylight hours or changes in the snow cover—whispers to the caribou that it is time. The pregnant females are the first to move. They struggle through deep, crusty snow. They swim rivers thick with drifting ice. They cross mountain passes and run from wolf packs and hunker down while storms turn them into lumpy snowdrifts.

Barren-ground caribou migrate farther than any other land mammal. Each year the caribou in the Porcupine herd wander nearly 3,000 miles from the coastal plain to the far reaches of their winter range and back again. The females near our camp are coasting now. They've reached their goal, the place of their own birth. A few lie down to rest, but soon they are back on their feet, too restless to linger in one spot.

I walk through the willows to watch the caribou cross the river. The water is swollen with snowmelt but clear, with just a hint of glacial green. While I'm waiting, I kneel down, lower my lips to the water, and drink. The water is numbingly cold, but I can deal with that as long as there is no worry about hepatitis or Giardia or PCBs. A land with drinkable water is a land worth fighting for. I hear the clatter of hooves on gravel. The lead caribou steps into the river. She doesn't realize that most of the world's fresh water is undrinkable industrial soup. She doesn't realize that the soup is boiling over and the toxic froth is creeping northward. I'm not going to be the one who tells her.

She walks into the water until she is chest deep and the swift current sweeps her off her hooves. She is naturally buoyant. Every one of her hairs is hollow and acts as a slender life jacket. She swims strongly, propelled by her hoofed "toes" that splay out like paddles. The remainder of the caribou splash into the river behind her. One of the calves is tiny, only hours old, and facing its first swim. It plunges in after its mother without hesitation, but the current washes it downstream like a big brown cork. Its mother races along the far bank, grunting and bobbing her head up and down. Finally the calf touches bottom and clambers onto the tundra with a flurry of spray. I take a last drink of water (that has a faint aftertaste of caribou) and walk back to camp.

"You ready for dinner yet? I'm starving." I upend a duffel bag and pour a jumble of zip-lock food bags on the gravel bar.

"Whatever," says Glen. "I'll set up the tent. Hey, guess what time it is in the land of the midnight sun?"

"Don't tell me! I don't want to know. One of the great things about being in the wilderness is not having to watch the clock."

"It's one in the morning."

"Thanks," I say sarcastically. "Now I know why I'm hungry."

"I knew that deep down you wanted to know the time."

As the nearest tree is hundreds of miles to the south, a cooking fire is not an option. I pull the stove from its bag, spit on the metal plug at the end of the fuel line, and wriggle it into the pump assembly on the fuel bottle. The saliva, which acts as a lubricant, is the only thing natural about this operation. I pump the stove, open the valve and watch as white gas dribbles into a metal ring. I flick a lighter and flames engulf the stove. After a minute of fiery priming, the stove splutters and hisses with wheezy fossil-fuel respirations. The noise and smell of technology makes the wilderness feeling retreat, like darkness disappears when you flick on a flashlight. I can no longer hear the white-crowned sparrow singing in the willows or the shrill chatter of the ground squirrel down by the river.

Heat waves distort the air above the pot, like mirage lines rising from sun-baked pavement. It's my latest contribution to climate change. I'm out here in the middle of somewhere, in the heart of the calving grounds of the Porcupine caribou herd, because I'm convinced that Big Oil should keep its toxic footprints out of the Arctic Refuge. Meanwhile I'm cooking over a gas stove.

I wish I could anesthetize my brain and forget life's contradictions. Others manage to. Even at some wilderness conferences nowadays, they pin plastic name tags on their shirts, drink coffee from Styrofoam cups, and eat pasta salad on throwaway plates with plastic forks. I'm a rebel who brings my own mug, but then again, I don't consider myself a *real* environmentalist.

Environmentalists work more than I do. They understand the deep inner life of GIS mapping, endangered species legislation, and conservation biology. They organize meetings in Toronto, Seattle, and Rio de Janeiro. They amass thousands of air miles points so they can go to more meetings. They write proposals when they should be sleeping. They write proposals when they should be canoeing. They spend so much time under artificial lights that they look like mushrooms. Maybe I'll be one when I grow up, but not right now.

Right now I'm too busy rationalizing. Too busy compromising. I turn the thermostat so low in the winter that I have to wear several sweaters and a wool hat to keep the blood circulating—but oil heats the house. I bicycle to the Yukon River, dragging my kayak behind on a makeshift trailer—but it's a plastic kayak. I write books about protecting wilderness—while they clear-cut the boreal forest for pulp and paper. Some days I wish I could forget the rest of the world and concentrate on the only person I know I can influence. Me. I see myself in a little cabin somewhere. Hauling my own water, squatting in an outhouse, reading by candlelight.

But if we all tramp down that idyllic little trail to the cabin in the woods, who will be left to speak for the caribou and spotted owls and newts? It sure won't be the CEOs of Big Oil. Their heads are filled with hydraulic pumps and titanium wheels. They believe that international trade and industrial wealthiness is next to godliness.

Fortunately, I know that my flights of fancy are "collateral damage" from the collision between a fast-moving civilized object (me) and a wilderness that moves at its own pace. Speed distorts my perceptions, and my brain is still whirling at airplane speed. My thoughts will become earthbound after I use my legs for a few days. I'll slow down. I'll concentrate on things that matter: whether I'm hungry, whether the first poppies have blossomed yet, whether the movement out on the tundra is a caribou. Or a grizzly.

There's a sudden commotion near the river, and my nerves jangle in full-twitch alert. Nothing to worry about. Just a couple of male ptarmigan. Just ptarmigan? These are not *just* ptarmigan. These are birds who live a life of no compromise. Birds who disdain migration and are superbly adapted to year-round Arctic life. In the winter they turn white and grow feathers on their toes. They eat freeze-dried willow buds and fly into snowbanks to hide from gyrfalcons. Now that spring is here, they are full of hormones. They burst out of the willows, wings beating furiously. They fly high above our tent, thrust out their chests, and glide across the river, each screaming that he has the fittest genes to pass to the next generation.

"Yes, dear," says Glen. "I'm listening, Alice."

"What *are* you talking about?"

"The ptarmigan sound like they're saying, *mo-tel, mo-tel, mo-tel.* They sound just like Alice. Whenever I want to camp she says, *No-way! Mo-tel! Mo-tel!*"

I pour a can of beer into a pot and add chopped garlic, dried mustard, and half a pound of cheese. I set the pot on the stove. I mix cornstarch with a couple of tablespoons of the Jago River, pour it in, and stir as the concoction bubbles.

"Is this our traditional first meal of fondue?" asks Glen.

"Yep, but we can't eat until after I take a picture of that grizzly."

"Grizzly? Are you serious?" He looks around. "Where is it?"

"It's across the river, just upstream."

I grab my camera and a can of "bear spray." Bear spray, an infusion of cayenne pepper that theoretically deters an attacking bear, is sold to discerning campers who either hate guns or are incompetent in their use. I fall into both categories. The instructions on the can are simple. It isn't like insect repellent; don't spray your kids. Remove the plastic safety clip and remain calm. Pray that the grizzly approaches from downwind. Wait until the bear is ten feet away. Blast pepper spray into its eyes.

I hope I'll never have to use it.

The grizzly's golden fur ripples over its muscular shoulders. Its legs are moose-brown. It meanders along the riverbank and rakes a ground squirrel's hole with long, powerful claws. It grabs a dead willow branch, rolls on its back, and tosses the branch into the air. The bear is upwind of us. It doesn't know that we've moved in and that property values in the neighborhood have plummeted.

"I'm going to let it know we're here," I whisper to Glen. "It's getting a little close for comfort."

"Do you have to? I came here to watch wildlife, not scare it away."

"Yo bear, look over here!" I shout, ignoring Glen.

The grizzly peers toward us nearsightedly and swings its great head sideways in search of our scent. I wave my arms, and instantly the bear spins and gallops away. The bear could handle Glen and me with two paws tied behind its back, yet it doesn't stop running until it is out of sight over the ridge. Why is it afraid of us? It must be *unnatural selection*. For thousands of years, the bears that haven't run away have been speared, skewered with arrows, or blown away by high-caliber bullets. This grizzly, even though it may never have encountered a human before, instinctively knows that we are poison.

I instinctively know the smell of burnt fondue. I run back and shut off the stove. I spoon lumpy fondue into bowls, trying not to rake up the blackened bottom layer. I cube a loaf of bread and chop broccoli. It tastes fine. At least I think so.

"This reminds me of the very first time Alice cooked me supper," says Glen, soaking up the last of the fondue with a chunk of bread. "It was delicious, simply delicious. There was a spot between the burnt and the raw parts that was simply delicious."

"Thanks for the compliment. I'm going to bed."

Sunlight slants into the tent door in the morning. Or is it afternoon? It's hard to tell, when the sun corkscrews around the horizon without setting for three months. Clouds still hover over the Brooks Range, and there is a fluffy line of fog to the north, but above us the sky is clear. I pull on a pair of pants over the long underwear I slept in, slip on sandals, and wander across the gravel bar to see what's happening in the neighborhood. Steam rises in the chill air when I pee.

The light is perfect for photography, but nothing will be in focus until after my morning fix of caffeine. I light the stove, put on a pot of coffee, and unwrap two cinnamon buns. I turn off the stove when the coffee starts boiling happily.

Wilderness coffee-brewing technology hasn't improved much since cowboys were at home on the range. It's still called cowboy coffee, although it's also known as camp coffee, or mud. I like dark roast, ground fine but not espresso fine. If it is ground too coarsely, chunks of coffee rise to the surface and stick in your teeth. The recommended allowance is one twenty-fifth of a pound per person per day, but I always bring one twentieth to make sure. Better too much than too little. Better too strong than too weak. I add the coffee to cold water and bring it to a rollicking boil. The grounds will eventually sink on their own, but I speed up the process with centrifugal force. I grab the pot and whirl it over my head a dozen times. This only works with a pot that has a sturdy, over-the-top handle and a tightly fitting lid. I bring cream for as long as it will last. Then I resort to dry milk powder. I use non-instant and mix it with a little water before adding it to my coffee. Otherwise, gritty white islands that taste like aspirin drift lazily across the surface of my mug.

"Breakfast is ready," I yell to Glen, who is watching a herd of caribou across the river. He puts down his binoculars and picks up a cinnamon bun.

"This thing tastes like iced home insulation," says Glen. "Well, as I always say to Alice, I hate to eat and run—but I think I'm going to throw up."

I gulp my coffee and drop my mug onto the gravel bar. I pack my camera and tripod in a day-pack and pick up the blind. My wife, Wendy, lovingly sewed it for me, using seven yards of camouflage nylon and four hula-hoops. It is light and portable and has a vertical slit to poke a telephoto lens through.

"What *are* you doing?" says Glen. "You aren't going out with the blind again, are you?"

"Just watch," I answer. "I'm going to get a poster shot of those caribou."

I pull the blind over my head like a ball gown and walk out on the tundra, which is covered by mushroom-shaped clumps of soil and vegetation called tussocks. Each unstable lump is topped with tufts of cottongrass and surrounded by soggy, spongy, moatlike crevices. There are two ways to deal with tussocks, which are the curse of hikers (although caribou prance through them as though they're born with steel-belted ligaments and tendons). You can try stepping on the top, but tussocks usually pitch you sideways in an ankle-wrenching lurch.

Stepping between the tussocks is more stable and is the preferred method, particularly if you enjoy continuous swamp-walking.

After a few minutes of tripping and staggering I hoist the blind's skirts above my knees. That works better, although I can only see a three-foot diameter around my boots. I trudge blindly across the coastal plain. When I hope I'm in position, I slide my lens through the slit and peer through the viewfinder. No caribou. The tundra is empty. I pull the blind over my head, fling it onto the ground, and sit on a tussock. Instantly, the bog wicks up through the seat of my pants.

Now that I'm at ground level I inspect a tussock. I can see the green leaves of Arctic dryad, willows, sedges, and cottongrass sprouting from a bed of moss and lichen. I can't see the complex mixture of live and dead tissues, insects, rotting berries, and microorganisms that make each tussock its own community. Sitting on the surface of the tundra is like floating in a kayak, surrounded by millions of tussock-whitecaps in a storm-tossed sea.

Arctic plants are studies in adaptation. Each must survive frigid winter temperatures and blizzards that blast scalpel-sharp ice crystals across the tundra. Each must take advantage of every second of the short growing season. Many plants have "wintergreen" leaves that develop late in the summer, survive the winter, and begin photosynthesis as soon as it warms up. Almost all plants grow buds that also overwinter and flower as soon as the sun warms the soil. The Arctic Refuge was under snow just a few days ago, but already there is a vibrant green blush under last year's golden grasses. This nutritious new growth is one of the reasons that the coastal plain is a critical habitat for female caribou at this time of year.

I pull out binoculars and scan the tundra for movement. Glen is watching me through his own binoculars. The only caribou in sight are browsing on a hillside across the Jago. I can see the outlines of their ribs under their shaggy brown coats. This time of year, the caribou are at the low point of their fat reserves. Most of the winter, they've been surviving on "caribou moss," a pale lichen that looks as tasty and nutritious as the shag rug in my living room. When they reach the coastal plain, they are ready for something fresh, something green, just like I'm ready for a huge salad after a month of dried camp food. When they reach the coastal plain, the pregnant females eat, and eat, and eat—about ten pounds of sedges, willows, and moss each day, the equivalent of what you could stuff into a couple of garbage bags.

The caribou need all the calories they can get. During the next ten days, 50,000 calves will slither onto the tundra, each a compact feeding machine. The calves may think that nursing is a free lunch, but the cows know better. Producing thick, rich caribou milk (with two to three times the fat content of cow's milk) is an energy drain. And so the cows keep eating. I pick up the blind and head back for another cup of coffee.

"The caribou took off as soon as you popped out of the willows," laughs Glen. "That blind is great for scaring away wildlife. Why don't you wear it around camp to keep the grizzlies away?"

"Laugh it up."

"You should have stayed in camp. I counted 127 caribou across the river a few minutes ago. Hey, they're running away! Did you wave the blind at them?"

"Give me a break. Look on the crest of the hill. Is that another bear?"

"It is," says Glen, focusing his binoculars. "It's a beautiful, dark grizzly, heading right toward the caribou."

A cow with a single antler lifts her forelegs in the air and leaps away, a bound that releases a warning scent from her hooves. The mothers with calves slip away over the hill, but not all of the caribou run away. The cow with the single antler turns and runs toward the bear. Other caribou dash back and forth like Christmas shoppers at a K-Mart. The distracted grizzly charges, but the caribou trot away gracefully. The bear soon realizes the futility of pursuit and stops to claw at the ground, as if she prefers roots to fresh caribou meat any day. Meanwhile, the vulnerable calves are long gone.

"Those calves followed their mothers right away," says Glen. "They're a lot more obedient than human children."

"If there is a predator around they won't get the chance to be told twice."

"Right," says Glen. "They probably tell them to listen up or they'll be dead. D-E-A-D-dead! I wonder if that would work with kids at a day care?"

The grizzlies that patrol the calving grounds do occasionally catch and kill baby caribou. Unless a bear surprises a calf at close range, though, even one a few days old can outrun a bear. It's a different story with wolves that hunt in packs and can run down even healthy adult caribou.

Like caribou, however, wolves must rear their young in the early Arctic summer. In one of nature's beautiful quirks, the coastal plain, which is the perfect place for caribou to raise their calves, is not a suitable denning habitat for wolves. If a wolf tried to dig a den it would hit permafrost—solid ice—just a few inches below the surface. Wolves are forced to den on south-facing slopes in the mountains and are almost entirely absent from the coastal plain when caribou calves are most vulnerable.

It is no accident that the caribou have returned here to give birth for tens of thousands of years. In a hostile world, the coastal plain is the safest place they will ever find.

"What about a hike?" asks Glen.

"Sure, let's pack a lunch and head upriver—" I'm interrupted by a honking *uhuuuh*.

"What's that? Sounds like a cross between a mallard and a warthog."

"It must be a duck or a goose in one of the wetlands. I'll check it out."

I snap my camera onto my tripod but leave the blind behind. I follow the croaking sounds through the willows and onto the tawny grasslands. I almost step on a caribou calf. Its coat is golden brown, like butter blended with honey, like sunlight on the tundra. It has long slender legs and huge dark eyes and is longer, but not much heavier, than the tortoise-shell cat that visits my backyard in Whitehorse. The withered stump of an umbilical cord dangles from its belly. The calf croaks, gathers its legs under its body, and leaps upright.

I look around, but there are no adult caribou nearby. Why is this calf on its own? A newborn caribou will flop down and blend into the tundra if it is too young to flee from danger. Like deer fawns, they have little odor and may escape detection by lying motionless. The calf wobbles toward me. I instinctively hold out my hand, as if it is an approaching Labrador retriever. The calf springs away in alarm when it gets a muzzleful of pungent human scent. I snap a few pictures, then turn and walk as fast as I can back to camp. The calf totters after me for a couple of steps, then sinks onto its belly.

"What was it?" asks Glen.

"An abandoned calf."

"I bet it was with the group of caribou that took off when we landed yesterday," says Glen. "Its mother was probably too frightened by the plane to come back."

"No way," I say out loud, but a sudden acid feeling in my stomach tells me that he is right. "Let's clear out of here. Maybe she'll come back if there are no people around."

I throw pita bread, hummus, dried fruit, and chocolate into a pack along with a rain jacket and my camera gear. Then we hike south on the tussock-free gravel bars beside the greenish-colored Jago River. The water was recently locked inside snow and ice crystals. It tumbles and froths downstream as if it's uncomfortable in its new liquid state and anxious to reach the frozen ocean. I turn several times to scan our camping area with binoculars, but the tundra is deserted. No caribou cow searches for lost offspring. A pair of Pacific loons looking for open water squawk overhead, flying across the bleached Arctic sky. A long line of caribou fords the river upstream.

After a couple of hours of hiking, we wander into a gallery of weathered boulders. They look like "glacial erratics," huge stones carried along by a glacier and abandoned when the ice retreated. If that's what they are, they were deposited more than 100,000 years ago, before the beginning of the latest ice age. At that time, much of the Earth's water abandoned its temperate ocean existence and accumulated in several-mile-thick sheets of ice that straddled the globe. Sea level dropped by more than 100 yards, and the shallow Bering Strait and northern coastal shelf was left dry by the retreating oceans. This land "bridge" became a vast grassland known as Beringia, which extended through what is now northern Alaska and Yukon.

Beringia was a refuge from the crushing weight of ice that smothered North America. It was plenty cold enough for glaciers, but there wasn't enough snow. Even now, much of the North is an "Arctic desert," receiving only a few inches of precipitation each year. Back in Beringian days, fantastic animals roamed the coastal plain: woolly mammoths, ground sloths, steppe bison, camels, giant beavers, scimitar cats, musk oxen, caribou, and the continent's first people.

The ice age is still alive and well in the Arctic. A couple of feet below me, the ground is frozen solid. The permafrost is more than 1,000 feet deep in places. From above, the coastal plain looks as if some insane giant has slashed intricate geometric patterns with a sword, but there is method in the madness of these "tundra polygons." The huge polygons are formed by the intense Arctic freeze-thaw cycle. The thin surface layer that thaws each summer contracts and cracks as it refreezes the following winter. Water seeps in and freezes. Ice wedges form and thicken, pushing up the soil into the bizarre linear patterns strewn across the Arctic.

Ten thousand years ago, at the end of the Holocene ice age, many Beringian animals became extinct. People and caribou were among the species that survived. When the ice retreated, plants and animals from Beringia slowly moved south, recolonizing the land that had been scoured by 100,000 years of ice. The Arctic, like warmer regions to the south of the ice sheets, served as a gene pool for the renewal of life.

We may need the Arctic to play that role again. This time it isn't glaciers that are smothering life, it is the *industrial beast.* The beast has the virility and soul of an HIV virus. The beast is a part of us all and is destroying the Earth's immune systems by trading the health of the environment for convenience and comfort. The beast's pulse throbs even here on the coastal plain. Maybe I'm feeling my own heartbeat.

It is warm among the boulders, and several hundred caribou are feeding and resting across the river. A couple of fat bumblebees drone around the pussy willows. I lean onto a smooth granite backrest and reach for my binoculars. A calf, still slick and wet from its birth sac, staggers to its feet. It lists to the side and collapses in a heap of gangly legs. It gathers its strength and tries again, this time wobbling determinedly toward its mother before crashing into her flanks. She licks it as it burrows under her belly in search of warm milk.

Another cow lies down, gets back up, and spins restlessly. She kicks out her hind leg and flops back down. It looks as if she might be having contractions, but what do I know? Maybe she's kicking at a bumblebee. If she is about to give birth, her labor will be quick and easy: no screaming, no sweating labor coaches, no morphine, no cesarean sections.

A fogbank slithers up from the coast. The orange rim of the sun sinks into the gloom, and the golden tundra turns gray. The caribou become fuzzy blobs that merge with the mist. Our solarium is now a refrigerator. I put on a jacket and a tuque. We pack up the remains of our lunch and walk downstream along the riverbank. Eventually our tents loom up in the fog. There is no sign of the abandoned calf.

The mist thickens until it feels like rain that can't be bothered to fall to the ground. Glen flicks water from his rain hood and mutters about how great it is to be in the Arctic desert. I boil a pot of water for noodles and chop the last of our fresh vegetables. When the pasta is almost done, I chuck in the broccoli and cauliflower. I drain the noodles and stir in a couple of spoonfuls of pesto. Glen inspects his bowl suspiciously. He's a meat-and-potatoes guy except when I'm in control of the stove.

"You called that stuff we had for lunch *humongous*, right? What is this?"

"That was hummus. It's a paste made from garbanzo beans, tahini, lemon juice, and garlic. This is pesto. This is totally gourmet. You'd pay big bucks for this at an Italian restaurant."

"Looks like what you find at the bottom of a parrot's cage."

"Doesn't Alice serve you this at home?"

"Last time Alice tried to cook something gourmet, I said, 'I know it's rude to ask for your recipe, but I'm afraid that I might need to tell my doctor.'"

Glen informs me that it is 28 degrees at 11:45. Always pleased to know the time and the latest weather report, I squirm into our tent, which is now rimed with ice. Glen crawls in behind me and falls asleep immediately. He breathes rhythmically. He must have a clear conscience. I toss and turn. I can't get the abandoned calf out of my head. I flip to one side, hoping its mother came back and led it to safety. Over to my stomach, seeing a white-hot image of the calf starving to death and being dragged away by a grizzly. Onto my back, sure that if we hadn't flown into the calving grounds the calf would be alive.

After eight months of writing proposals, sending endless e-mails, and groveling before funding agencies, I'm finally in the Arctic Refuge. I should be ecstatic. Instead, I'm depressed. After staring into the dark eyes of that calf for five minutes, the entire Caribou Commons Project seems sterile.

The fog is gone when I wake up in the morning, except in my head. I'm groggy from lack of sleep, but my depression has changed to good, healthy anger. Anger at the multinational oil companies who want to invade the calving grounds. If a couple of hikers who are trying to tread carefully disturb the caribou, how would they react to industrial beasts like British Petroleum or Exxon? I know how the caribou would react, and so do the oil barons—they can read biological studies as easily as I can.

They know that caribou during calving and post-calving periods do *not* become acclimatized to the sights, smells, and sounds of industrial oil development. They know that oil development in the Arctic Refuge would force the caribou to have their calves elsewhere. They know that the calf survival rate would drop. They know that even a five percent drop in calf survival would have a profound impact on the herd. They know that caribou are not the only animals that would be killed and displaced. Why should they care, when ecological health is not reflected in the bottom line?

My only hope is that Big Oil is cocksure about its own might. Why should a fossil-fuel Goliath worry about a puny David flinging pebbles? Some of the pebbles I'm collecting are photographs, so I'd better get at it. The blind was useless, so I pull a second secret weapon from my clothes bag. While Glen had been buying up a Fairbanks outdoors store, I had walked down the street to an Army surplus store. Behind the assault knives, night-vision binoculars, and canteens I found a camouflage outfit that once belonged to Private First Class Doucet of the U.S. Marines.

"What have we here?" asks Glen as I button up the shirt. "Wishing you were in boot camp instead of the Arctic?"

"There is no way to sneak up on the caribou, but they don't seem bothered if you stay still. I'm going to hang out somewhere and wait for them to come to me."

I load my pack with camera gear, food, and warm clothes and hike eastward. After an hour I reach a creek that curves lazily beside a series of alpine ridges. My boots aren't completely saturated from the tussock swamps, so I take them off, sling them over my neck and ford the stream with bare feet. I sit down and wriggle my toes in the hazy sunshine. Eventually the permafrost in my feet melts. I put my boots back on and hike up a slope that rises to a jagged ridge. There is a big boulder on the crest to hide behind, and the gully below is a perfect caribou ramp between the alpine and the tundra. I throw off my pack, find a flat spot, and lie down. After my restless night, I fall asleep almost instantly.

The soft splashing of rain on my face wakes me up. Low, dreary clouds squat above the coastal plain. At least my sleep wasn't haunted by the caribou calf and my brain is firing on most of its cylinders again. I look over the crest of the ridge and see a ghostly outline flickering in the mist. Before long, 30 cows and calves materialize.

I set up my tripod, focus my telephoto lens on the gully, and calculate aperture and shutter speed. I check my position to ensure that I'm invisible. I wait, motionless, decked out in camouflage and splayed out behind a boulder. Now that I'm fully awake, I start to shiver. My Marine-issue cotton pants are still wet from fording the creek. Icy fingers of wind massage Doucet's sweaty shirt against my back. Military clothing may be fashionable, but it isn't warm. I take off the shirt and put on a jacket.

Finally the caribou wander into the gully, but they are in no hurry to move into camera range. The wind whistles through the rocks. Lapland longspurs sing mating songs. Ground squirrels chatter across the gully to each other. A rough-legged hawk wheels overhead, and the squirrels plunge into their holes with outraged squeaks. I hear a faint whine. A jet above me is zooming toward Anchorage, or Tokyo, or Seoul. The passengers are at 33,000 feet and going 500 miles per hour. They're so high and moving so quickly they don't even know they are visiting the Arctic Refuge.

Something that looks like a giant ghost-moth flies toward me: a snowy owl. The owl swoops low over my head, with slow, deliberate wing-beats. It banks in a series of dizzying circles just out of my reach, its luminous, hypnotic eyes locked on mine. I swivel my neck to keep it in sight. Round and round it goes, like a carousel owl. It is silent, the shape and alignment of its wing feathers damping noise. Finally I lift my arm to let it know I'm not a large, juicy lemming. It circles a last time, then flaps back toward the Jago.

It's still raining. The caribou are still dithering out of camera range. I drape Doucet's shirt over my head and camera, as a cross between an umbrella and a blind. I suppose someone washed this shirt before selling it to me, but the detergent didn't purge the smell of Doucet's underarms mixed with bug dope. I peer through the lens. I have no peripheral vision. The lens is a periscope, and my field of vision is a narrow circle of tussocks. Finally I see a caribou, but her muzzle is in the air, her nostrils are twitching, and her hind legs are splayed out in classic alarm posture.

I freeze. I'm just another rock on the ridge. I wait as patiently as I can, but the air under this shirt smells like the bottom of a high-school gym locker. I need oxygen. Finally I can't stand it any longer. I pull the shirt off my head and gulp fresh air. I peer cautiously over the boulder, but the caribou are gone. The smell of Doucet's shirt must have drifted into the gully. Caribou rely mainly on their eyes to spot predators, but their noses obviously work too.

I'm too cold to crouch on the ridge any longer, so I stuff my camera into my pack and hike north. I wander along the ridge until I reach an escarpment 100 feet above the stream I forded earlier. Two hundred and fifty caribou are down there among the willows, feeding, resting, and nursing their calves. I drop my pack and wriggle into a comfortable position. Glen is also watching the caribou. He's a scarlet splash sitting on the tundra half a mile away.

These few weeks on the coastal plain are critical for the caribou, and not just for fattening up and avoiding predators. The cows and their newborn calves need a time of peace when they can bond. Through constant contact they learn each other's appearance, scent, and voice. A mother may abandon her calf if she is disturbed during this recognition period. Each cow has energy enough only for her own offspring. She will not adopt an abandoned stranger.

Before long, the caribou will congregate into the huge herds of summer and continue their endless migration. Biologists have counted as many as 100,000 animals in a single herd. If a mother loses her calf in the confusion of a river crossing, she must be able to find it among a milling throng. If a wolf pack scatters the herd, a cow must be able circle back and identify her own offspring among thousands of others. Survival in the Arctic is a tightrope walk above dangers, and each calf has only its own mother to teach it to balance.

A dozen caribou lie quietly in a clearing across the creek, except for a pair of calves who have no intention of resting. They bound up to each other, stand with stiff legs for a moment, and race into the willows. They chase each other until they are suddenly exhausted. They flop down and become tawny-colored tussocks. After a couple of minutes, one realizes that it is hungry. It bleats and approaches a caribou in a scene from the classic toddlers' book *Are You My Mother?* The cow lowers her head and drives it away. The calf cries piteously until its real mother grunts in response. The calf trots over, whacks its forehead between her hind legs to start the flow of milk, and suckles.

Suddenly the caribou jump to their hooves. The calf lets go of the upward-fleeing teat and scrambles onto its thin legs. They bolt across the creek. The calves shadow their mothers, their sticklike legs a blur. The caribou's speed and agility has been honed by thousands of years of eluding predators. During the ice ages it was American lions, short-faced bears, and scimitar cats. Today it's grizzlies, wolves, and wolverines. The Arctic Refuge isn't a Yosemite where the wolves and grizzlies are long gone and the living is easy for the fat deer who graze placidly in El Capitan Meadows.

The caribou race past Glen and bolt toward the Jago River. I wonder if I've unwittingly spooked the caribou again. I haven't moved in an hour but, as before, my scent could have floated into the valley. This time, though, it isn't my fault. A grizzly bursts out of the willows beside the creek in a fury of churning muscles and flying blond fur. The white tails of the caribou twinkle as they dash across the tundra. It looks as if they've escaped. But I'm still here. What if the bear smells me after its unsuccessful charge?

Bears are not only powerful, they're fast. Faster than an Olympic sprinter on steroids. I unclip the bear spray from my pack and look nervously for the grizzly. I can't see it anywhere. The slope below me drops away too steeply to see if the bear is climbing up. The only movement in the valley is the ripple of water flowing over a gravel bar. The caribou are gone. Glen hasn't moved. I pop the orange safety lid from the bear spray.

After a couple of long minutes of peering anxiously down the hill, I finally see the grizzly, a shrinking blond dot on the tundra. It must have stopped in midcharge when it slammed into a brick wall of human scent. My pulse drops slowly. The tundra is mammal-free except for Glen, who is walking back toward camp. Now that my adrenaline has gone back to wherever it goes, I'm hungry. It's time for stale bread and cheese and fresh creek water. I sit on my perch and enjoy the picnic. A watery sun trickles through the low clouds.

Uhuuh. I know that mournful sound. I couldn't get to sleep last night thinking about it. A calf stands up shakily in the willows and bleats for its mother. The grizzly would have had a warm lunch if I hadn't scared it away. It isn't politically correct to feel good about disturbing a wild predator-prey encounter, but the hell with political correctness. Maybe this live calf somehow balances out the one near our camp. At least I feel better—until I realize that this calf is also dead without its mother.

I scan the tundra hopefully, but nothing is moving. After 45 minutes of calling, the calf gives up and lies back down. I've almost given up hope when I hear the deeper snort of an adult caribou. We both hear the calf's answering grunt. The cow bounds across the creek, locates the calf, and smells its flank to make sure it is hers. The calf thrusts its head between her legs to nurse, but she is too nervous to stay still. She turns and walks away, dragging the calf like a shark drags a remora. The calf hangs on resolutely. It doesn't let go until they splash into the creek. They run across the tundra toward the Jago.

I pack my gear, wade across the creek, and set off across the tussock-field. I'm tired and soaked when I trudge into camp. Glen is curled up in his sleeping bag. I squat down to talk to him through the tent door.

"How long were you watching the caribou?"

"I was there all afternoon," he says, "and I finally saw a calf being born. It stood up after 45 minutes, although it fell over right away. It was walking after an hour and 20 minutes."

"Wasn't that an incredible scene? It's no wonder that this is a sacred place to the Gwich'in."

"Sure," he says, "you just need to explain that to Exxon and British Petroleum."

"Right," I answer bitterly. "Wall Street and Bond Street are their sacred places. Why don't they drill for oil there?"

I stand up and look around. A couple of dozen caribou are grazing across the Jago. I hear a raven croak and watch it fly across the river, above the caribou. It flies westward, as a crow flies, straight as a pipeline, straight toward Prudhoe Bay. Maybe it's trying to get there for tomorrow morning's smorgasbord breakfast. It's served daily in the garbage cans behind the Prudhoe Bay Hotel.

I suddenly scream as loud as I can, "Screw you, British Petroleum!"

Glen looks surprised at my outburst. The wind blows the words back in my face. The caribou across the river don't hear a thing.

Political Winds in Washington, D.C.

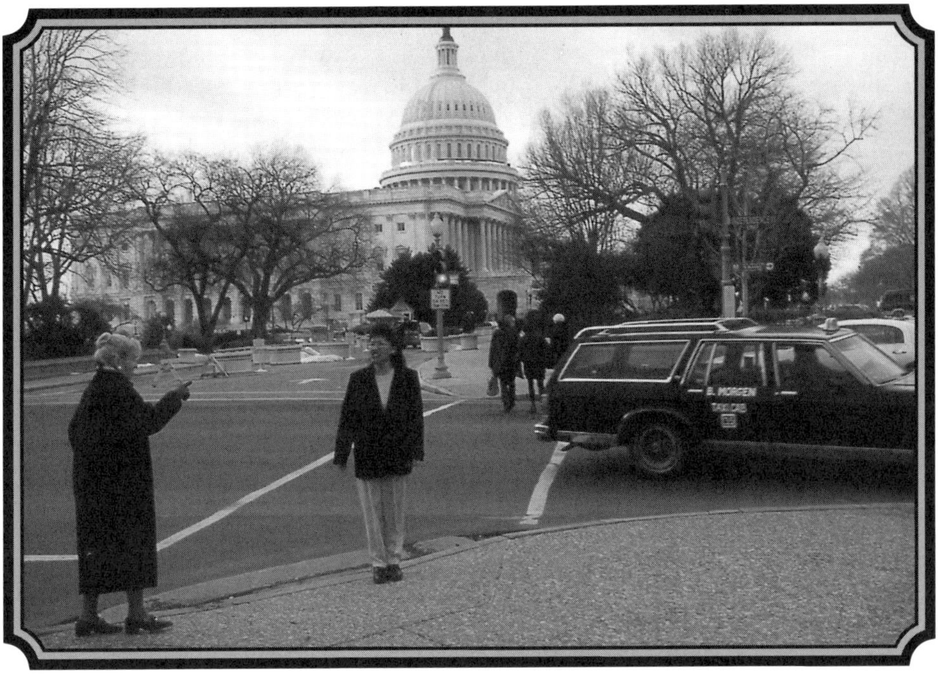

"We're here to ask your congressman to cosponsor the Wilderness Bill that would protect the Arctic National Wildlife Refuge," says Lorraine Peter. Lorraine is the representative of the Yukon Legislative Assembly from the Vuntut Gwich'in riding (administrative jurisdiction) of Old Crow.

"I believe that he supports protection of the Arctic Refuge," replies a young aide. He leans forward and fingers his blue paisley tie. "I'm sure he would cosponsor the Wilderness Bill…except for one thing. And that one thing is Don Young, the Alaska representative."

I squirm in a couch against the wall, wondering if the broad, pinstriped backside of an oil lobbyist last warmed the smooth, dark leather under my butt. The room has blue plush carpets, rows of leather-bound books in dark wooden bookshelves, and a poster of a vase full of daisies and roses. It's the best seat in the house to hear about political blackmail.

The congressman's aide is wearing tan pants with a crease sharp enough to slice bread and a green striped shirt with a polo player over his heart. He looks as if he just walked out of an Ivy League college where he was president of the Young Republicans. Like a chameleon, he blends in with the decor effortlessly. I can tell he has what it takes to succeed here in D.C. Like Tolkien's Frodo Baggins wearing his ring, he casts a faint shadow. He passes into elevators unnoticed. His keen peripheral vision allows him to absorb what Lorraine is saying while giving nothing back that will make a discernable wave.

"As you know, Don Young is the chair of the House Resources Committee," he continues. "It used to be the House *Natural* Resources Committee, before Mr. Young changed the name. Anyway, we have an important bill in front of the Resources Committee, a bill that would protect White Clay Creek. If my representative cosponsors the Arctic Bill, then Don Young will kill White Clay Creek. It's as simple as that."

I glance down the couch at Lorraine. She's here, with the blessing of the elders in Old Crow, to speak about the calving grounds of the Porcupine caribou herd and the survival of her culture. Lorraine stares intently at the young man with her dark brown eyes. Her eyes are like caribou eyes, eyes that mirror a long history of survival in the Arctic. I'm glad she isn't looking at me like that. The aide is oblivious, comfortable in the knowledge that he's at the center of the known universe. Political realism flows in his veins, full of antibodies that protect him from catching any empathy toward another culture.

"This has nothing to do with policy," says the staffer. "You've got me on policy. This has everything to do with politics. The congressman has his finger on the pulse of the political climate around here. When the political wind is blowing the right direction, he'll feel it."

I look above the aide's head at a framed photo of the congressman shaking hands with Ronald Reagan ("To Mike with Best Wishes…Ron"). He looks stuffed, as if a political wind would knock him on his ass. On his radar screen, the calving grounds of the Porcupine caribou herd are light years away, on the edge of some dark, frozen galaxy. Old Crow isn't even a blip on the screen.

A Visit to Old Crow

Does anyone know how many cosponsors the Wilderness Bill needs in order to bypass Don Young and the House Resources Committee?" I ask. "Is it possible—"

Boots clump up the outside steps. The door opens, and the wind blows in an old man. It isn't a political wind. The cold air hits the low-pressure area centered over the wooden table in front of me and turns into a fogbank of steam that swirls around the old man's feet. He bends over to take off his boots, smiles shyly, and shuffles to a chair leaning against the wall. He sits down and looks at us. He doesn't say anything. I hear the scraping of chair legs on the wooden floor and the hoarse squawks of ravens outside.

There are no crows in Old Crow, Yukon, but there are lots of ravens. The Gwich'in don't care about the niceties of bird identification, although they are birders from way back. In Old Crow, Arctic Village, and Fort McPherson, birds fit into two broad categories: those you can eat, and those you can't. Ravens are "crows." Scoters and harlequin ducks are "black duck." Long-tailed ducks (formerly old squaws) are *uh-un-lak*. Chickadees are "little ones."

A raven talks to itself on the roof of a log cabin next door. Its croak is as solid as a black feather drifting to the ground. It asks a guttural question, then answers, as if fascinated by its own voice. If I listened a little harder, I'm sure I could understand what it is saying. I know what the other ravens I hear in the distance are talking about. They are arguing with village dogs over bloody scraps of frozen caribou, moose, or black duck.

The meeting is at a standstill. We all stare at the old man. I don't know whether to repeat my question. Ferreting out the sordid details of Washington, D.C., political reality suddenly seems useless. Then Gladys Netro, the chair of our meeting, stands up and walks around the table to the old man.

"Everyone," she says, "this is Albert Charlie."

"Hello," says Albert, looking at the mostly pale faces sitting around six wooden tables arranged in a rectangle. Four of us represent Yukon conservation organizations; two are from foundations out of Toronto and Seattle. The rest are Gwich'in leaders who have been fighting to protect the calving grounds for longer than they care to remember.

Albert isn't in a hurry to speak. This is an example of "Indian Time," waiting until a thought travels from your brain to your lips before filling the air with words. White people sneer about Indian Time when natives skip work, are late for meetings, or don't jump through government hoops quickly enough. Indian Time is rampant when the salmon are running or the caribou trot over the mountains north of Old Crow. The manifestation of Indian Time that most annoys developers and government bureaucrats is when aboriginal people delay projects while they consider whether it will harm their traditional lands.

"I heard that you are meeting about the caribou," Albert says finally. "I want to tell you some things. I worked with an oil company for four years. I watch them. I know how they work. I see how they dynamite: blasting. They say it's good; it doesn't hurt. But I know it hurts. And garbage. They just leave it. I know oil companies don't care about the caribou. We're the ones who feed our children caribou meat."

When Albert says "we," he isn't only talking about the 7,000 Gwich'in scattered across Alaska, the Yukon, and Northwest Territories. "We" means his great-grandfather who hunted caribou in the spring up in Old Crow Flats and floated back down the river in a skin boat. "We" includes his ancestors of 12,000 years ago who lived down the Porcupine River at Bluefish Caves. "We" is his great-granddaughter who isn't born yet.

"Now the oil companies talk about going up to the calving grounds! They don't even come around to Old Crow and ask us. They're planning to come here and make scrambled eggs out of our land, leaving with a pocketful of money. They'll go back and get fresh fruit and vegetables. The caribou is *our* fresh stuff."

Albert's voice is soft and rocky, like the Porcupine River murmuring over a gravel bar. He's a little old man, bent and slow, but he looks as tough as an old willow. He talks with long pauses that give time for his words to form solid images in my mind.

"Old timers tell us that hard times are coming back. I know they are coming back. And what will happen if the caribou are gone? It's pretty scary. If they find oil, they're going to spill it. And what would the caribou think about that?"

Albert has said all he needs to say. He puts his jacket back on and heads out into the brittle March sunshine.

Most meetings I've been to have been ruled by an agenda, by protocol, by *Robert's Rules of Order*. Not this one. We're in Old Crow, and we're talking about caribou. Gwich'in are caribou people. Of course they come in to tell us what they think, especially the elders. That's their job. Besides the old ones, a scattering of young mothers and men wearing grease-splotched snowsuits pop in to tell us what's on their minds.

"Let's take a half-hour break," says Gladys. "Have some coffee or get some fresh air."

I decide on the fresh air. The sun is shining brightly, and I walk outside in my sweater. I last for one block and then put on my down jacket. The wind whips tendrils of dry snow across the frozen Porcupine River. The wood smoke dribbling out of chimneys bends northward, like gray pencils lying perpendicular to the log homes along the street. The houses are small and squat, as though they are trying to shrink down into the relative warmth of the soil. The trees in the boreal forest are too stunted and twisted to build and heat ranch houses.

If there is a Main Street in Old Crow, it is the Porcupine River, the river for which the caribou herd is named. It's early April—spring theoretically—but it's minus 20 degrees Fahrenheit outside, and the river is a sheet of ice winding for hundreds of miles through the wilderness. I walk down a steep embankment in front of the Northern Store and onto the river. I jump up and down at the edge to make sure the ice is strong enough to hold my weight. It doesn't quiver. It's as solid as concrete.

Old Crow is an isolated village in the heart of Gwich'in country. The only way to get there is by boat, snowmobile, dog team, or plane. The international border is downstream, between Old Crow and Fort Yukon, a village at the confluence of the Porcupine and Yukon Rivers. The Gwich'in Nation existed long before the U.S. and Canadian governments decided to run a line down the center of their traditional territory. Everyone has relatives and friends on both sides of the border. No one guards the border except caribou and moose, and they refuse to wear uniforms.

The school in Old Crow burned down last year, and during the winter the river was more than Main Street. The Yukon government bulldozed out a winter road that linked Old Crow with the Dempster Highway so they could truck in the materials for the new school. When breakup comes, the road will melt and flow to the Pacific, and that's the way the Gwich'in like it. They have rejected past proposals to build an all-weather road into Old Crow. Their way of life is changing fast enough as it is.

The first trickle of technological change arrived on the blue broadcloth coattails of English explorers like Alexander Mackenzie and John Franklin at the beginning of the nineteenth century. Traders followed the explorers like rats after a plague. Along with the spirit of free enterprise, the merry men of the Hudson's Bay Company and the Northwest Company brought guns, liquor, trade items, and deadly diseases.

Change was slow at first, but it has accelerated, especially during the past few decades. The Gwich'in don't reject everything about "progress." They race snowmobiles through the forest. They clamp 50-horsepower motors on riverboats and roar up the Porcupine River. They watch cable television, surf the Internet, and eat apples from Chile.

They've paid a price. A price of alcoholism. A price of loss of traditional knowledge and native language. A price of graveyards filled with victims of smallpox and influenza. A price of industrial contaminants that rain out of the sky and build up in the ecosystem. A price in empty fishing nets when the salmon don't swim up the Porcupine River like they used to.

More trouble is brewing for the Gwich'in, just across the Alaska-Yukon border, in the Arctic National Wildlife Refuge. Multinational oil companies and Alaskan politicians are lobbying the U.S. Congress for permission to drill for oil in the core calving area of the Porcupine caribou herd. Gwich'in on both sides of the border depend upon the caribou. They believe that oil development would hurt the caribou, a belief backed up by caribou biologists. Even a study completed by the U.S. Department of the Interior concluded that drilling would jeopardize up to 40 percent of the herd and drive caribou away from native villages and hunters.

This is not a price the Gwich'in can afford to pay.

I walk across the river into the stillness of the forest. A gray jay squawks and flutters into the top of a black spruce. A squirrel balanced on lower branches ignores it and chews a cone, rotating it in its paws like a kid with an ice cream. Bits of cone and seeds rain down into a mound at the base of the tree, which leans over at an odd angle. The forest grows on a thin layer of soil over an undulating sheet of permafrost. The trees tilt and sway like the patrons outside the Capital Hotel in Whitehorse on a Saturday night. The squirrel chatters shrilly when I approach its midden, flicking its tail in time with its outburst. I sit down in the pile of shredded cones, as big and soft as a couch.

A snowmobile bursts out of the drunken forest and speeds across the river. The growl of a ski-doo is as restful as a dentist's drill, and one is always revving up somewhere in Old Crow. I stand up, brush the wood off my pants, and follow the cloud of blue smoke back into town. Not many people around, but plenty of dogs: tethered sled dogs as well as the mongrels that slink behind woodpiles when you stare at them. The sled dogs jump onto their dog houses and howl mournfully as I walk past. Outside the community center, two little kids in oversized snowsuits wrestle with a fat husky pup.

I walk into the Old Crow Youth Center, a two-story high-rise (in Old Crow, anything over the first floor is a skyscraper). I take off my boots at the door. Low-angle sunshine streams through a tall bank of south-facing windows. The next order of business is for each of us to talk about our involvement with the caribou, and what we are going to do to help protect the calving grounds.

"I'm Marvin Frost, the chief of the Vuntut Gwich'in," says a broad-shouldered man across the table. I can barely hear him. His baseball cap is pulled low over his face, and he looks at his hands as he speaks, as if he wishes he was outside setting up a wall tent or changing the oil on his ski-doo.

"I was taught by the elders, by my grandma. They taught me how to use all parts of the caribou. Now I have five little children. I know how important it is to teach the children how to live out on the land. They are going to need the caribou just like our ancestors."

"Hell-o," says a woman with dark curly hair, "I'm Kathie Nukon." Each of her sentences ends with a lilt, a tiny question mark. She speaks even more quietly than the chief. I wonder if the Gwich'in are always this shy or if they only seem quiet when compared with the white people around the table.

"I'm Gladys' sister, and I'm one of the councilors for the Vuntut Gwich'in. I just want to thank you all for coming to Old Crow, and I also want to find out how I can help. I'm ready to travel down south to speak about the caribou if I'm needed."

"My name is Ken Madsen," I say when it's my turn. I describe the Caribou Commons Project: the four-month-long, 1,000-mile wilderness trip, our hopes for media coverage, our plans for extensive concert and slideshow tours.

Everyone nods politely. Inside my head the project is a great idea, but when I let it out into the fresh air it sounds bizarre, particularly when I describe it to the Gwich'in. I've been a wilderness campaigner for decades, but *wilderness* isn't even in Gwich'in vocabulary. We urban North Americans think of wilderness as areas with rocks, plants, wildlife, mountains, and rivers. Places where people are visitors (mainly wearing Gore-Tex). Gwich'in don't consider the Arctic *wild.* It is simpler than that: It is home.

We wind up our meeting in the late afternoon with a prayer. I've been uncomfortable during prayers ever since I was a kid growing up in California. My worst moment in school was in grade four, when my teacher decided to show us the importance of freedom of religion and the great American spiritual melting pot. She asked every kid in the class to say which church their family attended. I was the only kid whose parents were openly atheist. On the few occasions when I've been stuck in a church, I usually stand staring ahead during a prayer, which is OK since everyone else is looking down.

It's different here. An old woman speaks quietly in the Gwich'in language. I understand her words as well as I understand the ravens outside, but the prayer doesn't invoke some foreign spirit in the sky; it bubbles up out of the ground, like spring water. I stare out the window listening to her melodic words, thinking about caribou. Maybe I do understand her meaning.

After the prayer, a ski-doo roars up to the youth center, slows down, and settles into a hiccuping idle. A woman walks in, plops a baby on the floor, and takes off her parka. A young man wearing jeans and a beaded, caribou-skin vest tromps in, carrying a steaming stainless-steel pot. The baby looks at us with deep-brown, unblinking eyes. Gladys walks over, picks up the baby, and swings her in the air. The other two bustle into a small kitchen adjoining the main hall. The community of Old Crow is preparing a feast for us. This is the part I've been worrying about: The part where the Gwich'in share caribou meat with their guests.

I haven't eaten meat since 1976. I didn't stop because I was concerned about animal rights. I wasn't thinking about the pain and suffering felt by cows as they were shipped across the prairies in crowded cattle cars, pumped full of hormones and antibiotics, and slaughtered in bloody warehouses. I wasn't considering the energy loss as good healthy plant carbohydrates were transformed into animal protein.

I stopped eating steak, hamburgers, and veal cutlets because I hated walking in cow patties in alpine meadows when I went backpacking. I hated seeing tiger lilies squashed under a heavy bovine hoof. I hated hearing cattle bawling in the still mountain air instead of the whistle of hoary marmots and the chatter of chickadees. I wished that there were still wolves and grizzlies left to chase the "white-faced prairie maggots" out of the mountains. I stopped eating meat as a lonely protest against overgrazing and the loss of wildlife habitat.

I walk over to the sun-drenched windows to inspect a display of traditional crafts made from caribou: skin blankets, moccasins, baby belts, mittens, hats, fish hooks, parkas, and snowshoes. I pick up a pair of moccasins. The soles are soft and supple, useless for concrete but perfect for walking around the North when it's forty below and the snow is as dry and sticky as sandpaper. The moccasins are meticulously beaded with pink fireweed blossoms. They are tanned with caribou brains and smell like wood smoke. I put them down and wonder what to do if someone hands me a platter dripping with ribs or a caribou steak.

However, a long winter has gone by since the caribou last crossed the Porcupine River. As Grafton N'jootli had told us in the morning, "We haven't seen the caribou since September. My freezer is empty right now. If the caribou don't come back soon, I'm going to be one sore Gwich'in."

Even so, the people of Old Crow have scraped together enough caribou meat to boil up a vat of stew. Gladys hands me a bowl: broth the same color as her eyes, carrots, potatoes, and chunks of dark brown meat. I consider my options. I could fill up on buns and salad and get rid of the stew. There are no dogs under the table, but I could casually carry my bowl into the kitchen and dump it back in the vat.

Or, I could eat it.

I spread butter on a bun and bite off a chunk. Good homemade white bun. Warm and crusty. The butter melts into it and dribbles onto my plate. The salad is another story. The tomato in my bowl is faintly red, but it has the consistency and flavor of a croquet ball. The lettuce has had a long and sordid history. It grew up as an iceberg sproutling in southern California and grew strong on a diet of bright sunshine, chemical fertilizers, and water diverted from the Colorado River. It dreamed of growing up to grace the governor's table in Sacramento, but it started running with the wrong crowd: the bad-hearted romaine gang and brown-edged leaf lettuces. When things became too hot in California, it stowed away on a produce truck, then slipped onto a northward bound DC-3. Several weeks later, it ended up in a land where lettuces are not meant to live, in Old Crow, north of the Arctic Circle.

I stab a forkful of salad. It tastes like ranch dressing. Might as well be eating cardboard. I've heard Gwich'in elders say that a day is coming when the planes will no longer land with Diet Coke, Kraft Dinner, and lettuce. That's the day they'll need their dried caribou meat. The elders know that the Gwich'in have to hang on to their traditional ways.

I dip into the stew. A small chunk of caribou meat swims up and lodges on my spoon. Caribou meat isn't *my* cultural heritage; but when it comes down to it, I'm not willing to risk offending these people. They are sharing more than their meat. They're sharing a part of their life. I chew tentatively. Tougher and stringier than tofu, with an earthy flavor. As I chew, I think about what Gladys and Kathie's mother, Hannah Netro, had told us earlier in the day.

"The calving grounds, my dad's been there. He's seen it himself, a nice and green grass place. My dad, he prays over this place. And I pray over this place. And I feel sad; I don't know what to do. We need help from people like you."

I felt the weight of my consumptive culture pressing down on my head as I listened. Why should Hannah Netro need to ask help from people like us? Why should her culture be threatened by short-term oil money? Hannah pointed to the doorway where our high-tech, Merrell and Vasque boots were heaped up, where our North Face, Patagonia, and Sierra Designs jackets were piled on a bench.

"I remember no shoes like that, no jackets like those. We made all of our clothing from caribou—jackets, mitts, mukluks. I ask God to help us. I want the calving grounds to stay the way it is."

I wished I could grab the CEOs of British Petroleum, ARCO, Exxon, and Chevron by their pinstriped necks and sit them on wooden chairs between Hannah Netro and Albert Charlie. I know what the elders would do. They would offer them homemade buns and stew. They would watch them eat with their dark eyes, eyes that have grown old watching the caribou crossing the Porcupine River.

Maybe Albert Charlie would ask them to describe their plans for the calving grounds. I know he'd listen, but then maybe he would ask the same question he had asked us earlier in the day.

"What would the caribou think about that?"

A Vegetarian in Eugene

Aren't there any laws against drilling for oil in a National Wildlife Refuge?" asks a young man sitting next to the projectors. "I'm a philosophy major, and my understanding is that a refuge is a place where you go to get away from persecution and oppression. It seems to me that the caribou would become refugees from the Refuge."

"I agree with you," I answer. "Unfortunately there are no laws against drilling in Wildlife Refuges and a few Refuges do have oil and gas activity. However, there haven't been any new leases issued for the past 35 years. We believe that it would set a bad precedent to reverse that trend."

"I doubt if our current president would think it's a bad precedent," says a woman in the front row. "George W. was an oil man before he was a politician, and so was Vice President Cheney."

"They aren't the only ones," I say. "National Security Advisor Condoleezza Rice was on the board of directors of Chevron. She even has an oil tanker named after her! Are there any other questions?"

Sandra Newman and I stand in the front of a crowd of 150 in a lecture hall at the University of Oregon campus in Eugene. It's a lousy venue for a slideshow. The ceiling is low; the people at the back can only see the top of the screen. I'm surprised that they waited patiently until we turned the lights up for a question-and-answer session.

"I have a question for Sandra," yells a young man wearing a ragged brown sweater and a wool Rasta hat. "Have you Gwich'in people ever thought of becoming vegetarians?"

"Excuse me?" Sandra looks at me with a surprised look on her face. She has already explained the age-old relationship that the Gwich'in have with the Porcupine caribou herd. She turns back to the young man. "We are caribou people. We can't grow fruits and vegetables in the Arctic. Our elders tell us we have to hold on to the old ways. We can't feed our children oil when they are hungry."

"I think you should stop eating meat. There must be lots of roots and berries that grow up there."

"You know," I say. "I'll tell you a story. I'm like you. I don't eat meat, either. In fact, the only time I've eaten meat in the last 25 years was when I was visiting Old Crow. The community put on a feast to thank us for helping to protect the calving grounds, and they gave me a bowl of caribou stew. They were honoring me with a part of their life. I'd never hunt caribou myself, but the Gwich'in have a traditional right to live off the land, and for them that means caribou."

"Something like that happened to me, too," shouts the man. "I'm a vegan, but when I went to New Orleans for Mardi Gras someone gave me a bowl of shrimp gumbo. Guess what happened after I ate that shrimp?"

"I don't know," says Sandra.

"The very next day I got bitten by a pit bull!"

The crowd bursts out laughing. I look at Sandra. "It's a good thing there are no pit bulls in the Arctic," she whispers.

Prudhoe Bay: "No Impact" on Wildlife

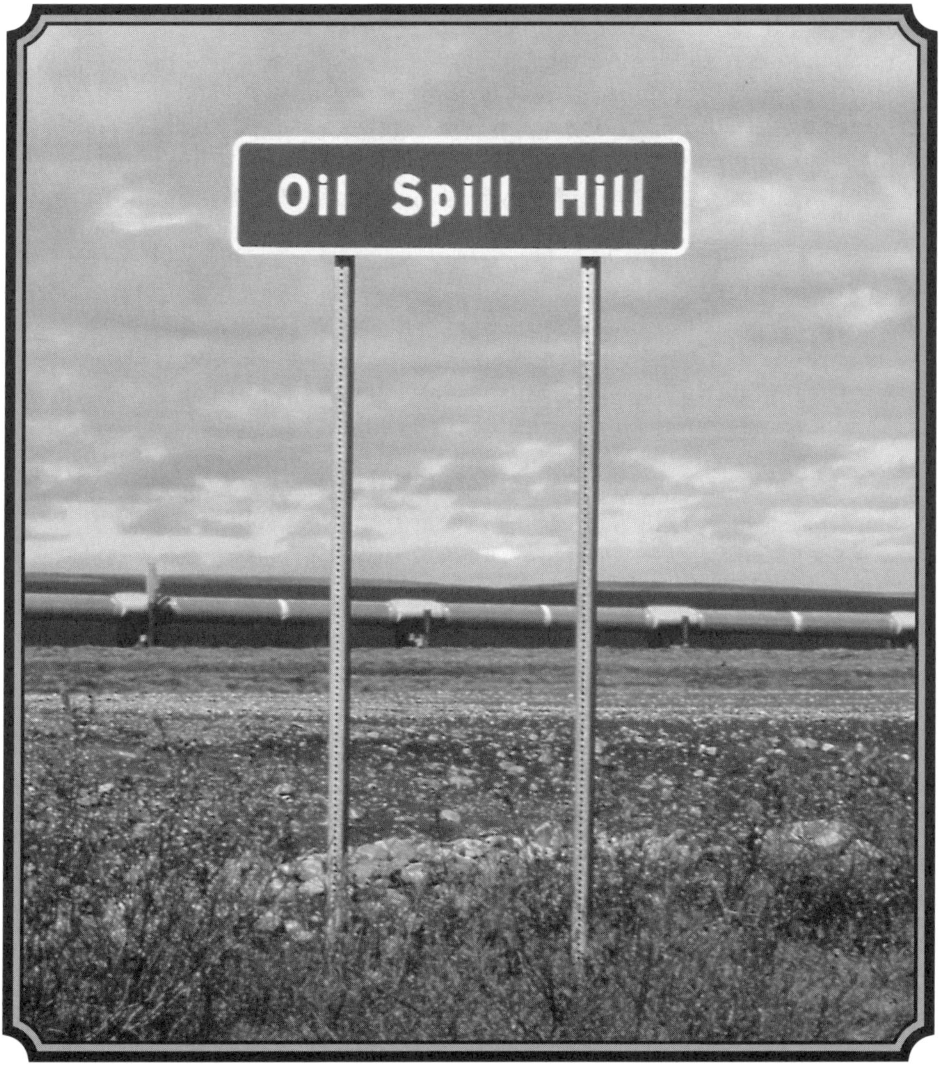

Look at that sign," says Glen Davis. "'Oil Spill Hill.' At least someone was honest."

"Honesty is a good thing," I answer. "Maybe British Petroleum will change its name to Pollution 'R' Us."

"Dream on," says Glen.

"Why don't you stop, and I'll take a photo of you with the pipeline. You can tell me if George Bush, Sr., was right when he said, 'The caribou love it. They rub against it and they have babies. There are more caribou in Alaska than you can shake a stick at.'"

"I wish we had his stick to shake at some caribou. We've covered a thousand miles and haven't seen one yet."

Glen pulls over on the shoulder of the gravel highway and scrambles up the bank to the Trans-Alaska Pipeline. It towers over his head. He looks like a small plastic toy, Captain Marvel standing under a huge python slithering over the tundra. The pipeline is an engineering marvel. Everyone says so. Through the miracle of modern technology and a "can-do" attitude, we can suck oil from below the Arctic permafrost, pipe it across Alaska, and spill it in the Pacific.

"I can't speak for the caribou," says Glen as we get back in the car, "but the pipeline didn't seem like an aphrodisiac to me."

Glen puts the car in gear and we follow the pipeline north to Deadhorse, the town on the edge of the Prudhoe Bay fossil-fuel empire. Big trucks circle endlessly on the perimeter road leading from Deadhorse toward the ocean. The trucks are comets, trailed by long plumes of gritty dust that drift lazily into the wetlands that flank the road.

We join the procession, but our journey is quickly aborted at a British Petroleum checkpoint with flashing orange lights. "Stop. Arctic Ocean Access Restricted. Private Vehicles Prohibited. This Means You." In the distance we see pipelines, burning gas flares, gravel quarries and towering drill rigs. Glen veers to the left, and we pass a complex of blocky green buildings girdled by dozens of pipelines. "Danger. Poison Gas. Hydrogen Sulfide May Be Present." I close my window, and we rattle back toward Deadhorse.

We park in front of the Prudhoe Bay Hotel and shell out $300 for a double room with all of the comforts of a Motel 6. While we're at the desk, we sign up for the official oilfields tour. It's another hundred bucks, but it's the only way to catch even a sanitized glimpse of the oilfields. We dump our backpacks in our room and head to the restaurant.

The hotel serves up all-you-can-eat, mining-camp-style dining. I load my plate with scalloped potatoes, peas and carrots, and an unidentified fish swimming in white sauce. I bypass the brightly lit display case with Day-Glo Jell-O desserts. Competing televisions blare at us from two corners of the room. We choose a table under CNN *Headline News* instead of Country Music TV. We eat in silence while a contestant in the U.S.

National Spelling Bee Championships spells "pagurian" and a woman reports the grisly details of a murder-suicide in Hollywood. We return our trays and head back to the front desk.

"Well! Looks like you are my only guests today!" Our guide is a clean-cut youth from Anchorage. "Let's start our oilfield adventure in the rec room with a video."

We troop into a long room where a couple of plaid-jacketed men are playing pool. I sink into a couch. The room is hot, and the click of the balls on the pool table becomes the rhythm beat to the narrator's syrupy voice. A procession of carefully edited sequences parades smoothly across the screen. Arial views of pipelines on the tundra. Men in hard hats and hydraulic-oil-splattered coveralls dancing with thick chains and bright metal. Happy caribou. Oil flowing southward through the pipeline. Oil liberated from its liquid bondage and blossoming into the products that define our civilization: computers, swimming pools, Pokémon toys, highways clogged with traffic, Styrofoam cups. All brought to us by British Petroleum and ARCO, with no impact on native people, caribou, or the Arctic tundra.

The TV flickers and fades, and we follow our tour guide's bright white shirt and spotless brown slacks outside. We blink like moles in the bright, hazy light. I don't know how the guide stays so clean. I've been in Deadhorse for just two hours, and already my jeans are mud-splattered from the puddles outside the hotel. We climb aboard an idling white minibus and bump down the dusty road.

"Can you hear me? Well great, I guess the microphone is working! We're off!" It's early in the season, and his cheerful patter hasn't settled into the tired groove of August. "This is downtown Deadhorse. You've seen the hotel. On your left is the general store. It looks small, but you can pick up just about any souvenir you want."

Deadhorse was spawned by the service industries that grew up around the oilfields. Besides the store, there are a couple of prefab hotels and the dingy offices of drilling companies. Many of the buildings are abandoned. A few are collapsing in Arctic-style planned obsolescence. Outmoded vehicles rust in parking lots. It's a ghost town in the making, waiting for the day when the oil gushing through the pipeline slows and becomes a trickle.

Deadhorse is a malignant melanoma on the landscape, but there isn't much point in surgically removing it. The cancer has spread across the coastal plain. Four thousand wells. Two refineries and 25 production and treatment plants. Thousands of miles of roads and pipelines. Fifty-five contaminated waste sites. Sixty million cubic yards of gravel mined. Twice the nitrogen oxide pollution of Washington, D.C.

"We have to check in with the guard before going into the main oilfields," says our guide. "I'll need to show him your photo identification."

We drive toward the flashing yellow lights of the guardhouse. The hairs on the back of my neck tingle with a cool shiver of paranoia, as though I'm a spy sneaking through Checkpoint Charlie into Cold War Berlin. Maybe they know we aren't ordinary tourists.

Arctic Power, a company funded by the oil industry and the state of Alaska, already has its eye on the Caribou Commons Project. Its website has a "Tracking the Opposition" section. It calls us "migrating musicians, trekking after the Porcupine caribou herd in the hopes of creating a campaign to show oil development as a force that will destroy wildlife and native culture."

We stop in a swirl of dust. Our guide slides open his window and passes our identification to a bored-looking guard. As he stares at it and makes a notation in a book, I think back to a visit I had with Lenny Kohm at his home in the Blue Ridge Mountains.

Lenny is a legendary figure in the struggle to protect the Arctic Refuge. Fifteen years ago he was in his mid-40s, living in the Napa Valley and making a living by selling promo photos for wineries. One day he was invited to go north to visit the Arctic Refuge. He saw migratory birds flying toward the coastal plain. He saw caribou. He visited Gwich'in villages and experienced a different way of living.

Suddenly Lenny realized that the compass course he'd been following through life was off by 180 degrees. He quit his job. He became a starving Arctic activist. He put together a slideshow and began traveling across the United States with it. He returned north whenever he could afford to. One day his Gwich'in friends started joining him as he crisscrossed the country. Lenny spoke about the need to protect the Arctic Refuge. The Gwich'in talked about their dependence on the caribou and their fears about oil development.

Lenny is still doing it. The list of cosponsors in Congress for Arctic Refuge Wilderness designation has grown steadily through the years. The oil wells might have already been drilled had Lenny not devoted his life to the caribou, the polar bears, and his Gwich'in friends.

"You ever worry that the oil barons are watching you?" I asked him.

"They probably don't know I exist."

"Multinational oil companies may be rich, powerful, and ruthless, but they aren't stupid. They know what you're up to."

Then I told him about an interview I'd heard years ago on the CBC Radio program *As It Happens*. The segment was aired during the aftermath of the *Exxon Valdez* oil spill. The radio host summed up the events that led to the oil spill and then dialed up an activist in Washington, D.C., who was trying to expose Exxon's negligence in the cleanup efforts.

"My memory is like a sieve," I told Lenny, "but this is how I remember it."

The story really began in 1968 when the Prudhoe Bay oilfields were discovered. Five years later, Vice President Spiro Agnew broke a tie vote in the Senate, and the Trans-Alaska Pipeline Authorization Act passed. Oil finally gurgled toward Valdez in 1977. Alyeska, the company responsible for the pipeline, promised that "no spill is likely to flow unnoticed for more than a few minutes."

Promises, promises. Before any oil reached Valdez, a bulldozer crushed a pipeline valve, and 80,000 gallons of crude oil spewed onto the tundra. In 1979, the pipeline ruptured at Antigun Pass and 210,000 gallons of oil gushed out. Leak detection alarms failed. Containment booms malfunctioned. Oil flowed down the Antigun River, leaving a slick of dead aquatic life and oiled birds. Over the next decade, thousands of spills occurred in the oilfields and along the pipeline corridor.

In Valdez, and along the Pacific tanker route, fishermen warned that a major disaster was inevitable. The oil industry countered with the best scientific reports that money could buy. They promised "zero spillage" in Prince William Sound.

March 24th, 1989, was a perfect night in Prince William Sound. The winds were calm, the stars bright, the booze strong. If only God hadn't put Bligh Reef smack in the path of the *Exxon Valdez.* The reef ripped the belly out of the single-hulled oil tanker. Eleven million gallons of crude oil gushed into the ocean. The oil, still warm from Prudhoe Bay, fouled a fragile seashore as long as the coast of California. The spill killed dozens of orcas, hundreds of harbor seals, thousands of sea otters, and hundreds of thousands of seabirds such as marbled murrelets, harlequin ducks, and cormorants. Prince William Sound still hasn't recovered.

After the spill the *Exxon Valdez* was banned from carrying oil in Alaskan waters. Like someone in a federal witness protection program, the tanker was given a new job, a new name, and sent where no one would know her. The *Exxon Valdez* was renamed the *SeaRiver Mediterranean* and now carries crude from the Middle East to Europe. Exxon is suing to bring the tanker back to Prince William Sound.

"The man interviewed by *As It Happens* was just like you," I told Lenny. "Nobody special. Just another idealist trying to expose Exxon's negligence in cleaning up Prince William Sound."

Most conservation work is not romantic. It is not watching wolves from an alpine ridge or counting caribou on the coastal plain. It is staring at a computer screen, enduring boring meetings, and writing tedious proposals. Fund-raising is the most soul-numbing of all. I didn't need to tell Lenny any of that. He and I both know what it is like.

"This guy was drowning in a sea of legal challenges from Exxon's high-priced law firms. Whenever he got his head above water another wave broke over him. One day, though, his luck changed. He got a call from a lawyer who told him he had heard about his fight against Exxon. He said he believed in the cause and offered to donate his firm's legal services. They arranged to meet at the lawyer's office. It looked like any other law firm:

solid, lawyerly furniture, soft carpets, a bookshelf with law texts, some diplomas on the wall. The receptionist had her hair in a bun and wore glasses. The partners were dressed in pinstripe suits and said words like 'affidavit' and 'tort.'

"The man put his faith in his new legal friends. After they went to work, though, nothing went right. There were unaccountable delays. Legal briefs disappeared in an impenetrable thicket of red tape. Exxon was as far from justice as ever. Eventually he became suspicious. He did some detective work and discovered that these guys were not real lawyers at all. They were actors who had rented the office suite and decked it out like a real law office. They'd been hired by Big Oil to throw monkey wrenches into his conservation work.

"Anyway, I wouldn't be too complacent if I were you," I told Lenny. "Big Oil has deep pockets. British Petroleum made a profit of nearly $12 billion in 1999. Exxon raked in almost $16 billion. I bet they're watching you."

"I doubt it," said Lenny. "I'm just a mosquito buzzing around that they can't be bothered to swat."

Up in Prudhoe Bay it is too cold for mosquitoes. The guard stares at us through the dusty glass, passes back our driver's licenses, and waves us on.

"Well, OK! Here we go into the heart of the oilfields. You might be surprised to learn that there are no permanent residents in Prudhoe Bay. Hardly any women. No family homes, kids, or dogs. These buildings on our left are where the workers live. They have recreation facilities, gyms, and movie theaters. Still, it's tough to work shifts and maintain a family life. There is an incredibly high divorce rate."

The tundra looks like an Isaac Asimov novel of a lunar settlement. Huge satellite dishes and telecommunication towers shimmer in an Arctic mirage. A spider's web of pipelines runs into and around massive buildings painted a uniform olive green. Gas flares flicker in the icy wind. We rumble down the gravel road until we see the sheet of ice that is the Arctic Ocean. There is a small lead of open water along the shore.

"This is the highlight for most folks," says our guide. "There isn't enough water for a swim yet, but this is your chance to dip your toes in the Arctic Ocean."

Glen and I aren't interested in exposing our flesh to the ocean. We'll have plenty of opportunity for that later in the summer. I set up my tripod and focus on a drilling rig out on the ice. Clouds fly along the coast just a few hundred feet above sea level. They look like ragged white sheep shedding their thick winter fur over the tundra. Snow pellets splatter on my telephoto lens. We get back on the bus.

"No takers for an Arctic dip? Well then, next stop, mile "0" on the pipeline! If you'll excuse the pun, you are just seeing the tip of the iceberg

Downtown Deadhorse, Prudhoe Bay, Alaska

when it comes to the oilfields. If you saw a map of oil development, you'd be amazed at how extensive it is."

"What do you think about the Arctic Refuge?" I ask.

"We all want to develop ANWR," he says. "We have a powerful lobby in Washington. It's just a matter of time."

People associated with the oil industry always call the Arctic Refuge "ANWR" (pronounced "Anwar"). It's a convenient acronym if you don't want to mention contentious words such as *National*, *Wildlife*, and *Refuge*.

"What about caribou and other wildlife?" asks Glen. "Shouldn't there be a place left for them?"

"Well, as one of our Alaskan politicians once said, we've never had a documented case of an oil rig chasing a caribou out onto the pack ice!" He waves his hand out the window toward the moonscape. "When the oil stops flowing, this will be returned to Mother Nature."

"I'm not sure that she'll want it back," I mutter to Glen.

We pull over at the beginning of the Trans-Alaska Pipeline. I take a picture of the "0" sign and the pipeline snaking toward Valdez. We get back in the bus and drive to Deadhorse. I ask the driver to let me out at the Prudhoe Bay Visitor Center. It is full of black-and-white photos, pipeline memorabilia, and dioramas of oilfield construction. A sign in large letters proclaims: "Oil Development in the Arctic has No Impact on Wildlife."

George Orwell would have been proud. There must be a Ministry of Truth in Big Oil's corporate headquarters. War is peace. Oil development has "no impact." BP stands for "Beyond Petroleum." There will be "zero spillage" in Prince William Sound.

Between July 1995 and June 2001, "no impact" meant 2,454 spills in the Prudhoe Bay oilfields and along the route of the pipeline. More than a spill a day from vehicle crashes, explosions, fires, hull failures, and pipeline ruptures. One and a half million gallons of crude oil and other toxic chemicals spilled into the fragile Arctic environment, according to the Alaska Department of Environmental Conservation.

The U.S. Army Corps of Engineers regulates the oil industry's "No Impact" in the Arctic. Across the United States, the Corps has destroyed more wetlands with dams and construction projects than any other developer. Giving them regulatory power over oil development is a classic case of the fox guarding the henhouse. The Corps has approved more than 1,000 oil-related permits on Alaska's North Slope. It has rejected only three. And the Corps has turned down *every* appeal made by the Fish and Wildlife Service in the past decade.

British Petroleum is the biggest player in the Alaskan oilfields. It advertises that it is a "green" corporation. The ads don't mention that, in February 2000, BP was fined $22 million for illegally disposing of hazardous drilling wastes at its Endicott facility near Prudhoe Bay. BP is also busily promoting Northstar, a controversial offshore development that boasts artificial islands and the Arctic Ocean's first sub-sea pipeline. Even the development-loving Corps of Engineers estimates the chance of a major oil spill at 12 to 25 percent. Critics say that an undersea spill will be difficult to detect and impossible to clean up. BP tested its cleanup equipment in two "spill drills" during the summer of 2000. It didn't work.

I walk out of the visitor center into a Deadhorse Saturday night. The trucks are still circling, and soon my hair is covered with a film of dust. I walk along the road beside a swamp. Plastic jugs and Styrofoam cups float lazily in a rainbow-colored oil slick where migratory birds should be nesting.

I wonder whether the floating junk was manufactured from oil pumped up from right under my feet. Maybe the oil began its long journey at mile "0" of the pipeline. Maybe it was pumped into a single-hulled tanker in Valdez and shipped to Japan. Maybe, like salmon, the plastic and Styrofoam migrated back to the place of their birth, to decompose and add their bodies to the Jurassic mush from which they were created.

Here I am in Alaska, the last frontier. The very last frontier until we fire off starships to look for petrochemicals beneath the red spot on Jupiter. Ninety-five percent of Alaska's North Slope is already available for oil development. The only chunk that we have the chance to save for the caribou and ptarmigan and polar bears is the Arctic Refuge.

I wish I were back there.

A Gwich'in in Oil City

John Hummel is the organizer for our slideshow in Oil City, Pennsylvania. He's full of energy, charged by the same batteries that power nonstop drumming bunnies. After a long drive from Delaware, I just feel like flaking out with a book. John has other ideas. Before we know what has hit us, Lorraine Peter and I are on a driving tour of "The Valley that Changed the World."

"This is the Transit Building," says John. "It was the nerve center of John D. Rockefeller's Standard Oil empire." We walk through a yellow brick archway gilded with intertwining pineapples and grape leaves. "Rockefeller started as a bookkeeper in Cleveland. Seven years later he was the world's first oil baron."

We walk into the lobby and John pushes the button of an ancient elevator, which begins to rattle and creak down from the third floor. John gives us a short history about Rockefeller, the birth of the oil industry, and the evolution of modern business ethics. The "law of the jungle" ruled the oil industry at the end of the 1800s, at least if the survival of the fittest is the same as the survival of the most ruthless. Rockefeller bought or created new engineering and pipeline companies that pretended to be independent but gave hidden rebates to Standard Oil. He secretly financed shell companies that spied on his real competitors. He sat in the Transit Building and spun far-reaching corporate webs based on deceit, fraud, special privileges, and force.

"The original antitrust laws in the United States were created to deal with the John D. Rockefellers of the world," John tells us. "Rockefeller set the standard for today's oil industry. Maybe that's why he called his company Standard Oil. Standard Oil's concentration of power hasn't been rivaled since the oil companies started merging recently: Exxon-Mobil, BP-Amoco, Chevron-Texaco. It means less competition for consumers and more political clout for a small number of multinational corporations."

"It's scary when you hear about their political contributions. Who is really running the government?"

"Ordinary ethics do not apply to making money," says John dryly.

The elevator doors lurch open, and John leads us through a rabbit's warren of offices. He introduces us to Marilyn Black, who works for Oil Heritage Region, Inc. Now that the oil industry has taken off with its money, Marilyn is trying to sell Oil City as a tourist mecca.

"Let me tell you about the region's oil heritage," says Marilyn. "Oil became commercially viable after whales were hunted nearly to extinction and whale oil became too expensive. The first commercial well was drilled by Edwin Drake back in 1859."

As Marilyn talks I look at the displays on the walls and thumb through brochures which are stiff with one-liners: "OIL: It changed the world with just a spark." "OIL: The driving force of our fast paced industrial world." "OIL: It changed our world in unimaginable ways."

"Oil: It destroyed our world in unimaginable ways," whispers John.

"The Transit Building was built in 1894," says Marilyn, "after a disastrous fire and flood swept down from Oil Creek and Titusville. The exterior walls were 22 inches thick, and there were bank vaults on every floor. Rockefeller had a water-powered elevator installed. The only other one in the world was in the Eiffel Tower."

"Can you tell me about the Native Americans from this area?" asks Lorraine.

"I know the Senecas hunted near here," says Marilyn, "but I don't know much about them. Verango County is 97 percent white, with a small African-American population. There might be a few Native Americans around, but most are in reservations up in New York State."

After we finish our tour, Marilyn gives us each a little vial of Pennsylvania crude oil. It is thick and rich-looking, like organic maple syrup from Quebec. "Try smelling it," she says. "It has a special Pennsylvania tang."

Lorraine holds the vial and sniffs tentatively. She jerks her head back as if she's inhaled pure ammonia. "Can you imagine thousands of gallons of this spilled in the calving grounds?" she asks.

We thank Marilyn for the tour, lurch down the elevator, and get in John's car. He drives north along the Allegheny River, steering for the site of the original oil strike.

"We've been working to reintroduce otters to the Allegheny," says John. "So far it's been a success."

"Can you imagine a time when someone will have to reintroduce animals to the Porcupine River?" I ask.

"No," says Lorraine flatly.

"Have a look at the Monday edition of our local paper, the Oil City Derrick," says John. He passes a newspaper over his shoulder to the back seat.

"Local crude refining ends today," I read out loud. "It's like Detroit without cars, Akron without rubber, or Milwaukee without beer. Only here, it is even more difficult to imagine—*Oil* City without oil."

"What about Old Crow without caribou?" asks Lorraine.

John turns off the car in a deserted parking lot outside the Drake Well Museum. We pay our entrance fee, and while John chats with the curator, Lorraine and I drift quietly through the museum. We stop in front of a diorama about "oil smellers," diviners who used witch hazel twigs to sniff out oil.

"Looks less destructive than the "thumper-trucks" they use for seismic exploration on the tundra," I say.

John joins us in front of a display about the first oil-shipping schemes. Water was impounded behind dams. Barrels and flat-bottom barges were pumped full of oil and floated in the reservoir. Then they opened the floodgates. The fleet jostled, collided, and smashed downstream toward Oil City. At the beginning only one-third of the oil made it to market. The rest ended up in the river.

"Imagine sending oil down a flooding creek," I say.

"That was modern technology at the time," says John. "Just imagine what people in the future will think when they look back on today's cutting-edge technology: leaky pipelines and single-hull tankers like the *Exxon Valdez.*"

"I guess things haven't changed that much," says Lorraine.

We meet Wendy and Malkolm for an early supper and drive to the Knights of Columbus building in Oil City. It's on Petroleum Road. We put out 100 folding metal chairs in the auditorium. The room fills up quickly and, as 7:00 approaches, we need to rustle up a few more chairs from a back room. Then I weave through the crowd to double-check my equipment.

"Are you the fellow giving the talk about oil development in the Arctic?" asks an old man in a plaid shirt sitting near the projectors. He grabs my sleeve and pulls me closer.

"Yes, me and Lorraine Peter. She's a Gwich'in speaker from Old Crow."

"Not too many people happy with the oil industry in this audience tonight," he says.

"Why?"

"Pennzoil-Quaker State just announced that they're closing down the last refinery. They sucked the oil out of the ground, sold it for billions, and took the money to Dallas and Houston."

"I wondered what people around hear thought about oil companies."

"They didn't leave anything but problems here," he says bitterly.

"The cancer rate in Oil City is abnormally high," adds his wife, leaning across from the next chair. "A dear friend just died of cancer. She had twins in grade one."

The man asks if I'd heard of the fiasco at the local franchise of a major fast-food chain. "They built it on the site of the old Empire Refinery. We had some big floods a couple of years ago, and toxic tar started bubbling up in the parking lot. They roped off the sludge and kept frying burgers."

"I wonder how many more will end up with cancer?" asks the woman.

"Are you ready to start?" asks John.

It's standing room only when I turn on the projectors. Lorraine sits quietly at the front, looking at the images: an antler next to a patch of yellow blossoms on the coastal plain, a female caribou suckling her newborn baby, a polluted wetland in Prudhoe Bay. She looks tense, but it isn't fear of public speaking. She isn't used to looking at pictures of the calving grounds of the Porcupine caribou herd. The Gwich'in don't ever go there. The coastal plain lives only in their imaginations, not right in their faces, on a big screen in the Knights of Columbus building in Oil City. Lorraine doesn't move until I've finished talking about the political storm battering the Arctic Refuge. Then I introduce her.

She walks to the microphone. She's wearing a white caribou-hide dress and moccasins. Around her shoulders is a fringed black collar with bright blossoms that Lorraine beaded by hand. She stands quietly for a moment, as if she needs to gather strength. Then she speaks.

"*Hah tzat gween zee.* In my language, that means "Good evening." I just want to share with you the time and place when I was born. The home I was born into, my mother's place, was a wall tent, and the size of that tent was 10 feet by 12 feet. I come from a family of six girls. We just celebrated my mother's 82nd birthday in April.

"When I was growing up, from the first time I could eat, caribou was my food. The caribou are very important for our people. We use it for clothing, we use it for tools, and, of course, it is the main source of food for the Gwich'in.

"When I was growing up, school started in July and ended in March. In April we would get ready to go out to my mother's trapping area. It was springtime, the snow was melting, and the birds were coming back. It was a time of great joy and excitement for our people. It was a time of freedom.

"It was during these times that our parents and our grandparents taught us about taking care of the land and the animals. It was a time of learning our responsibilities. A time to learn what my mother had learned from her mother and was now passing down to me.

"I'd like to share a story with you. It happened when I was about 10 years old. Our wall tent was close to the trails where the caribou migrate, heading back from their winter range to the calving grounds. One day my mother was out on the land with my older sisters and I stayed home to look after my youngest sister. We were home in the tent. The floor was made of spruce boughs. My sister was taking her afternoon nap. I was cleaning up, putting things away. And I heard a noise, so I crawled quietly to the doorway and lifted the flap.

"I looked out onto the lake, and just outside our tent were 150 caribou making their way up to the Arctic Refuge. And they were taking their time, eating along the way. And for me, that moment was normal and natural. I never realized that one day that would be at risk.

"I have never been up to that area, the calving grounds. That is a sacred place for my people. My mother has never been to that place. My grandmother has never been there. My great-grandparents never walked on those lands. The reason we never go there is that we hold great respect for animals during their birthing time.

"I look around and see that there are many women here tonight. I have a son. He is 20 years old. One day when my son was in high school he got on the phone with my mom, who was 79 years old. He came in all excited.

"'Mom,' he told me, 'in the springtime I'm going out on the land with Grandma.'

"'Yes, like Grandma is going to go out there,' I kind of laughed at him. 'I don't think so.'

"My mom makes her way around her home with a cane. Well, I'll tell you what happened. The last laugh was on me. Come March, the two of them were back and forth on the phone making plans. They left in April and didn't come back to town until June. The two of them spent the whole spring out there in that area where I was raised. They spent two and a half months living with the caribou. And that was one of the greatest teachings that my son will ever have. That is how much our animals mean to us.

"I came south for my first tour last spring. I went to Washington, D.C. And for me, that was one of the scariest experiences I ever had. I was in a foreign land, and I was talking to people who didn't know anything about me. When I got to Washington, D.C., I had no idea what to expect. I found myself sitting across the desk from a senator. I had five or ten minutes to explain to him how important his decision would be. It was then that I realized that the lives of my people, our land and our livelihood, lie in the hands of another country, of another people—people who have no idea who we are.

"Then I understood what my grandmother had asked me to do. She passed away a few years ago at the age of 106. That man you saw in the slideshow, Johnny Charlie, he was my uncle. He passed away last summer. He came down here, too, to tell people about the caribou. He gave his life to this issue and asked us to carry on. I understood why our elders asked us to travel, to tell the outside world about the caribou and our way of life.

"After being in Washington, D.C., I toured the state of Indiana. And I realized that we do have hope. In these rooms there are many wonderful people who care. I believe that it is my responsibility to be here on behalf of my people. Not only for myself. This is not about me anymore; it is about my 20-year-old son. It is about the children who are still unborn.

"The elders asked us to talk to people in a good way, without any violence. And I take that very seriously. My ancestors took care of that land for 20,000 years. And now the oil companies want to come into that land and destroy it and everything that goes with it. The oil companies tell us we'll be a richer people. They tell us that we will have more money and a better way of life. Better jobs and bigger homes. My people believe that we already are a rich people. We're rich because we still have our animals and our land and our way of life. We don't need their destruction. We need to hold onto what we already have.

"It is really difficult to travel this far from home. These presentations are really emotional for me. But it is why I am here today, to ask you for your support. Every letter counts. And I want to let you know that my people appreciate everything you can do. I'd like to thank Ken and Wendy and Malkolm for looking after me on the road. And I'd like to thank all of you here tonight for taking the time to come out and listen.

"Massi cho. 'Massi cho' in my language means thank you very much."

"You keep fighting for your land," says John as we load up the van after the slideshow. "In Oil City they thought that land is only valuable if there was oil under it or if it had trees you could cut down. You don't want what happened around here."

"My son's got to feed his children on our land," says Lorraine.

"Good luck," says John. "You do your part and we'll bird-dog the politicians down here. Tell your people about Oil City. I know they don't want this."

We wave goodbye to John and drive south. We pass the fast-food franchise, but we don't stop for a burger.

Lorraine Peter, Oil City, Pennsylvania

Caribou Pass

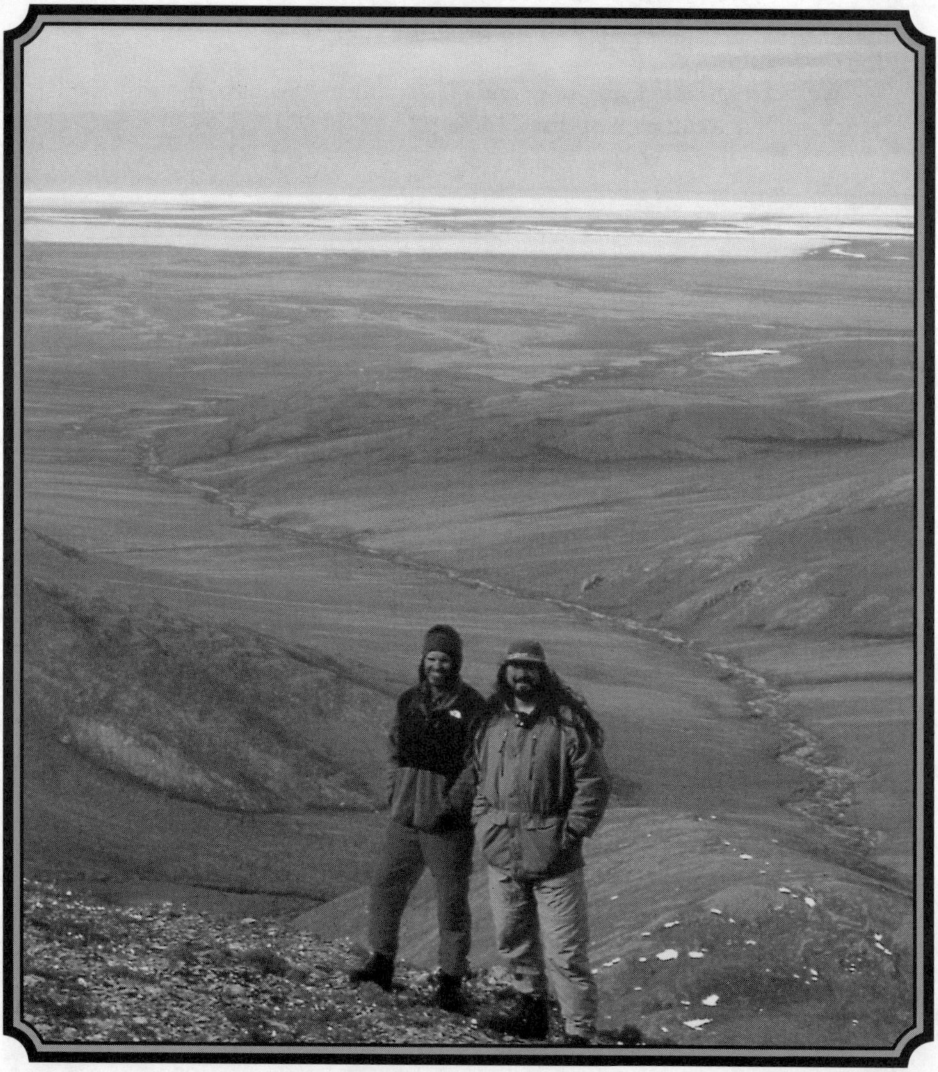

Hooves clack on water-polished stones. I wake up and groggily poke my head out of the tent. A dozen phantom caribou float through the fog and vanish in the willows. There are no clues in the dull fog-light as to how long I've slept. Could be four in the morning. Could be four in the afternoon. I wriggle down into my sleeping bag and fade back to sleep.

"Listen to that rain," says Glen when I wake up later. "It's another fine day in the Arctic desert." Glen doesn't believe a good joke is ever completely worn out.

"It's not raining as hard as it sounds," I answer, "but Don isn't going to be able to land unless the clouds lift."

Two days ago, Don Ross plucked Glen and me from our camp beside the Jago River and dropped us here at "Caribou Pass." Today he is scheduled to bring in the first installment of musicians who are working with the Caribou Commons Project. I put on my rain suit and crawl outside.

Fog curls around the willows and drifts lazily across the river. I walk down to wash my face and a mew gull rises up, screaming that the enemy is approaching. A fat ground squirrel scurries over to a food bag next to our tarp. It grabs a strap and begins to gnaw on the plastic as if it's the tough shell on a monstrous seed. I yell and toss a stick in its general direction. It dives into a Swiss-cheese network of holes under a gnarly old willow.

Forty caribou graze calmly beside a knoll that overlooks Caribou Pass, a broad valley east of the Kongakut River. The bulls are funneling through the pass now. They are several weeks behind the females, drifting northwestward at a leisurely pace. The biggest bulls browse together, surrounded by an entourage of smaller animals. It'll be a different story during the autumn rut, when raging hormones rule the bull's behavior and their antlers harden and become lethal ivory weapons.

Caribou are the only members of the deer family in which both sexes have antlers, although they grow in different rhythms. The females retain their antlers throughout the winter, shedding them during the spring migration or after they arrive in the calving grounds. Their new ones don't start to grow until later in the summer. This time of year the cow's excess energy goes toward producing milk for their calves, not toward growing antlers. The bulls, however, lose their antlers after the autumn rut and begin growing new ones in late winter. The biggest bulls in Caribou Pass already have rounded, velvet-covered antlers that curl high above their heads.

The caribou drift toward the river, and I hike up to take their place on the knoll. The tundra is a uniform green from our camp, but up close it is covered with wildflowers. The blossoms look fragile, but they are Arctic survivors, as tough as old leather boots. I find a dry patch under a rock outcrop and sit down, surrounded by magenta rhododendrons called Lapland rosebay, deep blue lupines, and forget-me-nots the color of the sky.

A solitary Arctic poppy shudders in a light breath of wind. Its lemon yellow face searches for the sun, unsuccessfully. On days that aren't thick with cloud, a poppy's teacup-shaped head acts like a parabolic reflector, catching sun-rays that bounce around inside, warming it and attracting insect pollinators. Each blossom rotates its head on its skinny stalk, following the circular march of the sun around the horizon. Since sunlight inhibits the production of growth hormone, the sunny side of the stalks grows more slowly, and the poppies grow straight and true. Despite their constant head-twisting, poppies don't get dizzy, and their stalks don't corkscrew until their heads fall off.

It's quiet on the knoll. There are a hundred caribou higher up in the pass, but they're too far away for me to hear their grunts and hoof beats. The cloud and soft rain mute the river's murmur. A dome of silence presses in around me, until it is shattered by the angry growl of an engine. Somehow Don found his way through the mist from Arctic Village. A cloud spits out the plane like a watermelon seed. It bounces to a stop on the primitive runway. Before long, a second plane pops out. Don is so busy he's hired another pilot, Dirk Nickisch, to bring in the rest of our crew.

I pull out my binoculars, and the red and blue dots grow arms and legs. Matthew Lien has his head inside a huge black Pelican case. Matthew went to school in San Diego but spent summers with his dad in the Yukon. Concrete and exhaust for ten months, beavers and bush for two. He is an exceptional musician who is passionate about the environment. Through the marvels of the global village, he has become a superstar in Taiwan, where he wears shades and stays in five-star hotels with extra security so he isn't besieged by fans. It doesn't look as if Glen is besieging him, although he does have his camera dangling around his neck.

I leave the wildflowers to their business and hike toward camp. The two airplanes are gone by the time I get there, and our campsite looks like a FutureShop warehouse. Steve Philp, who plays saxophone and flute with Matthew, is setting up his video camera. Paul Gatien, a sound man and the technical guru for our project, is fiddling with a satellite telephone. Scattered on the gravel bar are battery belts that look like diving weights, a digital tape deck, a car battery, wires, adapters, plugs, and a solar panel that's taller than I am. Richard Mostyn, a journalist for the *Yukon News*, looks like a throwback to the Stone Age with his pen and pad of paper.

"What a flight!" says Richard. "We couldn't see much except mist and shadowy mountain ridges. Then Dirk cranked up a cassette tape of Diamond Rio. There we were, hurtling through the clouds, listening to freakin' country twang on the headsets."

"Dirk's a great name for a pilot," says Steve, "like something out of a Harlequin Romance."

"He's a good guy," says Richard. "He used to be a crop duster, spreading pesticides and herbicides over the Midwest."

"He's cool," says Paul. "He's changed his ways. He's even gone to Washington, D.C., to lobby for protection of the Refuge. "

"It's 36 degrees in the Arctic desert," says Glen. "If you want help getting your tents up, let's do it now, otherwise I'm going back to my book."

The rain is now streaked with white sleet, like the first gray hairs I found on my temples last year. We pile the gear under the red tarp and dig out the tents. I've never liked putting up a tent in the rain, watching the tent sponge up water like a dish rag, knowing that you'll be spreading a dry sleeping bag on a wet floor. It isn't so bad, though, when it's someone else's tent.

"We flew over a musk ox about a half a mile upstream," says Richard. "I wonder if it could hear Diamond Rio blasting out of the sky?"

"The pole goes through that sleeve," says Glen dryly.

"Hey Matthew," yells Richard. "Could you believe that waiter at the restaurant in Fairbanks?"

"You wouldn't believe that guy," says Matthew. "Paul orders the number-one special without ham or bacon, and the waiter looks at him like he asked for roasted penguin."

"Try to keep the zipper out of the mud," says Glen. "Let's get the fly on before this tent turns into a swamp."

"What about that burger in Beaver Creek?" says Richard. "They wanted 11 bucks for a burger! Eleven bucks! Double cheese, double meat patty, bacon, and—get this—a wiener! A wiener! I couldn't believe it. Who would pay 11 bucks for a freakin' burger? Even if does have a wiener in it?"

"You guys want go for a walk?" I ask when the tents are finally up. "Maybe we can find that musk ox."

"There are a couple of things I musk do first," says Steve.

"Geez," says Paul. "I didn't come to the wilderness to listen to puns."

"All I ox is that you let me put my sleeping bag in the tent before it starts to snow."

"It's dropped to 35 degrees," says Glen. "You can have your musk ox. I'm heading for the tent."

"Any chance of something to eat?" asks Matthew. "It's been a long time since the number-one special."

"I have a bag of chips I bought in Tok," says Richard. "Freakin' four bucks for a bag of chips."

"How about some bread and cheese and a cup of coffee?" I suggest. "A freakin' cup of coffee costs five bucks in the Arctic Refuge, though."

An hour later we walk upriver and ford the creek that drains Caribou Pass. My senses quiver when I'm in the wilderness, as though I'm suddenly aware that I'm made of flesh and blood, and there are large predators with fangs and claws nearby. My hearing sharpens, and all sounds become relevant: the moan of the wind, the song of a white-crowned sparrow, the rustle of a large body in the willows. Other noises are cluttering up the airwaves today: the idle chatter of people talking because silence is uncomfortable.

"Remember that guy at U.S. Customs?" asks Richard. "I didn't think the freakin' guy was going to let us through. I thought he'd send us back to Beaver Creek for a burger."

"We were fine until we started talking about protecting caribou," says Paul. "That's when he brought out the sniffer dog."

"The caribou don't have problems at the border," says Steve, "and they're protecting themselves."

"No they aren't," says Matthew.

"Yes they are."

"No they aren't."

"Are!"

"Aren't, aren't, aren't!"

"There was a grizzly here not long ago," I say. When Matthew and Steve get going, it's best to divert their attention.

I point to a set of velvet-covered antlers and a hoof protruding forlornly from a mound of earth. Caribou fur and bones are scattered over an area the size of my living room. The sour smell of decomposing flesh rises up from the mound. I squat down and pick up a thigh bone streaked with red.

"It's a bloody scene," says Paul.

"It's bloody," says Matthew, "but somehow it isn't violent."

"Who do you think killed it?" asks Steve.

"It was a grizzly that raked up all this soil and buried the carcass," I say. "Either it surprised the caribou in the willows, or wolves killed the caribou and the bear chased them away. There isn't much meat left here, but bears often bed down near a kill. Let's clear out of these willows."

Suddenly everyone is quiet. Not long ago they had both feet firmly planted in civilization. They were rattling with engine vibration, thinking about burgers and customs agents, wired to Diamond Rio. A couple of minutes ago they were like swimmers testing a lake with their toes, not sure whether to stay on shore or dive in. Suddenly they know that they have no choice. They are up to their necks in the wilderness.

We climb to the top of a hill and look upriver. No musk oxen in sight, although a dozen caribou are swimming across the river. I hear the harsh croak of a northern shrike. Rain drums on my hood. We turn around and hike back to camp. It is too wet and cold to cook, so we eat brownies and dried fruit.

After everyone else retreats to their tents, I putter around outside, making sure everything is safe and dry under the tarp. I see movement out of the corner of my eye and look up on the hillside. A pair of wolves trots toward the knoll. The black one is clearly etched against the tundra. The gray one looks like patch of mist. They stand and look out over Caribou Pass for a moment, then disappear over the hill. I head for my sleeping bag.

The chatter of rain on the tent lulls me to sleep. When I wake up later its patter is gone, but the tent sags ominously. I reach up and push at the nylon above my head. A mini-avalanche hisses against the fly.

"What are you doing?" asks Glen, sitting up.

"This is a three-season tent, right?"

"Yes."

"Well, it's winter outside. We'd better clear off the snow so it doesn't collapse on us."

Glen grabs a walking stick and rattles it around the top of the tent. Before long the tent is clear, but the snow keeps falling. We sleep for a while, clear the snow, then doze again. After a while I can't sleep anymore and I'm bored with being horizontal. I sit up and pull on my thickest long underwear.

"Could you be quiet?" says Glen. "I've only had 18 hours of sleep."

I ignore him and head out into the storm. The snow is melting as it hits the ground, although solid white walls line the edges of the tents. The Kongakut River is no longer innocent blue-green. The water is curry-colored and rising quickly. I move the kitchen to higher ground and sling the tarp between a new set of willows. I fire up the stove and make life-restoring coffee.

"Frosty the snowman was a jolly, happy soul." My singing voice is more irritating than the worst alarm clock, especially for musicians. I can carry coffee, but I can't carry a tune. I set steaming mugs outside Matthew and Steve's tent. "Anyone interested in eating?"

A hand creeps out, curls around a mug and scurries back inside. "What was that noise? Is it morning already?" asks Steve.

I squat down and sip my coffee, knowing that musicians move grudgingly when they first wake up, no matter how long they've slept. I set a pot of water on the stove and dump in a bag of noodles when it bubbles. Glen crawls out of the tent, but other than that it is quiet in the neighborhood. Thirty bull caribou are lying on the hillside, patiently, like boulders. Bedding down on snow is the norm in their lives. If there are calves being born out on the coastal plain, their first sensation after a warm, wet womb will be cold, wet snow. A rough-legged hawk flies over the river. A mew gull flies up to chase it away. I drain the noodles and stir in what's left of a jar of pesto.

"At least there are no mosquitoes," says Matthew as he unzips his tent and peers out.

"You're in luck," says Glen, looking over my shoulder. "Ken scraped out the bottom of the parrot's cage for dinner. Or is it breakfast?"

"It's what was on the menu last night before the storm spoiled the party."

As we're eating, the clouds break, and sunshine pours into the valley. The snow melts furiously. A million rivulets ripple across the tundra, swell the creeks, and pour into the rivers. The Kongakut, now a brown torrent, crawls threateningly toward our tents, then finally retreats; the floodwaters surge out toward the ocean. Wildflowers peek out, undaunted after spending a day smothered by snow.

"I hope I can get close enough to record the caribou," says Matthew, looking longingly at the bulls on the hillside.

Caribou are noisy. They bleat and croak and grunt and snort. They trot with a distinctive "clicking" as their wiry tendons slide up and down in their lower legs. Matthew hopes that a herd of caribou will stampede within range of his microphones. He wants to record environmental sounds to blend with the music inside his head.

I load my camera gear into a backpack while Matthew readies his recording equipment. He fixes a pair of microphones onto a telescopic boom, slings his digital tape recorder around his shoulder, fits headphones over his ears, and tightens a thick, heavy battery belt around his waist.

"Going scuba diving?" asks Glen. "You forgot your mask."

"Very funny," says Matthew, picking up the microphone boom.

We wander off in different directions. I head up the slope to try to photograph a willow ptarmigan perched on a tussock. It's a male with bright white feathers, shining like a beacon on the verdant hillside. He clucks complacently, as though it is still winter and his white plumage is invisible against the snow. He doesn't know it, but he is an evolutionary sacrificial lamb. Female ptarmigan molt much earlier than males. After the snow melts, they blend in perfectly with the tussocks. The glowing white males are lightning rods for the ptarmigan's chief predator, the gyrfalcon. Heaps of white feathers dot the tundra like early-blooming cottongrass.

The ptarmigan clucks, flicking its head from side to side as I approach. When I'm about 10 yards away, the tundra under my feet explodes in a flurry of feathers and a female flies away, croaking angrily. I back up a step and examine the ground, but I can't see the nest. I keep looking and finally I see them, four cream-colored, brown-speckled eggs in a shallow depression lined with dried plants. The mottled, grayish-brown female scolds me loudly, the cadence slowing at the end like a Christmas toy whose batteries are thankfully running down.

It's just as well for people of the male persuasion that the ptarmigan's "expendable-mate" evolutionary quirk doesn't apply to humans. Maybe it does, though. Just think about teenage boys in fast cars, men with snowmobiles and bottles of Wild Turkey, and the preponderance of men shooting and dropping bombs on each other around the world.

I leave the ptarmigan to their nest and hike onto the ridges surrounding Caribou Pass. It's a perfect spring day in the Arctic Refuge, calm and 50 degrees, which seems hot in the intense sunshine. Groups of caribou flow through the pass like a river. They occasionally eddy and drift upstream, but they always rejoin the main current and stream inexorably toward the coastal plain. A short-eared owl flaps over the creek and drops silently onto a vole. Lapland longspurs, tiny tundra troubadours, fly up from tussocks and float slowly down to earth, singing their liquid breeding song. A few hundred yards away, four golden lumps sprawl on a meadow: a sow grizzly with three small cubs. I backtrack and hike back toward the braided river, 2,000 vertical feet below. It glitters with veins of gold in the late evening light.

Glen is the only one in camp when I return. I cook dinner and leave the pot of macaroni and cheese to congeal for the latecomers. I crawl into my sleeping bag and am almost asleep when Matthew yells, "Ken, you have to come and look at this."

I crawl outside and throw on my boots. A bull moose lumbers over the Kongakut's shallow braids and swims across the deepest channel. It stops on a gravel bar and shakes like a huge Labrador retriever. Flying water droplets glitter in the midnight sun. Then it walks toward us. Stops, stares. Moves one step at a time on legs that look too thin to support its battleship body. Unlike the caribou who float gracefully over the tundra, moose are solid and of the earth. He approaches to within 50 yards of camp, then turns and crashes into the willows.

In the morning the holiday is over. It's time for our interviews.

Matthew and Steve's six-person circus tent is the nerve center of our communications empire. The satellite phone looks like a laptop computer and sits on Matthew's briefcase. The lid doubles as an antenna and points toward invisible satellites floating over the mountains. Wires lead to the car battery. More wires spaghetti out of the tent door to the solar panel. Steve's digital video camera and Matthew's recording gear line the edges of the tent. Their sleeping bags look like afterthoughts.

During the winter the satellite phone sounded like a good idea. The point of our project is to draw attention to the threats to the Arctic Refuge, and so we've hyped our plans to the media. We've invited the living rooms of North America into the living room of the caribou. We've wired the wilderness and, in the process, transformed it into something else. I accept that we should do it, but I don't have to like it.

We warm up with CKRW-Radio Whitehorse, the *Whitehorse Star*, and CBC Inuvik. Then it is time for *As It Happens*, CBC National Radio. My voice, live from the Arctic Refuge, beamed across Canada, to member stations in the United States, and around the world on shortwave. This is my chance to jumpstart our publicity. Steve dials up Toronto, chats to a producer, and hands me the telephone. I hear a couple of beeps, a faint hum, and then Mary-Lou Findlay's familiar voice. Her words, beamed through the atmosphere and bounced off a satellite, sound flat and tinny. Matthew and Steve stare at me expectantly from other side of the tent.

"Come September," she says, "Ken Madsen will be wowing people when he describes how he spent his summer vacation. For four months, he will be traveling with the Porcupine caribou herd across the Arctic wilderness. The herd of 150,000 caribou travels thousands of miles every summer. Mr. Madsen and his companions will journey from the Arctic National Wildlife Refuge in Alaska to Old Crow in the Yukon. They will cross daunting wilderness on foot, by sea kayak, and by canoe. We reach Ken

Madsen by satellite telephone in the Arctic National Wildlife Refuge in northeastern Alaska."

The interview starts slowly. Mary-Lou asks where I am, what the conditions are like, whether I'm surrounded by caribou. At my best, I am a mediocre interviewee. Today I am not at my best. Words that I don't say in normal conversation jump to my tongue unbidden, words like "literally" and "actually" and "interesting." Not just "interesting," but "*really* interesting." I "*um*." Sentences charge out of my mouth like unruly dogs. Once they are off the leash, they go where they want, out of my control. Frankly, I'm lousy—but at least I don't say "frankly."

"Can you go where the caribou go?" asks Mary-Lou.

"Well, I'm not strictly following the caribou, because that would be impossible to do. What's really interesting, just watching the caribou, the calves when they are first born, they have to try to stand up really quickly because you never know when a predator is going to be around. They literally have to be moving within half an hour, and within two hours of birth there is absolutely no way you could catch them on the ground . . ."

I ramble on for several more minutes in this vein until I see Matthew waving his arms at me, like a grease monkey in the pit signaling a race-car driver to pull over. I switch to the story of the grizzly that charged into the group of cows and calves near the Jago River. I describe the bear sprinting away and the mother returning to find her calf.

"The bear ran away from you?" asks Mary-Lou.

"Yes. The bear caught my scent. We've run into ten grizzly bears in the ten days we've been here, and every one of them has done what wild bears usually do, which is to take off. They have an instinctive fear of people."

"Unless they eat you!"

Now I've done it. I want my words to paint a picture of a land with natural predator-prey relationships, a rare jewel in our industrialized world. I want listeners to understand the age-old relationship between the caribou and the Gwich'in. I want to talk about how oil development would forever change this wilderness. Somehow though, I've blundered into the quicksand of a discussion about how frightening it is to be in grizzly territory. I try to get my foot out of the quagmire by explaining that I'm not worried about being eaten. And that we are not armed. And that the land of the grizzly is not a guerrilla war zone.

"You're going to be out there for a few months?" she asks. "Maybe we can call you again and check in with you a little bit later?"

"Shit!" I think in a panic. "She's about to end the interview! I haven't talked about the musical side of the project. I haven't told her about Matthew's creative genius and his digital recording project. I haven't even mentioned the other musicians working on the project. They'll kill me."

"One thing I should mention is what we are trying to do." I launch into a last-ditch effort to highlight the Caribou Commons Project. "A group of musicians are traveling with me, including Matthew Lien, who is sitting in the tent here with me. He is an incredible composer...and he's recording the sounds of the land and the sounds of the caribou...and we'll put together this live concert which we are planning on touring across North America...and we're hoping that we'll convince people across the continent that this area is too wonderful to be tampered with."

"OK," says Mary-Lou. "Thank you very much. Take care, now."

"Let me out of this tent," I say. "I'd rather face a dozen grizzlies than another interview."

"You did fine," says Steve, who is always charitable.

I squirm over the wires and out of the tent while Matthew and Steve shut down the satellite phone. Now that the confounded interviews are finished, we can go hiking. Glen packs up our tent. I stuff my sleeping bag and four days' supply of food into my backpack. A ground squirrel watches in disappointment. We hoist the packs and start walking. *As It Happens* is a distant memory by the time I'm halfway up the first hill. We trudge under our heavy backpacks, gasping and soaked in sweat.

A flash of color hovers above a patch of wildflowers. At first I think it's a hummingbird, but they don't migrate anywhere near the Arctic. I walk closer and see that it's a sphinx moth. The last one I saw was 35 years ago, 32 degrees to the south, 3,000 miles as the moth flies. It makes me think about my father and about how the way we value wild creatures has changed over the years.

My dad was an entomologist at the University of California. He loved butterflies, but it was a possessive love. They weren't just quicksilver patches of rainbow; they were trophies. He traded butterflies with collectors around the globe. He studied catalogues that listed rare ones at $40 or $50, which seemed like a fortune to me. He taught me to capture a butterfly with a swish of a net and a flick of the wrist. He showed me how to squeeze its abdomen gently until it stopped struggling. He taught me to spread butterfly wings on a Styrofoam mat and pin them firmly in place. When rigor mortis set in, I hung them on the wall in glass mounts with black frames. I spent countless afternoons down by Walnut Creek chasing monarchs and elusive black swallowtails.

On warm spring nights, my dad would hang blue fluorescent light bulbs to tree branches and sling cyanide bottles underneath. In the morning, the bottom of the jar would be a mound of dead beetles and moths. The sphinx moths were by far the biggest, the size of hummingbirds. The outside of their wings were drab brown, but when you pinned the wings back, the insides were inset with hot pink flashes. The sphinx moth in front of me is very much alive, a flicker above a scarlet patch of moss campion blossoms. Its wings are a blur as it hovers, sucking life from the blossoms and giving it back. Then it is gone. I take another step forward, my heavy pack digging into my shoulders.

Late in the afternoon we straggle to the top of the pass. We drop our leaden packs. It feels as if we're floating as we walk up a ridge to a high point overlooking the coastal plain. The sea is still frozen. There's nothing but ice from here to Siberia. A golden eagle rips past, trying to get away from a bullet-shaped peregrine falcon that is dive-bombing it. I sit on a boulder while my friends wander along the ridge.

The coastal plain is too far away for me to see movement, but I know there are migratory animals out there: polar bears shambling out on the ice to hunt seals, red-throated loons circling to land on newly-melted tundra ponds, bowhead and beluga whales swimming toward the Mackenzie Delta from the Bering Sea, Arctic char and wolves and tundra swans. If all of the migratory species that come to the Arctic Refuge left a trail, the land would be covered by interlocking lines, great curving paths radiating in all directions. One species, though, does leave evidence of its travels.

The foothills below me are scored by caribou trails. In the low-angle sunlight, the intricate pattern of the paths is shadowed in bold relief. The last time I'd spoken to my friend Norma Kassi, she had told me about the trails. "They look like the wrinkles on an elder's face," she said, "like the smile lines on Grandma's face."

The Arctic Refuge was not covered by glaciers during the last ice age. The mountains have been sculpted by wind, rain, and snow. And by the footsteps of the caribou. A hundred thousand years of hooves cutting through a dense mat of vegetation and roots. The caribou are a biological force; their bodies shape a vast ecosystem. They are a geological force; their hooves shape the ridges that we are hiking on. They are a spiritual force; their migration shapes the Gwich'in culture.

"I forgot to tell you," says Steve, coming up behind me. "You have an interview with the *Washington Post* tomorrow morning. I've got the satellite phone in my backpack."

"Yeah, right. It's a good thing I know you don't have enough room for the damned thing."

We scramble down to the pass where we dropped our packs. No one mentions the price of potato chips along the Alaska Highway. Steve and Richard follow a caribou trail down the steep slope toward the coastal plain. Glen, Paul, and I take a last look over the frozen ocean and hoist our packs. Matthew appears over the ridge, in no hurry.

Every step carries us farther from the satellite phone, which is fine with me.

Radio Key Largo

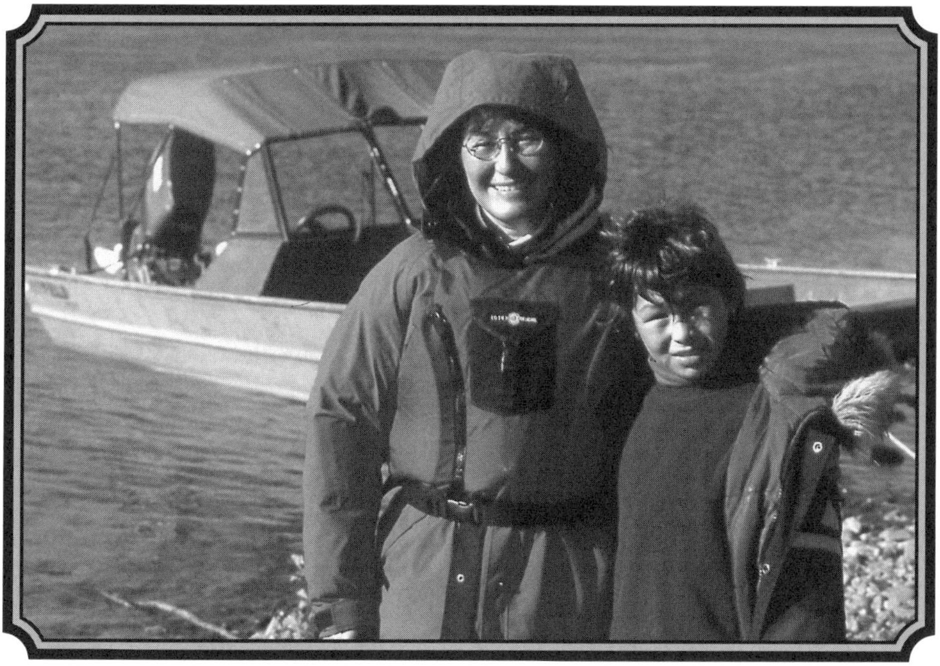

"This is JD, and you're listening to SUN 101. Big Richard and I are coming at you from the deck at Snapper's Restaurant in Key Largo."

JD pauses and pulls at a Budweiser long neck. He's dressed in Key Largo casual: Bermuda shorts, a green polo shirt, and a ball cap that says "The Extenders—Big Dick." Big Richard has on a chartreuse Hawaiian shirt and a toothy grin. JD doesn't tell us if the Big Dick on his hat is in honor of Big Richard.

"This is Turtle Club Radio," drawls JD. "Don't forget, Snapper's gives a 20 percent discount for card-carrying turtles!"

The salt breeze carries the sour tang of the tropics—decaying plants, fish guts, and rotting garbage. Listening to JD is as informative as sitting down with a vacuum cleaner, but his AM-radio patter doesn't entirely drown out the background tinkle of glasses from Snapper's—and the rapid footsteps of Norma Kassi's 8-year-old son, Yudii. Yudii doesn't walk; he darts, like the quick little geckoes scrabbling along the deck.

Yudii is a Gwich'in word that means the Big Dipper. In ancient times, this most familiar constellation was known as Ursa Major, the Great Bear. The cold lands of the North were understood to lie below Yudii's constellation. The Greeks called the North *Arcticos*, the land of the Great Bear. It's a good thing the Greeks didn't live in Key Largo. When I look to the north I can't see many stars; the Big Dipper is bleached by the bright haze of Miami's light pollution.

"Look, Mom!" Yudii says urgently. "Mom, look! There are huge fish over there by the dock."

"Shhh, Yudii," says Norma. "We're about to do an interview."

Yudii is gone by the time the words leave her lips. He is over at the dock, splayed out on the edge next to Malkolm, staring down at a school of tarpon. The fish are shadowy, like big torpedoes hanging in the pool of yellow light below a lamppost. Some of them are bigger than Yudii. The boys have been getting an eclectic education here in Florida. Earlier in the day, we had watched hotel workers illegally attracting manatees by spraying fresh water into the sea. In order to reach the fresh water that they loved to drink, the manatees had to swim through dangerous waters thick with zooming high-speed boats and sea-doos.

Malkolm and Yudii had heard that many manatees were killed in collisions with boats. One manatee we saw floating near the dock had deep propeller scars on its back. The boys dragged me along on a protest visit to the hotel manager. They had a secret plan to set up pickets outside the hotel, but the manager squelched that idea. He told them that they were the first people to ever complain and promised that he would stop his workers from baiting manatees.

"OK," says JD, "This is going to be a big change from our last guest. Big Richard and I aren't talking music festivals and partying anymore, we're talking caribou and icebergs. Norma Kassi and Ken Madsen have come way down from the North to talk to people about the Arctic National Wildlife Refuge. They did a slideshow last night at the Key Largo State Park, and on Saturday they'll be at the Natural History Museum in Miami. Ken, tell us why the folks of South Florida should care about caribou."

"Sure, JD," I say. "The coastal plain of the Arctic Refuge is known as America's Serengeti. This area is the calving grounds for the Porcupine caribou herd, and Norma will tell you how critical the caribou are for the Gwich'in. The coastal plain is much more than caribou, though..."

I'm not sure how long the interview will last, so I spew facts randomly onto the airwaves. I explain why biologists agree that the coastal plain is critical habitat for caribou. I talk about polar bears, bowhead whales, and migratory birds. I prattle about Prudhoe Bay, Washington, D.C., and Arctic Village. I drone on about air pollution, loss of wildlife habitat, and oil spills.

"We know all about the oil industry down here in south Florida," interrupts JD finally.

My mouth is still open. I look like one of the tarpon below the dock, or the stuffed grouper in the restaurant, or Big Richard, who appears to be asleep with his eyes open.

"We've had our own battles to stop oil development along Florida's coast. Senator Bob Graham was governor when Florida said 'no' to offshore oil development. I'm surprised he isn't supporting wilderness legislation for the Arctic Refuge."

"That's why we're here," says Norma. "The calving grounds are in our lands, but it is your politicians who will make the final decision."

"OK," says JD briskly. "Let's shower Senator Graham with letters about the Arctic Refuge. *Let it rain, let it rain, let it rain.* It'll help if you tell the senator you're a card-carrying turtle. Norma, tell us why caribou are important for the Gwich'in."

"Back in 1988 we had a historic gathering of our nation, the first time we had come together since anyone could remember. The elders chose me and a few others to travel south to tell the outside world how important the caribou are to us."

"Wow," says JD, "you've been at this a long time! What is the message that you bring from the North?"

"At our slideshows," says Norma, "I tell people what it was like to grow up on the land. In the spring, the people from my village would hitch up their dog teams and mush out to Old Crow Flats . . ." She tells about the excitement of waiting for the herd, and the celebration and cultural renewal when the caribou arrived.

"I can understand why you want to protect your Arctic home," says JD. "South Florida used to be clean and healthy. Now it's nothing like it used to be."

He's right. Sixteen million people are already jammed into Florida, not counting the illegals and tourists, and more pour in every day. They suck back millions of gallons of water and urbanize hundreds of thousands of acres of rural land every year. The Everglades are drying and dying because water is being shunted away along its northern border. You can't eat the fish because of high mercury levels. Florida panthers, American crocodiles, manatees, and wood storks are on the brink of extinction.

"Maybe you'd get people's attention if you were trying to sell the Arctic Refuge to the Disney Corporation," continues JD. "You could name it SerengetiAmerica."

Yudii is suddenly beside Norma, leaning against her side. I didn't see him come over. He materialized like Norma's voice in homes from the Florida Keys and up through Miami. Norma talks about the natural world and an ancient culture living close to the land. It's a way of life as far from DisneyWorld, Universal Studios, Wet'nWild, Sea World, and Pleasure Island as you can get.

"A long shadow hangs over our lives," says Norma. "Oil development threatens the caribou and our way of life. The elders tell us that a day is going to come when the transport trucks will stop rumbling up the Alaska Highway and the planes will stop landing in Old Crow with processed food."

"I guess you don't drive to the mall to get your groceries," says JD.

"The tundra and the forest are *our* grocery stores," says Norma. "The caribou move through our villages in an endless circle of life."

"Driving to Safeway and back is kind of a circle," says JD, "but I guess it's not the same."

Hiking Through a Nursery

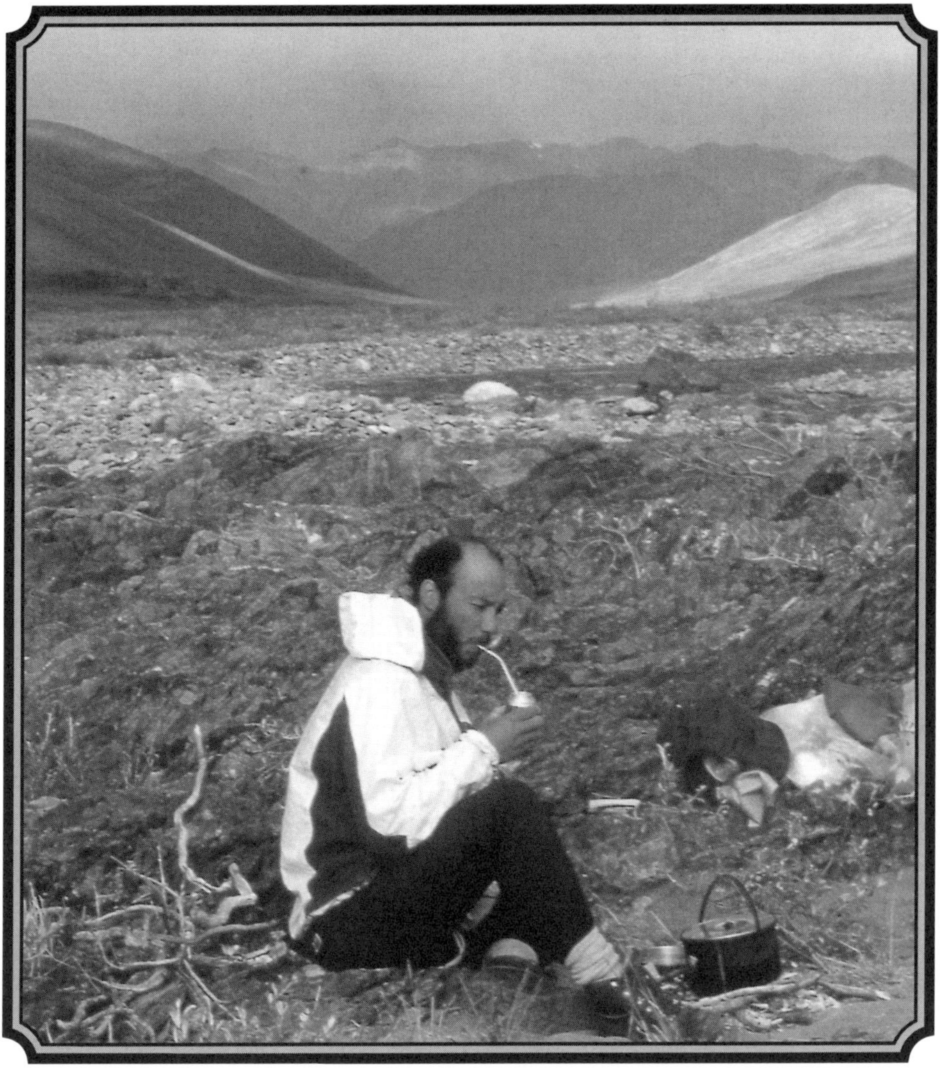

"See you on the Firth in a few weeks," I say as Matthew and Steve squeeze into the plane.

"You'll see us on the second, not the Firth," says Steve looking at his watch. "That's exactly 18 days."

"Wow, you aren't even on the plane yet, and you are already back on a schedule."

Matthew and Steve roar off with Don Ross toward Arctic Village. They are taking a circuitous route to the Firth River. They'll fly from Arctic Village to Fairbanks and drive back to Whitehorse. Then they'll jet to Ottawa, where they have a gig to play music for Prime Minister Chrétien at the Canada Day music festival. Finally they fly to Inuvik, Northwest Territories, and into the Firth. Glen is already down in Arctic Village, ready to fly back to Toronto. He'll languish in the Ontario humidity for a couple of weeks before he, too, will join us on the Firth.

My logistics are simpler. I'm walking, along with my wife, Wendy, and two friends, Alex Frid and Joyce Majiski. They flew in with Don when he landed yesterday to pluck Glen out of the wilderness. We load up our backpacks while Paul and Richard pack up their tent to get ready for Dirk and the last shuttle flight back to civilization.

"I hope he has something other than Diamond Rio," says Richard.

The first mosquitoes of the season hover lazily in the sunshine. They are big and dopey and easy to evade. Several dozen bull caribou circle around the commotion at the airstrip and swim across the Kongakut just upstream. A pair of ground squirrels burrow into Paul and Richard's food bag, which is temporarily unguarded.

"We aren't going hungry on this hike," says Alex, watching the squirrels with a predatory eye. Alex is a biologist who loves foraging from the land. It's partly a hobby, partly a spiritual quest, partly a way to stuff more food into his lean body. Back home he collects wild herbs for tea, edible plants for salad, and fresh road kill from the Alaska Highway for barbecues.

We shoulder our loads and hike north through the mountains. Three days later, we reach the Arctic Ocean. It is June 21, the summer solstice, and the sea should still be frozen. In this era of climate change, however, the ice has already withdrawn over the horizon, except for a 100-yard strip of icebergs jammed against the shore. A chill wind whips up steep waves that splinter and pulverize what's left of the ice. The pressure of the surf has bulldozed the nearest bergs out of the ocean and onto the tundra. Chunks of ice the size of transport trucks sprawl on the shore. We hike east along the beach, past an Arctic fox den, a short-eared owl's nest, and the U.S.-Canada border.

We find semi-level tent spots in the tussocks and haul our food to the kitchen down by the beach. Joyce lights a small cooking fire in the lee of a big, sun-bleached log. There isn't a live tree in sight, but driftwood litters the beach. The wood has come a long way. The bigger chunks grew tall in the relatively mild climes of northern British Columbia or Alberta, toppled into a stream, and floated 1,000 miles down the Mackenzie River system.

A pair of long-tailed ducks swims through the ice chunks, relentlessly yelling their breeding calls. They sound like Swiss yodelers with nasty colds. My Gwich'in and Inuvialuit friends call them *uh-un-lak*, which, coming from aboriginal lips, sounds just like their quavering call. The male is dark brown with a bronzed back, a white splotch over his eye, and a long pointed tail. He is courting a brown female with a short tail. A second male flutters over an iceberg, but three's a crowd, and he is as welcome as Senator Jesse Helms at a cocktail party in Havana. The first male Hovercrafts over the water toward the intruder, his wings frothing the surface. The two males disappear behind an iceberg in a flurry of outraged squawks and flying salt spray.

"Try this coltsfoot," says Alex, "it's awesome." While I've been watching the ducks, Alex has been foraging. He pulls a frying pan off the fire and stirs it with a wooden spoon. "Coltsfoot sautéed in olive oil with a dash of Parmesan cheese!"

Alex was born in Mexico City and still speaks with a Spanish accent. He is wearing black hiking pants, a woven South American vest, and a conical woolen hat. With his deeply tanned face, he looks as if he's washed up on a beach in Baja, not on the shores of the Arctic. He shovels half a dozen thick stalks into my bowl, each with four white blossoms radiating from its central stalk. I poke it doubtfully with my spoon, but it has a crunchy texture and fresh taste that had been missing during several weeks of dried food.

"It tastes just like asparagus," says Joyce. "Now it's time for the main course."

The wind blows the smoke into a thin white thread that vanishes before it reaches the tundra. Joyce kneels in the sand and stirs a pot of reconstituted dried tuna, potato flakes, peas, grated cheese, and spices. She dribbles olive oil into the frying pan, squishes a handful of the tuna mixture between her palms, and flops it into the pan. As the oil hisses and spatters in protest, we hear an otherworldly squawk.

"What is that?" asks Wendy. "It sounds like an archaeopteryx."

"How do you know what an archaeopteryx sounds like?" asks Alex.

"Sandhill crane," says Joyce nonchalantly, flipping a tuna cake. If Joyce were a bird she'd be a crane. She is long and thin and usually flies south for the winter. Like many Northerners, she migrates between career choices. She's sometimes a wildlife biologist, sometimes a wilderness guide, always an artist.

I grab my camera and hike up the creek that dribbles through our camp. A pair of cranes dances beside a pond in the midst of a courtship display. One spears a freeze-dried seedpod with its beak and tosses it into the air. They lift their heads and leap up with outstretched wings and a raucous bugling cry. The last cranes I saw were beside the Platte River in Nebraska, near I-80 and the 18-wheelers rolling endlessly on the treadmill between Denver and Chicago. If a crane gets flattened by a truck, the Arctic ecosystem feels the impact, like a storm out in the Pacific spawning waves that break on a beach thousands of miles away.

I see a bleached white skull on the tundra, sharp little Arctic fox's teeth grinning from a cobalt-blue patch of forget-me-nots. The skull is surprisingly small, not much longer than my index finger. Yesterday we saw two foxes shambling across the tundra with a curious lope. In the winter they are pure white and make their living by following polar bears, scavenging scraps of seal meat on the ice. This time of year they raid birds' nests and pounce on lemmings and voles. In their brown and white summer coats, they remind me of skinny raccoons.

"Your tuna cake is ready," yells Joyce.

As I walk back, a whimbrel with an improbably drooping beak springs up, spreads its wings, and flies toward the coast. I stroll into camp to see Wendy and Alex hovering around the frying pan like vultures. They have already inhaled their first tuna cakes and are hoping for more. It hasn't taken our appetites long to figure out that we are burning more calories than we are eating.

"Today is the solstice," I say through a mouthful. "At the Arctic Circle, the sun would be right on the horizon at midnight. We're three degrees north of the Arctic Circle, so the sun should be three degrees above the horizon at its low point."

"Maybe," says Wendy, doubtfully.

"Don't ask me," says Alex. "I'm a biologist, not an astronomer."

"I'm going to get up at midnight to check. Except we have to add an hour for daylight saving time."

"It doesn't matter anyway," says Wendy dryly. "We don't have a watch."

In the night, the wind rises in sharp moaning gusts. If we were in Washington, D.C., Budweiser cans would be pinging down the gutters and plastic Starbucks lids skittering across Pennsylvania Avenue. Up here, Arctic poppies lie flattened on the tundra, and our tent balloons inward. We huddle in our sleeping bags, which are zipped together for various reasons. When I think it must be the middle of the night, I crawl out of the tent, naked except for a compass. The wind whips the heat from my skin, raising instant goose bumps. I take a bearing on the sun, which is at 358 degrees. I hold my arm outstretched to see how many fingers' widths the sun is from the horizon, an amateur astronomer's rude calculation of angle.

"The sun is almost due north," I say as I crawl back in the tent, "and its still three fingers above the horizon. That's five degrees, right?"

"Keep away from me," says Wendy. "Your feet are icebergs."

"If you loved me you'd let me put my feet on your stomach."

"I wouldn't follow that thought any further if I were you," she says. "I'm going to sleep."

In the morning I choke down my allotment of granola, a whopping half a mugful. At least the granola gives the illusion of fullness as it hits the acidic stew in my stomach: strong coffee gurgling with lumpy powdered milk and brown sugar. My digestive system fizzes and pops like a high-school science experiment with potassium and water. I'm ready for my first judo match of the day with my backpack.

The pack glowers at me from the tundra, 90 pounds of trouble. It's as heavy as a bad conscience. I breathe deeply, like a Russian weightlifter. I grab the shoulder straps and jerk the pack to my bended knee. I contort my arms through the straps, hoist the monster onto my shoulders, and secure the waist-belt. My body feels brittle. One misstep and I'll be writhing on the ground with a sprained ankle. We weave through the tussocky labyrinth of wetlands that hug the coast, steering for the Clarence River where we hope there is firmer footing.

Arctic terns fly jerkily over a pair of lakes, dipping down to snap up small fish in their dagger-sharp beaks. A pair of tundra swans standing on shore turns their graceful necks and stares at us. When we approach, they slip into the water and sail away like tall ships with a following wind. Red-necked phalaropes poke among the aquatic plants for insects. They look like sandpipers but float like ducks.

Only 11 species of birds live year-round in the Arctic Refuge, birds such as snowy owls, gyrfalcons, and ptarmigan. The other 170-odd species that have been seen here are, like us, migrants. They come from every continent and all 50 U.S. states. Unlike us, they don't come to the coastal plain to thumb their beaks at British Petroleum, Exxon, and Alaskan politicians. They migrate great distances to get here, like the caribou, because nothing is more important to a species than reproductive success.

"It's time for Smart Ask, the trivia game for backpackers," I say cheerily. "Today's category is Arctic Refuge history. For ten points, who said this? 'Running a pipeline across the coastal plain of the Arctic Refuge would be like running a razor blade across the Mona Lisa.'"

"Buzz!" yells Wendy. "Robert Redford?"

"Wrong! It was Senator Ted Stevens of Alaska. How about this one? 'Perhaps Senator Moss of Utah put it best when he said, "I cannot get overly upset about the ritual mating season for Alaskan caribou when in the city of Denver last weekend it was impossible to find gas".'"

"Ronald Reagan!"

"George W. Bush!"

"Attila the Hun?"

"Wrong, that was Ted Stevens again, swaying in the political wind. Consistency is not his strong point."

We trudge through the tussocks until we reach the level gravel bars beside the Clarence River. A semipalmated plover shrieks a warning, *too-li, too-li.* Its mate suddenly flies up from under my feet. I step back so I don't crush four brown-flecked eggs on the gravel, their narrow ends pointing inward like the petals of a rock jasmine. The plover writhes on the ground in front of me as if a caribou just stepped on her, crushing her wing. I acknowledge her Oscar-winning performance and follow as she leads me away. When I'm well away from her nest, her wing miraculously heals, and she launches into the wind.

The Gwich'in call the coastal plain a birthing ground, and not just for caribou. We're hiking through a nursery for hundreds of animal species. This is the season when the coastal plain lives up to its nickname as "America's Serengeti." And so it is *not* the time of year when Alaska's federal politicians invite fellow senators and representatives to inspect the Arctic Refuge. They come during the winter, when there is no danger of seeing a caribou calf, swans, or wildflowers. They come in military aircraft, knowing that speed and altitude turn mountains, rivers, and plains into a toylike wilderness. The politicians hurtle over the snowy tundra and on to Prudhoe Bay for much-needed wining and dining. What harm could a few little pipelines do that frozen wasteland?

With their enormous packs dwarfing their thin legs, Wendy, Joyce, and Alex look like hermit crabs scuttling through meadows that are thick with flowers whipping in the wind: lupines, poppies, oxytrope, vetch, and hedysarum. When we stop for lunch, Joyce and Alex sit down in the blossoms and thumb through a well-worn plant book. Wendy often joins their quest for botanical knowledge, but today she nestles into the wind shelter of her pack and falls asleep.

"There's more qiviuq here," says Alex, pointing to a willow that is sprouting gray, white, and brown cotton candy.

For most of the year, musk oxen are swathed in a thick layer of *qiviuq*, the best insulating wool in the world. They are the only mammals that regularly remain above snow level on the coastal plain in the winter, facing blizzards with equanimity. In the early summer, musk oxen shed their qiviuq parkas. When a herd lumbers through the willows, the gnarled branches strip the wool from their hides like sheep-shears. We've been following a qiviuq trail for days. We've been plucking it from the willows and stuffing it in our pockets to spin and knit in the winter. I hold a chunk against my thumb and feel an instant glow of warmth.

"We're bound to catch up to them sometime soon," says Alex. "It even smells musky here."

He's right. Before long we see them on the other side of the river, the wind rippling their dark guard hairs like a nun's habit. They range in color from midnight black (not Arctic summer midnight) to chocolate with blond waves. The calves look like short-legged tapirs without the snout.

"Have a look through the scope," says Alex. "I count 30 of them, including six calves."

A long-tailed jaeger swoops over us as we set up camp. The mountains are clear and bright, but the coast shimmers in an arctic mirage. I anchor our tent to stout willows while Wendy prepares dinner. She pours a water-bottle full of rehydrating vegetables into a pot and simmers it with dried *gado-gado* (spicy Thai peanut sauce). My share, even with a dollop of rice, looks pathetically small after a day of hiking.

"This gado-gado tastes great," says Alex, diligently scraping his bowl for the last grain of rice.

"It's goodo-goodo," adds Joyce.

"This evening light is perfect," I say when further licking of my bowl is futile. "I'm going to take some pictures of the musk oxen."

The others join me. I take off my boots and put on sandals to ford the river. The water is like liquid ice, and after a few seconds it burns like liquid fire. I splash across to the other side and sit on a sun-warmed rock. I rub my feet until the feeling returns and put my boots back on. The musk oxen graze placidly. If they were caribou, they'd be over the horizon by now. A bull peers toward us, like a nearsighted old man.

I snap my camera to my tripod and walk a little closer to the musk oxen. Joyce, Wendy and Alex stay back in the willows. Suddenly, as if I've stepped across an infrared sensor, the musk oxen stampede in frenzied circles. A cloud of dust glows yellow in the evening light and billows toward the mountains. In seconds, the herd is bunched in a tight ring, the calves in the center, the adults facing outward, their lethal horns lowered menacingly.

"I can't believe how fast they are," I whisper.

"That's defensive posture number one," says Joyce.

Musk oxen have survived since the Pleistocene Age. Twenty thousand years ago, in their bristly defensive circles they warded off scimitar cats and short-faced bears. Ten thousand years ago, they warded off wolves, grizzlies, polar bears, and stone-age hunters. During the past couple of centuries, however, musk oxen have discovered that defensive circles don't work so well against bullets. Musk oxen were slaughtered by "sportsmen," by zookeepers trying to capture calves, and by native hunters who bartered the meat with whalers and traders.

In Alaska, expanding Inupiat populations with shiny new weapons played a large role in the demise of the musk oxen. By the end of the nineteenth century, there were none left in Alaska or the Yukon. Musk oxen were reintroduced to the Arctic Refuge in 1969, and now several hundred live in the coastal plain. They have also spread eastward into the Yukon. A couple of years ago I saw a lone bull beside the Peel River, well south of the Arctic Circle.

"I wouldn't get any closer," says Joyce. "You don't want to see defensive posture number two. That's when they charge."

I snap a few more photos, then we retreat across the river. When we reach the tents the herd stampedes again. They charge in a frenzy for a few seconds, then suddenly settle down to graze peacefully again.

"They're like sheep," says Alex, who has spent the past few summers studying how Dall sheep react to airplanes and helicopters, "one gets skittish and spooks the whole crowd."

In the morning, fog shrouds the coastal plain, and the valley where the Clarence spills out of the mountains looks like the entrance to a cave. Two cow moose skirt along the edge of the coastal plain. The fog splinters, and shards of blue sky appear overhead.

"There's an ungulate up the valley," yells Alex, slipping into biologist-speak (why say animal when you can say ungulate?). He focuses his binoculars. "Sorry. It's not an ungulate. It's a grizzly."

The grizzly, a rich golden-brown, ambles across the valley and jumps onto a massive sheet of ice. The ice builds up in the winter when the river continually overflows and freezes. The "Clarence-sicle" is 10 feet thick and several miles long, with a bear on top. We wait until the grizzly climbs the ridge on the other side of the valley, then follow its route across the ice. We set up camp in a meadow near the river.

Now that we are away from the coast and sheltered by the mountains, the wind drops and the temperature rises. Mosquitoes flock to join us, like carload after carload of unwanted relatives arriving for the summer holidays. The bugs rise up from the vegetation like morning mist and begin their jerky vampire-dance. We put up our tents in record time. Wendy, Joyce, and Alex dive inside and zip up the netting. It's my turn to cook, so I put on armor: a bug-jacket with a proboscis-proof fabric and a head-net.

"Who do these mosquitoes torment when we're not around?" I yell as I light the stove, brushing mosquitoes off my hands.

"They feed off plants," yells Joyce from the safety of her tent. "They just need a blood meal to reproduce."

"But if the caribou migrate through different valleys each summer, how do mosquitoes get blood meals during the off years?"

"Maybe they feed on ground squirrels, or voles, or grizzlies," shouts Alex. "Maybe even birds. This year it's us."

Mosquitoes can "smell" tiny increases in carbon dioxide concentrations and detect small rises in temperature from miles away. When I lift the pot lid, they swarm into the rising steam. I amuse myself by counting the mosquitoes that dive-bomb into the boiling water. Thirty-six by the time the pasta is *al dente*.

"Dinner's ready," I yell, "and tonight we have plenty of protein."

The mosquitoes follow us for days as we hike up the Clarence, over a barren alpine pass, and down to the Malcolm River. It is warm and windless. We walk with our head-nets zipped tight. The fine netting keeps the bugs out but retains heat and sweat. It's like hiking in Costa Rica. My body is a sweat watershed: waterfalls pour off my face, streams bubble out of my armpits, rivers flow into my boots.

We have lunch in a mosquito fog. I don't feel like eating, but I reach for a cracker because I need some energy. I forget that I'm wearing a bug-jacket. The cracker bounces back from the netting across my open mouth. Joyce chews on a dried apricot and stretches out a bare arm. Then, pouncing like a cat, she swats her wrist.

"Sixteen with one swipe," she says proudly.

The mosquitoes drop in for dinner. They join Wendy and me for an evening walk along the Malcolm River, which is abruptly cut short by a massive grizzly digging for roots. The mosquitoes ignore the bear and follow us as we sneak back to camp. We take turns diving into the tent, zipping the netting for each other, minimizing the time the door is open. Even so, dozens of bugs sneak in. We pin them against the nylon walls and slaughter them unmercifully.

In the morning, several hundred mosquitoes are perched on the netting at each end of the tent, like vultures on a cactus waiting for something to die. Hundreds more lurk between the tent body and the fly, battering relentlessly against the fabric. It sounds like rain.

We pack up camp and hike down the Malcolm River. The high-pitched buzzing of the mosquitoes is like Chinese water torture: mildly bothersome at first, then irritating, then suddenly intolerable. They whine like tiny dentist drills, boring not into your teeth, but into your brain. I walk with my head down and my hands in my pockets, wishing that an Arctic hurricane would scour the valley. We develop a morbid fascination with the mosquitoes, and our conversation turns entomological.

"I've heard that mosquitoes have the biggest total biomass of any animal species," says Alex.

"I wonder how many mossies it takes to equal a blue whale?" asks Joyce.

"Hey Wendy, you're a doctor. If mosquitoes transmit malaria," asks Alex, "then how about AIDS?"

"I don't think they can," she replies, "but I'm not sure why."

"When they transmit disease," I ask, "do they bite an infected person, then immediately bite someone else, like junkies sharing a needle?"

"I don't think so," she says. "I'd have to look it up, but I think part of the malaria life cycle is inside the insect."

At the end of a long day of hiking we set up camp near a rapid that ends in a deep pool. It is so hot that we shuck our clothes and dive into the icy water. The mosquitoes are disoriented for a few moments when we climb out. Maybe their heat-seeking sensors are confused when our skin is super-chilled. Maybe goose bumps taste lousy. The sun dries us quickly, and the mosquitoes regain their purpose in life. We sprint for the tents.

If mosquitoes drive us crazy, what is it like for the caribou? They have not evolved bug-jackets or repellent or tents. Biologists call the caribou's reactions "annoyance responses," although I'm sure caribou would choose a stronger word.

Caribou quiver and stamp. They scratch with their antlers and their hooves. They jump and dance jerkily as if a giant, palsied hand has marionette stings attached to their vertebrae. Suddenly they start running. Caribou in a stampeding herd are sometimes injured, and a lame caribou has little chance of escaping wolves or grizzlies. Calves, exhausted by trying to keep up with their mothers, are more vulnerable to predation and may be abandoned.

A single caribou can donate a quart of blood per week at the mosquito blood-donor clinics, but mosquitoes are not the only insects that torment caribou. Nasal bot flies lay their eggs on caribou muzzles. When the larvae hatch, they journey up the nose and hang out for the winter, cloistered and warm in the sinus cavities. In the spring the caribou snort and spew the mature larvae back out into the tundra. Warble flies settle onto a caribou's hide to lay their eggs. When they hatch, the maggots squirm under the skin. They mature over the winter, then pop out like a bursting pimple and drop to the ground.

Insect-tormented caribou can be too harassed to eat. The cows, drained after giving birth and suckling their calves, are in urgent need of calories. They don't have long before the snow flies and frozen lichen replace the green summer smorgasbord. Survival during the winter depends upon feeding success during the brief summer.

The coastal plain of the Arctic Refuge plays an important role in helping the caribou avoid bugs. When the mosquitoes attack, the caribou walk or run into the wind, getting instant relief. Since the wind typically blows out of the north, it leads the caribou toward the ocean. The coast is often breezy, and when the wind drops the caribou wander onto shelves of ice where there are fewer bugs. There are also high-quality food sources along the coast.

During the mosquito season the caribou bunch up into larger and larger groups, eventually forming the great herds of summer. This isn't a case of misery loving company; the caribou in the center of a herd are bothered less by mosquitoes than those on the outer edges. The caribou usually stay on the coastal plain until early July. Then they migrate toward their summer range in the interior.

I'm groggy when I wake up in the morning. It is tough to get to sleep when the sun doesn't sink behind the mountains until midnight, and impossible to sleep in when the sun blasts into the tent at four in the morning and turns it into a sauna. There are a dozen fat red mosquitoes inside the tent, vampires who hid during last night's slaughter and crept out to suck our blood in the night. I reach up lazily to squash one. It explodes in a red blossom of hemoglobin and body parts.

A zipper whines in the distance. Probably Alex, ready for his morning fix of yerba maté. Yerba maté is a greenish herb that he discovered while he was traveling in South America. Alex swears that its mystic caffeinated jolt makes coffee seem like herbal tea. I tried to drink some down at the coast, but it tasted like an infusion of moldy alfalfa.

"I'm getting up," I shake Wendy. "Get ready to zip up the tent after I jump out."

"Hey, leave me alone. I'm sleeping in. It's Sunday."

"OK, but don't blame me if a thousand mosquitoes join you."

I pull on my clothes and bug jacket, jump out, and zip the tent up behind me. Alex is down by the river, pouring boiling water into a small metal pot that looks like a hookah pipe. He lets the yerba maté infuse for a couple of minutes, cradles the pot between his palms like a prayer, and sucks contentedly. Steam swirls around his face like hashish smoke.

"There's a little hot water left in the pot," he says. "You'll need to heat up more if you want coffee."

He squats cross-legged and closes his eyes like a mystic. Maybe he's entranced, his spirit traveling back 50,000 years, quivering to the thunder of ancient caribou hooves. Maybe he has gone back 100 million years and is cowering under the ferns, hiding from the thudding footsteps of duck-billed dinosaurs or allosauruses. Maybe he's asleep.

I walk to the river, strip down, and dive in. Instant wakefulness. I dry off in the sunshine, fill the pot, and carry it back to the kitchen. I spoon coffee into the pot and light the stove. While I'm waiting for a boil, I look up at the mountains. Nothing is moving. The brown of the rocky summits merge with the olive of low-lying willows and brighter green patches of grasses and sedges.

When the coffee is ready, I add powdered milk and brown sugar. I realize that I'm cradling my mug devoutly, just like Alex does with his yerba. Each of us is worshipping the caffeine god at our own altar. I take a sip and look back up into the alpine. The coffee must have an incredible jolt: the flank of a mountain is now alive with swarming brown dots. I put down the mug and rub my eyes, as if that will clear the spots. Caribou are swarming over the hillsides.

"Look at that!" I say to Alex.

"By the way your mouth was hanging open I thought you'd seen a bear," he says.

I yell to Wendy and Joyce. Alex snaps his scope to my tripod. The edge of the herd breaks away in a ragged stampede, swirling and eddying like smoke rising from an extinguished candle. Individually they are jumping, snorting, and flicking their tails to shake off mosquitoes. Collectively they flow over the tundra like a flock of sandpipers.

"Have a look through the scope," says Alex. "They look like bacteria in a petri dish."

"Or bees swarming over a honeycomb," says Wendy, taking her turn.

I peer through the scope, and the dots on the hillside become caribou. Several weeks ago, the bulls wanted nothing to do with the cows and their newborn calves. Now they are jammed together in a jostling mass of bodies.

"Your turn at the scope, Joyce," I say. "How many do you think there are?"

"Thousands," says Wendy.

"Who knows? Maybe 10,000?" says Alex. "Look at that! We're seeing geologic forces at work. The herd is a giant rototiller. They're churning up the hillside and fertilizing it as they go. They affect the vegetation, the hydrology, the wildlife."

"It looks like the caribou might cross the river upstream." I say. "I'm heading up there."

I toss my camera gear into my pack and run up the riverbank. The caribou trot down the slopes into a valley that is hidden from view behind a knoll. It is unnaturally quiet except for the background hum of mosquitoes. It is as though the land is holding its breath, waiting for the herd. I hike a little farther and set up my tripod in the willows. A ground squirrel races to the entrance of its hole, stands upright like a sentry, and scolds me.

"Sorry," I answer. "But if you're worried about me, you'd better keep your head down. Trouble's coming."

The last caribou trickle out of sight. The herd pools in the valley like a stream dammed by an obstruction. Maybe the caribou are reluctant to descend the open hillsides toward the river bottom, where predators could be lurking in the willows. Then four young bulls trot down to the bank, skitter back and forth beside the river, and retreat. Half a dozen more appear on the edge of a cutbank, look down at the river, then gallop along the bank to the west. I hear a clatter on my side of the river. A solitary female plunges into the shallow river, wades across, and trots up toward the massed herd.

Kwee-dle, kwee-dle, calls an American golden plover urgently. Its mate sings the same refrain from a separate tussock. The confusing stereo melody bewilders predators searching for the nest, but I'm not sure it'll deter 10,000 caribou from scrambling plover eggs. The mating pair has come a long way to find a safe nesting site. Their incredible migration to wintering grounds in South America includes a 2,500-mile, nonstop flight over the Atlantic at altitudes of 20,000 feet and speeds of 50 miles per hour. They are about to encounter the great migrants of the mammal world.

Suddenly the dam bursts, and the herd spills over the crest of the hill in a line 50 caribou wide. They stampede toward me, the bull's antlers like naked tree branches whipping in a winter wind. For a moment I panic, wondering irrationally if I'll be trampled. A willow ptarmigan flies up, squawking in protest. The caribou splash into the river and keep coming.

The lead caribou see me. They swerve, leaving a buffer of 10 yards on either side of me. I'm a rock in a flowing river of caribou, creating an eddy just big enough for me, a few willows, and the ground squirrel that is chattering indignantly. The caribou have changed since I saw them in the calving grounds. All of the females have dropped their antlers. The bull's antlers are thick and tall but still rounded and covered in velvet. The adults are shedding their winter coats, dropping bundles of hollow brown hair on the ground. Most are ragged looking, and some are entirely black. The calves are bigger, ranging in color from blond to tan to chestnut.

The ground squirrel is still chattering, but I can barely hear it above the clamor of the herd. Tendons click. Hooves drum on the ground. Caribou splash in the shallows and plunge into the deeper water beside the near shore. Bulls snort and grunt. Cows call to their calves. A butter-colored calf walks up to me. It honks like a sea lion that swallowed a mallard. Since I am not its mother, it trots back toward the river, bleating mournfully.

I look back toward camp and see Wendy, Joyce, and Alex wading through the herd. Now that the caribou are at the river, many of them are relaxing, as if it's a Sunday afternoon in Central Park. The caribou on the fringes are moving restlessly, like cars looking for parking places, but the ones around me are calm. Calves suckle. Adults lie down, browse on willows, cool off in the river.

I feel calm, too, and finally I realize why. For the first time in days, there are no mosquitoes plaguing me. No dentist's-drills around my ears. I take off my bug jacket. No stinging bites on my bare arms. I'm sharing the bugs with 10,000 other warm bodies. It's great to be part of the herd.

I have no idea how long I'm among the caribou. Three hours? Five hours? Gradually, though, they cross the river and trot southward up the slopes. Finally the last of the caribou disappear over the crest of the hills between us and the Firth River. I'm alone except for the ground squirrel, which is finally quiet. I feel as if I've just woken up from a vivid dream. Evening light pours on the willows like honey, and caribou still thunder between the synapses in my brain. I haven't eaten anything all day. I don't hear the plovers. I hope their nest survived.

Then I hear a grunt. A lone cow trots along the river, calling for her calf. I hear an answering call, and a calf stands up in the tussocks. It bleats anxiously and trots toward the cow. She sniffs its flanks. The calf tries to jam its head under the cow's hind legs to nurse, but she skitters sideways nervously. It doesn't look like a joyful reunion to me. The cow runs into the willows, the calf at her heels. I follow, since they are heading toward camp.

After a couple of minutes I hear the calf bleating again, calling for its real mother. The cow it was following must have driven it away. The calf walks along the river toward me. It halts and stares at me. Its dark eyes look resigned to its uncertain fate. Then it turns and walks slowly away, as if it doesn't have the energy to run. I follow it with my eyes until it reaches the spot where the herd crossed the river. It bleats one last time. Then it melts down into the tussocks to wait.

THE BUFFALO COMMONS

Matthew Lien and I hand our boarding cards to the flight attendant and walk onto the DC-9. The jet isn't crowded so we claim seats at the back where we can stretch out. Matthew, like every self-respecting musician, has been burning the candle at both ends. He falls asleep before we're in the air. I leaf through a *National Geographic* magazine and find an article about prairie dogs. Seems like farmers and ranchers hate the little rodents. They pay exterminators big bucks to poison them, dynamite their burrows, drown them, and flatten entire prairie dog towns with bulldozers.

"Oh, isn't that adorable," says a flight attendant, looking over my shoulder at a prairie dog pup. "They should make a Beanie Baby of that!"

"A what?"

"A Beanie Baby. I bought Pinky the flamingo and a platypus at our stopover in San Francisco last night."

"Beanie Babies aren't just cute, they're an investment!" chimes in a gray-haired woman from the row in front of us. "Last year I bought Princess Di, the Beanie Baby Bear. She's holding a tiny rose. Princess Di cost six dollars and now she's worth eighty!"

I return to National Geographic to see why the Great Plains aren't big enough for both people and prairie dogs. The gist of the article is that most ranchers and farmers believe that a just God wouldn't have made corn and cattle if He didn't intend them to take over the prairies.

"Here's coffee," says the flight attendant, "and I brought my platypus to show you. Her name is Patty."

Matthew eyes slit open at the smell of coffee. "Maybe the Beanie Baby corporation could make 'Boo' the caribou calf."

"What a cute name!" she says. "Why a caribou though?"

Matthew explains about the calving grounds and oil development. I stare out the window at a checkerboard pattern of farmlands below, wondering why people don't care about wild creatures and their habitat as much as they do about pets and plush toys. Maybe it's because wilderness just isn't cute and cuddly, no matter how many pictures of baby polar bears and seals you see. Wilderness is predators and parasites and putrefaction. It's abandoned caribou calves, wolf fangs covered with saliva, and blood-sucking insects. Wilderness is cold and wet and dirty. To top it all off, it's uncivilized.

Tyler Sutton meets us at the Omaha airport. I'd become friends with Tyler after he'd read an article I'd written about the Peel River watershed in the Northern Yukon. I was in the midst of a cross-Canada slide tour when I starting getting phone messages from Nebraska. I eventually called back, and Tyler invited me to bring my slideshow to Lincoln. The idea of bringing a Yukon wilderness slideshow to Nebraska was so bizarre that I couldn't resist.

Tyler is an attorney who, like many of the breed, specialized in raking in money. Recently, however, he had stepped off the treadmill to spend more time with his family. He also wanted to work on conservation and social issues—Like chauffeuring a couple of scruffy Yukoners searching for the soul of the prairies.

"This is the Platte River," says Tyler as we motor southwest toward Lincoln. "They say it's a mile wide and an inch deep. You Yukoners heard of the Platte River before?"

"Who cares about the Platte?" answers Matthew. "What about the Niobrara?"

Tyler had promised to take us canoeing. He had mailed me an article from *Backpacker Magazine* that said the Niobrara was one of the Lower 48's "ten best" canoeing rivers. We're looking forward to getting out and experiencing a little slice of what the prairies were like in the old days.

Tyler swings off I-80 into a sea of suburbs. Waves of single-family dwellings stretch to the horizon. The plains don't have mountains or oceans or forests, but they do have space. Even that has limits, though: ask a prairie dog. We bump over a set of railway tracks and into a belt of trees beside a creek.

"This is Wilderness Park," says Tyler dryly.

"You call this a wilderness?" splutters Matthew. "The interstate is wider."

"You need to learn how we do things here on the prairies," says Tyler, his eyes crinkling with amusement.

We drive through a subdivision with lots of big brick houses. The third little pig made a bundle as the general contractor here. We carry our packs into Tyler's house, but he doesn't give us time to relax.

"Come on," he says. "You wanted to see buffalo. Let's go see buffalo. We have some right here in Lincoln."

We drive westward through the suburbs to Pioneer Park, an oasis of playgrounds, picnic tables, and acres of lawn where kids toss footballs and frisbees. Tyler parks near a stout, 10-foot-high fence. Two yearling buffalo plod listlessly along a dirt road behind the wire. A pair of lean young men wearing overalls and baseball caps drive behind the buffalo in a dusty green pickup. One of the buffalo objects to being herded. It turns and trots toward us. A man hops out of the truck and runs behind the buffalo, waving his hat and yelling.

"Sorry," he grins at us. "We gotta move these fellows. They keep trying to escape to where they don't belong." He windmills his arms. "C'mon buddy, let's get on home."

The man in the pickup blasts the horn. The buffalo leans against the wire fence and rubs its flank. If I took one step, I could reach out and touch it. Its hide is coarse and tough, evolved for charging through thorn bushes and repelling the swat of a grizzly's claws. It stops scratching, looks back at the buffalo herder, and trots into a pasture where a dozen other docile-looking buffalo are grazing.

"Is that what people *think*?" snorts Matthew in disgust. "They've got to move the buffalo to where they *belong*? This entire land belongs to the buffalo."

"Let's go," says Tyler. "I want to show you Nine Mile Prairie. It's the largest piece of native tallgrass left in Nebraska."

Tyler drives a few hundred yards and parks outside a nature center. I walk into the middle of Nine Mile Prairie. I sit down in a patch of big bluestem and switch grass and let the warm breeze wash over me. A black beetle crawls over my shoe, drops off the laces, and climbs up a dried stalk of grass. I try to imagine what the prairie used to be like, but it is like trying to visualize the ocean by staring at a glass of saltwater. A meadowlark flutes its mating song from a fencepost, a melody that seems too liquid to float through the air. A flock of European starlings descends in a cloud of purple-black wings. The meadowlark flutters away. We get back in the car.

"Why is it called Nine Mile Prairie?" asks Matthew. "It sure isn't nine miles long or wide."

"Who knows?" answers Tyler dryly. "Maybe it's nine miles to the nearest McDonald's. It's about 250 acres. Only about one percent of the tallgrass biome is left, mostly in the Flint Hills in Kansas, but even that has been severely overgrazed. Let's get going. I have a surprise for you Arctic-lovers."

We hop in the car and drive to the University of Nebraska. I haven't been on a campus for years, and the students look impossibly young. Instead of the crop of God-fearing young Republicans I expected here in America's heartland, I see plenty of metal-studded ears, noses, and lips, and a smattering of orange, blue, and magenta hairstyles. Tyler leads us up the steps into Morrill Hall, which hosts the university's natural history museum.

"Look at that," says Tyler, pointing to a mural on the far wall. "That's the Platte River, ten thousand years ago."

It's a sunny Pleistocene spring morning. Last year's grasses are newly emerged from snow cover and gleam like tarnished gold. A snowdrift near the river hasn't melted yet. Woolly mammoths splash across the river, spooking a pair of sandhill cranes. In the distance, half a dozen caribou stand on a bluff, watching.

"I was amazed when I discovered this mural," says Tyler. "I had no idea that caribou once lived in Nebraska. Now we're going to talk to Mike Vorhees. Mike is the foremost paleontologist in Nebraska."

Mike Vorhees wears glasses with thick lenses and has a big head so he can fit in all his brains. When he talks, his magnified eyes stare into the distance, or into the past. We follow him into a back room bristling with old bones and fossils.

"Caribou haven't changed much in the last 10,000 years," he says, picking up a pair of antlers. "They filtered down to the Great Plains through the Mackenzie corridor. Back then we had a similar climate to what the Arctic has today."

"This is so cool," says Matthew, picking up an ancient musk-ox skull. "The Arctic Refuge is 3,000 miles away, but we're connected."

During the last ice age, caribou strayed as far south as the Gulf of Mexico. Musk oxen grazed on prairie grasses buried under this campus. The ancestors of the buffalo lumbered across the "land bridge," the broad grassland that formed in the Bering Strait between Alaska and Asia. Like caribou and musk oxen, the buffalo spread south. Eventually the climate warmed. The range of caribou and musk oxen, animals superbly adapted to the ice age, shrank with the melting glaciers. The buffalo stayed on the prairies.

The connections between the Great Plains and the coastal plain of the Arctic National Wildlife Refuge aren't all in the prehistoric past. Sandhill cranes still flap into the air from the shores of the Platte River, although nowadays they are flushed by transport trucks rather than woolly mammoths. The cranes migrate north, and many nest in the range of the Porcupine caribou herd. And not just cranes: white-fronted geese from Texas and red-throated loons from Minnesota and northern shrikes from South Dakota. Migratory birds connect every state in the United States and every province in Canada to the Arctic Refuge.

"Look at this," says Mike. "Mammoth tusks have daily growth rings. It is possible to tell, not only what year, but what day they died."

Mike tells us that evidence suggests that Paleo-Indians, in part, caused the extinctions of large mammals such as woolly mammoths. Of course, climate played a role, but there had been many ice-age advances and retreats. The new factor 10,000 years ago was people.

"If humans with stone tools could cause extinctions," says Mike, "just imagine what people with bulldozers can do. It scares the heck out of me."

"Me, too," says Matthew.

We drive back to the brick subdivision to get ready for our river trip. We load the back of Tyler's car with tents, sleeping bags, a cooler of food, pots, paddles, clothes, and cameras. In the morning we lash two canoes to the roof racks and cruise north on Highway 77 through Wahoo, Freemont, and Winslow. This isn't the quickest route to the Niobrara River, but we have an appointment in Winnebago first.

The name "Winnebago" was adopted by an RV company and is a symbol for indulgent consumption on American highways. Winnebago, Nebraska, is a dusty little town on another planet. We park off the highway and walk into the unassuming office of the Little Priest Tribal College. Louis LaRose, the president of the college, is wearing jeans and a red T-shirt that says "Intertribal Bison Cooperative." His face is the color of mahogany.

Louis tells us about the Intertribal Bison Cooperative. It was formed on a frigid February day in 1991. Representatives of 19 tribes met in the Black Hills of South Dakota: Lakota, Crow, Shoshone, Gros Ventre, Assinoboine, Blackfeet, Pueblo, Choctaw, and Winnebago. Many of these tribes were former enemies, but they put aside historic bitterness to work toward a common goal: to restore bison to the Indian Nations.

"It's too nice a day to sit and talk inside," says Louis. "Let's go see some buffalo."

"Cool," says Matthew.

"Wait a minute, I need to go lock up my little pickup before we go." Louis leans toward us and whispers, "I don't like to leave it unlocked. There are white folks around."

We hop into Tyler's car and drive past the high school. A billboard says it's the home of the Winnebago "Indians." As ramshackle homes and barbed-wire fences flash past, Matthew and I tell Louis about the oil industry's plans for the calving grounds of the Porcupine caribou herd. We turn onto a dirt road north of town and jostle up a hill.

Tyler parks on a hillside overlooking the Winnebago buffalo enclosure. The air is mild and full of the trills of red-winged blackbirds. The pen is bigger than the one in Pioneer Park, but not much. Several buffalo stand right beside the fence. They don't budge when we walk over for a closer look.

I hear the soft chewing of the buffalo and a deeper rumbling in their guts. Louis says that more than 60 million buffalo used to migrate across the Great Plains in the days before industrial agriculture, interstate highways, and barbed wire. He says that reintroducing buffalo on tribal lands will heal the spirit of both Indians and buffalo.

"If you don't mind," says Matthew, "I'd like to record your thoughts about the loss of the buffalo. We'd like to compare that to what we hope doesn't happen to the caribou."

"That's fine," answers Louis.

Matthew pulls out his recording equipment and holds out a microphone. "Why do you want to re-establish buffalo herds?"

"We were experiencing an extreme epidemic of diabetes on the reservation and the Government doctors would say, 'Well, this Indian has diabetes and has poor circulation, so we better cut his toes off.' Then they'd cut the feet off, and the next thing they'd be at the knees, and then you had all these Winnebagos rolling around in little wheelchairs. That's the way they dealt with diabetes."

Winnebagos rolling. Louis' image is starkly different from what you see on the cover of tourist brochures: shiny Winnebago RVs rolling past Old Faithful in Yellowstone or parked in front of the Grand Canyon.

"People diagnosed with diabetes took it like a death sentence," says Louis. "The more research we looked at, the more we saw a direct connection between diabetes and the Federal Government's surplus USDA food program. We made the *discovery* that the best diet for our people was our traditional native diet. We needed buffalo meat for medicinal reasons. That's how we got started on the return of the buffalo."

"Back in grade school we were fed a sanitized version about the killing of the buffalo," says Matthew. "What do your people think about it?"

"The Europeans wanted to take the land that the Creator allowed us to live on. They had this control problem. Anything they couldn't control or dominate they had to kill. So they destroyed the native wildlife and brought in animals they could control, like pigs and cows and sheep. Also, in order for General Sherman to defeat the Indians after the Civil War, the Army saw it was necessary to destroy their food supply. And so they killed off the buffalo, and also a lot of Indians."

"Doesn't sound like what I learned if fifth grade," I say.

"I imagine not," says Louis, "but I'm sure you've heard about the Sioux. Before the Indian Wars, the bison was their economy, their grocery store, their hardware store. They used everything from the buffalo except the gas, and, from what I understand, if you gave them enough time they would use that, too."

Matthew starts laughing, a laugh that rumbles up like the gas we heard in the buffalo's guts.

"I see you got my one-liner," says Louis dryly. "You're turning colors. Only non-Indians can do that."

We leave the buffalo to their digestion and drive to Louis' house. He goes inside and brings out glasses of soda and ice. Moisture beads on the outside of my glass, and I hold it against my cheek. Matthew sets up his microphone and tape deck.

"After your people's experience on the plains," says Matthew, "what advice would you give the Gwich'in?"

"They have to prepare themselves to fight, and to fight and to fight as long as they live. Somebody up there is looking at the land and seeing oil."

A loud, metallic squawk from the field interrupts Louis. *Kork-kok.*

"That bird squawking is a pheasant," he says, "an imported Chinese bird with a red neck."

"It isn't the only imported species around here with red necks," says Tyler.

"The same thing happened in the Black Hills. The Europeans came and looked around. What they saw was gold. They came in talking about money and progress and civilization. They didn't understand that money is sometimes too expensive for us to afford."

We finish our drinks and thank Louis for his hospitality. Tyler drives north through endless fields of corn stubble. We camp out in a state park near the Missouri River, and in the morning we head westward toward the Niobrara River.

"Hey Tyler," I say. "Can we stop at Carhenge?"

"Carhenge?" says Matthew. "What the hell it that?"

"It's some tourism operator's answer to Stonehenge," explains Tyler. "Instead of standing stones they've put up standing cars, painted gray. Don't get your hopes up, though—we won't be going within a hundred miles of it."

Cornfields, barbed-wire fences, hog farms, and overgrazed pastures roll past the windshield. Matthew frowns at the passing scene. It looks as if the pressure is building up in his head, like a dormant volcano about to become active. Suddenly he erupts.

"Someone should rip out all of these fences and let the buffalo return! The plains need to be plowed up under buffalo hooves and cleansed with buffalo shit."

"You talk like that in any of these small towns," says Tyler, "and the locals will run your sorry ass straight back to the Yukon."

Matthew and Tyler debate tirelessly about the scars on the Great Plains and what should be done about it. Matthew sees the ghosts of buffalo stampeding across the land, passing through the barbed wire as if it wasn't there. Tyler talks about the sanctity of the small farmer and what is possible under the present political landscape. I listen and stare out the window.

Buffalo, Nebraska

The first wave of white settlement washed over the prairies on the heels of the Civil War. By 1880, the Indians had been routed and all but a few hundred buffalo slaughtered. The settlers strung up barbed wire and tried to impose their will on a countryside prone to drought, hailstones as big as cherries, locusts, and incessant winds. They turned over the prairie topsoil with steel plows and prayed for rain.

The Indians looked on in dismay. A Pawnee chief in northeastern Colorado watched the settlers plowing up the native plants that gripped the topsoil with their intricate root systems and said, "Grass no good upside down."

The settlers thought they could control the prairie, but they couldn't subdue the climate. Years of drought baked the land. Gradually, the Great Plains changed from a grassland to a desert. By the 1930s the land was critically ill, infected with a virulent case of agri-cancer. Then the Dust Bowl years arrived.

I've experienced sandstorms but nothing like the dirty '30s in the Great Plains. The wind sucked up the earth and tossed it into the air. The blowing grit stripped the whitewash from houses and smothered children. The topsoil flew into the sky in clouds higher than the Rocky Mountains. The dust clouds floated east, and the prairies rained down on ships far out in the Atlantic. Farmers fled their homesteads. John Steinbeck picked up his pen and wrote *The Grapes of Wrath*.

The massive topsoil loss is not just ancient history. During the 1980s, soil erosion reached proportions similar to the Dust Bowl years. New irrigation techniques are sucking the aquifers dry and exposing even more marginal lands to industrial agriculture. Some climatologists think that the plains have had a relatively stable pattern of rainfall during the last half of the twentieth century. Droughts could be more severe as climate change heats up the Earth during the next few decades.

In the late afternoon we drive down a dirt road to a state park beside the Niobrara. We set up our tents on a broad lawn with fire pits, water faucets, and electrical outlets. We hike over the river on a wooden footbridge and scare a pair of wild turkeys scratching around in the dead leaves. A red-tailed hawk circles lazily overhead. We follow a trail to a waterfall, and when we return to camp, a blue compact car is parked by our tents. A dapper little man in his early sixties, wearing gray slacks and a tweed jacket, sits waiting at a picnic table.

"This is my canoeing partner, Fred Thomas," says Tyler. "Fred is a reporter for the *Omaha World-Herald*."

"Please don't hold that against me," says Fred. "I'm semiretired now. I just write a weekly column about quirky people and places around Nebraska."

"Is Tyler your next quirky subject?" asks Matthew.

"Tyler might be a bit controversial for the *World-Herald*," says Fred. "It's a conservative paper. It was the last major daily in the U.S. to call for Richard Nixon's resignation."

"Don't let Fred's mild manner fool you," says Tyler. "He was the driving force behind this section of the Niobrara becoming designated as a Wild and Scenic River."

"Was that controversial?" I ask.

"The locals don't necessarily trust the federal *guvmint*," he says.

In the morning we pick up a shuttle driver and drive through Valentine. We turn on a dusty dirt road and eventually find the put-in, which is fenced off by a rusty barbed-wire fence. We slide our canoes under the barbed wire and climb over the fence. Tyler and Fred are nervous about trespassing, but I'm an old hand at sneaking through restricted areas with boats. In Canada, we don't hold with blocking folks from getting to the water.

We load the canoes, climb aboard, and dip our paddles in the Niobrara. We paddle for a while, but the current is sluggish and so are we. We float downriver while vultures circle lazily above us, silhouetted against a veil of cirrus clouds. Evergreen trees march up the steep banks set back from the river, and there are birch trees, farther south here than anywhere else on the continent. The Niobrara's unusual prairie forest is a leftover from the last ice age. Mammoths and caribou once hid in the shadows of the trees. Now there are cattle.

"Listen," says Matthew, scowling at the barbed wire and cows. "You can hear the land crying out for the return of free-ranging buffalo."

"Are you talking about that 'moo' sound," asks Fred, "or do you hear something I don't?"

"I agree that we need a reserve for wild buffalo," says Tyler. "It would be good for the prairies and good for the tourist economy, but it isn't going to happen without local support."

"Things have to start happening *now,*" says Matthew. "Cows and fences don't belong here, buffalo do—"

"Paddle backward," I yell as I see a glint of silver above the river just ahead. "Paddle hard!"

We dig our paddles in the water and backpaddle furiously. Fortunately the current is sluggish. The canoe slows and we angle toward shore. We grind on a gravel bar and hop out.

"Holy shit!" says Matthew. "It's a strand of barbed wire!"

"You see what I've been telling you?" says Tyler as he and Fred pull in to shore. "The locals don't like city folks canoein' down their rivers and talking about the return of the buffalo."

"Did anyone bring wire cutters?" asks Matthew.

"Is that legal?" asks Fred.

"What? Legal to cut it?" splutters Matthew. "I don't care if it's legal. That wire almost took my head off!"

"No," says Fred, "I mean, is it legal to string wire across the river like that?"

"I believe it is," says Tyler. "Now you are starting to see how things work out here."

Matthew and I would have chopped the wire first and discussed private property rights second, but we didn't bring wire cutters. I lift the wire and we slide the canoes under. Cattle watch us placidly, as if there is no question about who is the logical endpoint of evolution. We paddle until we see a dilapidated bridge in the distance.

"We can camp here," says Fred. "I know the people who own this land. Otherwise it's private property all the way to the KOA Kampground at Highway 97."

None of us is in the mood for KOA Kamping so we unload the Kanoes and set up our tents in a Kottonwood grove. When we wake up in the morning, rain is dripping through the trees and pattering on our tents. We pack up our soggy gear and set off downstream. Matthew and I paddle under the bridge and pull into shore behind a rusty blue lump in the water. It turns out to be an Edsel with a sod roof. Weeds poke out of the broken windows. The river eddies around the wheel wells and flows through the radiator.

"Be careful," shouts Matthew to Tyler and Fred. "There's a Ford Fairlane downstream."

"Looks like we're heading into Car Canyon," I yell.

Geologically speaking, Car Canyon is not a real canyon, although the derelict vehicles do rise above the flat banks. I have paddled though some of North America's wildest canyons: the Grand Canyon, the Stikine Canyon, the Nahanni Canyons, Turnback Canyon on the Alsek. Each of them is magnificent, but Car Canyon is unique. We parallel park behind a '57 Chevy and get out to survey the canyon from dry land. A dozen Herefords chew their cuds beside a rusty red Oldsmobile.

"I've seen many of Nebraska's odd corners," says Fred, "but this is something."

"Tyler, is this the outskirts of Carhenge?" I ask.

"I wonder if they were trying to stabilize the banks," says Tyler, ignoring me, "or if it was just a convenient way to junk old cars?"

We climb back into the canoes and glide through the deepest part of Car Canyon. Even Tyler and Matthew are temporarily speechless. Finally the automobiles thin out and only scattered Chryslers and Buicks remind us of what lies upstream.

"Was it you who said the Niobrara was one of the top ten canoeing rivers in the United States?" asks Matthew.

"Don't blame me," says Tyler. "That was *Backpacker Magazine*!"

"The only way to make this a decent river is to get rid of the cows and replace them with buffalo."

"You're dreaming to think that free-ranging buffalo could be established in the near future," says Fred.

"Well, remember what Black Elk said," says Tyler, "Sometimes dreams are wiser than waking."

"Fred, you have to listen to something Louis said," says Matthew. "I have it on tape here somewhere." He rummages in a dry bag, pulls out his tape deck, and twirls the knobs. Louis' voice floats up out of the canoe.

"I remember the first day we brought the buffalo back. They were afraid because they just got unloaded from a truck. They were out running around in this pasture and checking everything out. Finally they calmed down when these birds flew over and landed on their backs. The birds were checking the buffalo out for bugs, and they were really busy and the buffalo didn't care. It was like the birds were saying: *Where you been for the last 150 years? What happened to you? You're home now.*"

Matthew clicks off the tape deck. Cattle moo in the distance. We paddle toward the KOA Kampground.

The Firth River: Just as it Should Be

Steve Philp walks up to a solar panel beside Parks Canada's outpost in Ivvavik National Park. The solar panel electrifies the bear fence that encircles the buildings. At least it did, until Steve disconnected it and hot-wired it to Matthew's battery pack. He rips off the duct tape that holds the wires in place and reconnects the bear fence. The park wardens would not approve, but the wardens aren't here.

"I hope this works," says Steve. "I can't believe we left the car battery behind."

While Wendy, Alex, Joyce, and I were hiking, the rest of our Firth River team was mired in logistical quicksand. They were trying to reach Inuvik, the jump-off point for flights into the Firth. A few people flew to Inuvik, but most were driving up with our rafts, kayaks, and equipment. The ground convoy was stranded in Dawson City after a rainstorm washed out the Dempster Highway. In the confused rush when they finally got to Inuvik, they forgot to load Matthew's car battery into the Twin-Otter bound for the Firth River. Then, when the plane landed on the rutted runway, Steve's solar panel shattered.

The Twin-Otter carries Wendy and Joyce back to civilization, but Alex stays to paddle down the river with us. Our tent camp is now a small city with a population of 15: musicians, raft guides, and friends who are helping with the Caribou Commons Project. Thanks to Steve's ingenuity and Parks Canada's solar panel, our batteries are fully charged. Matthew is ready to record the thundering hooves of the caribou herd. Steve's video camera is set to roll. We have juice for the satellite phone. All we need are caribou.

"Any signal from the lookouts?" asks Jay Burr, a trombone and tuba player.

"Not that I can see," I lower my binoculars.

Darcy Weavers, Hal Jordan, and Danette Readman, three of the musicians working with Matthew, are bivouacked on a mountain flanking the river, where they are scanning the horizons for caribou. If they see the herd, they will signal us by waving a red tarp. They've been up there for 24 hours and it is time for the changing of the guard. We hoist packs full of food and water and follow a caribou trail through a belt of stunted spruce trees. The forest grows only in the sheltered valley bottom, a strip-forest that shadows the Firth River like WalMarts, McDonald's, and Burger Kings crowd along Interstate, USA.

We wind along the trail, occasionally catching a glimpse of polished bedrock cliffs near the head of the Firth River's 50-mile-long canyon. We break out of the forest. Just upstream, the ice-blue river plunges over a ledge into a difficult-looking rapid. We clamber down to the water to cool off.

The hot spell that started as we hiked up the Clarence River is still spread, like an invisible down comforter, over the range of the Porcupine caribou herd. The sun is blurred by smoke. Forest-fire smoke regularly drifts across the Arctic in the summer, from as far away as Siberia. A large shorebird balances on the top of a spruce, flicking its tail in rhythm to its staccato calls.

"Lester, is that you?" asks Matthew.

"What *are* you talking about?" asks Glen.

"That's Lester Yellowlegs, right Ken?"

"Most people call it a lesser yellowlegs."

"Yeah, well, we call him Lester, right Stevie?"

"Right," says Steve, "We heard him a hundred times when we were working on that Southeast Yukon video project."

"Look at all this caribou hair at the waterline," I say. "A herd of caribou must have crossed the river upstream."

"It looks like a ring around a bathtub," says Glen.

"We haven't seen a single caribou since we got here," says Steve. "Where do you hide 100,000 caribou?"

"Hey," yells Matthew. "Look at this."

Matthew stares somberly at a dead caribou calf, wedged in a crevice. The calf's legs splay out, and its muzzle rests against cold bedrock. A tear-shaped ear droops against the gray stone. Flies hover above the calf's dark eyes and muzzle. I sit down and stare at the calf, my hands idly brushing the water-polished rock, which feels as smooth and slick as the marble corridors in Washington, D.C.

"What happened to it?" asks Steve.

"It must have drowned in a rapid," I answer. "Calves are good swimmers, but they aren't designed for whitewater."

I've read about "calf survival rates" and the rise and fall of the herd's population, but reading a sterile printed page is not the same as staring at a dead calf. This isn't a Disney movie set; this is the real thing.

In the late 1980s caribou biologists estimated that the population of the Porcupine caribou herd was 180,000. The numbers have dwindled since then. A caribou census in 2001 put the herd at 122,000. Caribou biologists believe that this variation is within the "normal" ebb and flow of the herd's population. Survival in the Arctic is an endless tightrope walk through a dangerous world of predators, storms, and raging rivers. A small misstep means death. Still, there is balance. Caribou are superbly adapted to their harsh Arctic home. They have survived as a species for more than a million years, populations rising and falling in rhythm with weather and climate. They lived with Pleistocene predators. They adapted to subsistence hunting when the first people emigrated across the Bering land bridge. Industrial man, however, is more lethal than anything they've faced in the past.

We leave the dead calf and trudge toward the lookout. Arctic poppies and lupines quiver in the mild breeze. A horned lark with a hidden nest nearby flies low over the alpine. She lands on a lichen-encrusted rock on the summit ridge and watches us closely. The river below is a blue thread.

"That's where you hide 100,000 caribou," says Matthew, flinging his arms at the endless peaks and valleys that fade into a distant blue haze.

We take shifts at the lookout, returning to the tent city in the valley when we are off-duty. The beach scene looks more like Maui than two degrees north of the Arctic Circle. Sunburned, mosquito-bitten people splash in the river. Danette and Tiarra Hillis, a relative of Glen's, lounge on the rocks in underwear and wide-brimmed hats. Jay, naked except for gumboots and a fishing rod, reels in an Arctic char.

The herd stays hidden despite the keen eyes of our mountain scouts. Kids in Omaha or Kalamazoo have a better idea of the herd's whereabouts than we do. They sit placidly in front of computers, logging onto an Internet site with the latest data from radio-collared caribou who are unwittingly sending signals into space. We've planned our trip at the most likely time to find the herd, but all we can do now is to scan the horizons. The Firth's bathtub ring of hair will tell us when it is too late, when the caribou have crossed the river upstream somewhere.

After four days of waiting, we abandon our high camp and load up our armada of four rafts, two whitewater kayaks, and a "rubber-ducky" inflatable kayak. The heat wave continues. The sun broils the permafrost. Moisture rises into the sky. Cumulus clouds drift lazily around the mountains. In the late afternoon they mushroom into thunderheads, dark anvils of cloud clawing upward toward the stratosphere. Lightning blasts the mountains. Thunderclaps reverberate in the canyon. The director of this movie is foreshadowing something.

A couple of days later I'm in my kayak, floating in an eddy, the Firth's sheer canyon walls rising 100 feet above me. I stare at a long, complicated stretch of whitewater. I'm feeling unaccountably nervous, although the rapids are not particularly challenging. I'm worried about my friends. Most of them are much less experienced than I am and wouldn't be here if I hadn't launched this Caribou Commons nonsense. The butterflies in my stomach started to flap at breakfast this morning.

"I don't like canyons," said Tyler Sutton, mopping up the maple syrup on his plate with a forkful of pancake. "If something goes wrong, you have no options."

"Come on, Tyler," said Matthew. "You survived Car Canyon on the Niobrara, and it's way scarier than this. You can paddle with us in the musician's raft if you want to."

"Are you crazy?" said Tyler. "Ride with you? I have a family to think about."

The first two rafts run the rapid safely. Jim Wischmeyer floats into the rapid next, in his "rubber-ducky." Jim prepared for this trip by flying his airplane from his home near Chicago to Alaska. Jim in his rubber-ducky is proof positive that natural selection is still at work. He braces wildly into a breaking wave and flips, grinning from ear to ear. I paddle out and tow him to shore.

The musician's raft careens around the corner. Musicians, nocturnal creatures, are more commonly observed in smoky bars than on wild rivers. Matthew's hair flies around his face as he leans out to steer. "Paddle hard," screams Matthew. "Hard, hard!" The raft hits a rock and rebounds into the current. "Spin right! Paddle hard!" They smash into a cliff, bounce off, and pirouette downstream, facing backward. I can hear Matthew yelling, "Hard, hard!" long after they are out of sight.

Alex shoots out from behind a rock to catch a wave. The river flies downstream, but the wave is steep enough for gravity to counterbalance his kayak with the current. He surfs back and forth, having too much fun to look upstream at the raft bearing down on him. Jody Schick, who is guiding the raft, has been paddling since he was 12. River water flows through his arteries, but he can't do the impossible. A raft in swift current is as maneuverable as a train on its tracks.

Alex finally hears Jody's shouts. He tries to surf to the side, but leans upstream and flips. The raft pounces, like a cat on a mouse. The end of Alex's kayak protrudes from under the raft. His paddle twitches feebly. Glen and Tyler lean out of the raft and stare down at the red underside of the kayak. Jody yells at them to back-paddle. The raft grudgingly releases its prey, and Alex wallows upright in a slow-motion Eskimo-roll. Blood gushes from a gash on his forehead. We find a beach, patch the cut, and continue downstream.

We camp early. A golden eagle circles overhead and a family of red-necked mergansers float downstream. A dozen Dall sheep, silhouetted against the bright sky, traverse across a ridge high above our camp. A lone bull caribou clatters between our tents and swims across the river. We run for our cameras and sound-recording gear, but the herd doesn't follow. In the morning we declare a "rest day" and hike into the mountains. A north wind carries the cool breath of the ocean and a change in the weather.

Clouds spit at us when we break camp the next day. We paddle through a tricky stretch of whitewater, then stop for lunch on a small sandbar. A creek tumbles through a gash in the canyon walls. We hike up the stream and scramble up a steep hillside to look for the remains of an ancient caribou fence. A pair of golden plovers shrieks in protest as we hike over the rise.

It doesn't look much like a fence. It is hard to see a pattern in the rounded white stones scattered across the tundra. Thousands of years ago they were piled up, supporting poles draped with animal skins, strategically placed to funnel caribou toward waiting hunters. I sit down beside a ground squirrel burrow and let the breeze wash over me. I try to think like an aboriginal hunter, waiting for the caribou. I can't do it. I'm too impatient, tethered to the twenty-first century by a leash of technology. In the old days, missing the herd meant hardship or starvation. If we don't find the caribou, all we lose are a few photos, sound effects, and memories. I stand up as Matthew and Tyler wander over.

"What is the evidence here?" asks Tyler. "Why do archaeologists think this was a caribou fence?"

"Use your imagination," says Matthew. "Slow down and listen to the land. You can feel the hunters waiting here."

"Seriously," says Tyler, ignoring Matthew. "I'd like to know what scientific evidence indicates that this was really a caribou fence. And why are all the stones white?"

"That was an enterprising archeologist," I answer. "He wanted to photograph the stones from the air, so he painted them white. Unfortunately he didn't use something that would wash away. He used latex."

"I'm surprised he didn't paint them neon red!" says Matthew. "I can't believe these so-called scientists. Archeologists paint stones. Medical researchers torture laboratory animals. Wildlife biologists harass wildlife."

"Are you saying that scientists shouldn't carry out research?" asks Tyler. "Where would we get the information so we can manage parks and wildlife refuges?"

"Why do we need to *manage* everything?" snorts Matthew. "Didn't the wilderness *manage* to survive before scientists arrived with tranquilizer guns and radio collars?"

I leave them to their wrangling and wander toward the edge of the canyon. Our high-tech, Gore-Tex gear on the sandbar looks as out of place in the ancient canyon as the latex on the caribou fence. Our rafts in the river look like foreign bacteria floating on the lifeblood of the land. The environment has antibodies to purge infestations such as ourselves: mosquitoes, rain, difficult rapids, sand in our food, and the ultimate defense: winter. It is easy to dispose of wilderness travelers. We'll be gone before the snow flies. Humans with dollar signs in their eyes are more persistent, and more likely to be cancerous.

We gather at the rafts and shove off. We drift downriver slowly, still hoping to round a corner and see a throng of caribou. Rough-legged hawks soar and screech as we float beneath their nest. A grizzly digging for roots on a hillside seems unaware of our passing. A lone musk ox stares at us from the willows. We're catching glimpses of the creatures that live here, like glancing into bright living room windows as you walk along a dark sidewalk. We imagine what life is like the other side of the curtains, but we don't really know.

The river carries us out of the mountains. The canyon walls shrink and eventually disappear. The narrow coastal plain is a different neighborhood, with its own character. A yellow-billed loon arrows overhead, commuting to the sea. She is a shift worker, leaving her mate on the nest while she takes her turn fishing. Glaucous gulls rise up in the air screaming, then attack our boats in graceful, swooping dives. Long-tailed jaegers fly jerkily over the tundra searching for lemmings or unattended nests. A handful of caribou waver in an Arctic coastal mirage. We paddle across a saltwater lagoon and beach our boats for the last time on a long, narrow island called Nunalik Spit. In 36 hours the Twin-Otter will land on the gravel bar to scoop up my friends.

A cold north wind whips up whitecaps and steep waves that lash the ocean-side of the spit. The wind feels Siberian. It picks up sand that stings like a thousand tiny wasps. I carry my pack to a wind-shelter that a previous traveler built from driftwood. I lash my tent to a sun-bleached log so it doesn't blow away.

"Hey Ken," yells Steve. "We found a little caribou calf down the beach. It's all alone. I wonder if it was abandoned."

I walk up the beach. Dozens of Arctic terns swirl in the wind and plunge into the ocean. A yellow-billed loon surfaces in the midst of the feeding frenzy, extends its neck, and swallows a wriggling fish. I see Matthew walking toward me.

Abandoned caribou calf, mouth of the Firth River, Arctic National Wildlife Refuge

"Did you see the calf?" he asks.

"Not yet."

"I found its mother. She's dead, but she wasn't killed by a predator. She's just lying on the sand as though she's asleep. I'll walk back with you."

We walk westward down the spit. The sun shines from a brittle blue sky, but the wind snatches its warmth and swirls it toward the mountains. A male snow bunting dances across a driftwood log, then hops onto a round, weathered whale's bone. It cocks its head toward us, then spreads its wings and blows down the beach.

"That vertebra is huge," says Matthew. "It must be from a bowhead."

"There's the calf," I whisper, "just past that log."

The calf stares at us wearily. Its eyes look like dark bruises. It lowers its head listlessly and grazes on a patch of vegetation with bell-shaped lavender blossoms. Fine, windblown sand swirls and eddies around its hooves. Six weeks old and its future is written in the pattern of ribs protruding from its dull, lusterless coat. I can't think of anything to say except inane regrets about not being able to bottle-feed the calf, teach it to migrate, and return it to the herd. Or things we've said before about calf-survival rates, oil development in the calving grounds, and the delicate balance of life. And death. Matthew is quiet, the fate of the calf becoming music in his head. We turn and walk back to camp.

At midnight a three-quarter moon hangs in the sky over the mountains, and a pod of beluga whales swims eastward, toward their own calving grounds near the Mackenzie Delta. White backs break the surface in a shimmer of reflected sunlight. My friends cluster around a small fire, reluctant to go to bed, trying to stretch out their trip. As I walk toward the firelight I hear Matthew begin to sing:

Relentlessly, the Arctic Sea resounds upon the shore
Mew gulls court, the waves report, just as ten thousand years before
Coming through, the caribou renew the ancient round
And as they do, a chosen few return their bodies to the ground

It is tragic, it is pure
To survive is to endure
And all is just as it should be
The coastal plain, the Arctic Sea

Summer herds move on towards the call of distant lands
Leaving only memories, and cloven hoof-prints in the sand

And the ocean glimmers gold tonight, bathed in Arctic light
Somewhere a tern takes rest from flight
Somewhere a calf will die tonight

It is tragic, it is pure
To survive is to endure
And all is just as it should be
The coastal plain, the Arctic Sea

A Caribou Calf in London

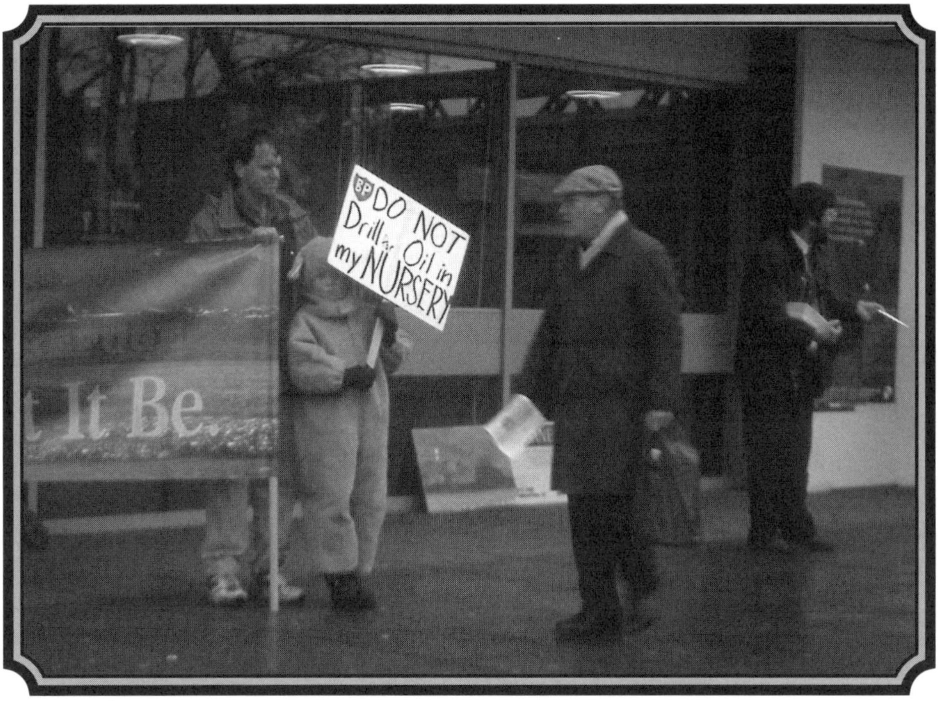

Prologue

In Tulsa (or maybe Toronto or Tokyo), a meteorologist stares at her computer. Her eyes glow red-rimmed and blurry in the monitor-light as she assesses the latest climate-change projections. During the past decade, the Earth sweltered under nine of the 10 warmest years since we started to record data. Climate change isn't just warmer temperatures, however. Extreme weather will become more extreme. Storms will be bigger and bolder, droughts drier and grimmer.

At present, the Arctic has a moderating influence on global warming. That may soon change. The western Arctic is heating up three times faster than the world average. Arctic ice is 40 percent thinner than in 1960, and a Massachusetts-size chunk of the ice pack is melting every year. As the polar ice cap shrinks, less of the sun's radiation is reflected back into space. More heat is absorbed. Meanwhile, permafrost is simmering on the climate-change stove, becoming permasoup. When the climate is cold, tundra peat is a "carbon sink," but when it warms and dries it will decompose, releasing carbon dioxide and methane, both greenhouse gases.

The inexorable drift toward warmer global climate will be confused by a higher variability of regional weather. We are opening a Pandora's Box of high- and low-pressure systems, tornadoes, nimbo-cirro-strato-cumulus clouds, rain, snow, sleet, hail, and wind. Who knows what will pop out next? More frequent and violent hurricanes? Worse flooding? Forest fires in Alaska in January? Many people believe that climate change belongs in a science-fiction future. They don't realize that the Pandora's Box is already open and that caribou and Arctic peoples are already feeling the impact.

It is the first year of a bright new Arctic millennium. All winter, blizzards howled across the northern boreal forest. Snowflakes swirled through stands of stunted black spruce and drifted across frozen rivers and lakes. By spring, snow lies thick and deep in the winter range of the Porcupine caribou herd, like the soft white down on a ptarmigan's breast. The elders in Old Crow and Arctic Village have never seen so much snow.

Biologists think that dwindling snow cover is a signal for caribou to begin their spring migration to the calving grounds. This year, the thick mantle of snow melts reluctantly, blanketing the boreal forest through March and April. The snow stays put and so do the caribou. The pregnant cows don't start north until the middle of May, weeks later than usual.

Who knows what caribou think about? They know nothing about fossil fuels, internal-combustion engines, traffic jams in Los Angeles, greenhouse gases, or climate change. Eventually, though, they must realize that *something* is wrong. Especially the pregnant cows. One day they know that they aren't going to make it to the calving grounds before they drop their calves.

London, England

"Mind the gap," says a dead electronic voice. "This is Bank Street, on the Piccadilly Line. Mind the gap."

The doors hiss closed. Snow is still falling in Alaska and the Yukon, but the air under the streets of London is warm and smells of sweat and diesel. I hold on to my projectors as we accelerate into the subterranean maze. If I let go, the projectors could slide down the aisle and knock over the suits, like pins in a bowling alley. Yesterday the "tube" was jammed with soccer fans heading for the FA cup semifinal at Wembley Stadium. They wore black-and-white-striped jerseys, swilled beer from bottles in brown paper bags, and belted out the Newcastle club song. Today is Monday, and the train is a forest of dark trousers and black shoes.

The train sways gently as we hurtle forward, but it is eerily quiet inside this insulated bubble. The only sound is the rustling of many *Financial Times*. The suit next to me turns the front page. I look over his shoulder and see a large ad with familiar photographs: caribou, Gwich'in, and a polar bear. The headline reads in bold black letters, "BP—Stay Out of the Arctic!" The man stares at the ad pokerfaced, then flips to the stock market quotations.

I get off at Bond Street and lug my projectors to the Canadian High Commission. I'm due to present the Caribou Commons slideshow here on Wednesday, and I'm worried that my projectors will explode when I plug them into an English electrical socket. But globalization must be a reality: the projectors work as though they were born with a cockney accent.

Wendy, Malkolm, and I are in London to take part in a week of activities leading up to British Petroleum's Annual Shareholders Meeting. The North American contingent consists of Gwich'in from Alaska and Canada, a scientist from the Canadian Wildlife Service, activists from U.S. conservation groups, and representatives from a "socially responsible" investment firm. Our British hosts are Greenpeace and the World Wide Fund for Nature (WWF).

I leave my projectors at the High Commission and walk into the London drizzle. I've been traveling mainly underground and now I feel like a mole, blinking in the light and sniffing at the wet air. London's air, a noxious mixture of coal smoke, carbon monoxide, and who-knows-what-else, makes Los Angeles smog seem fresh and pure. A bright green truck rumbles down the road trailing a vapor trail of greenhouse gases. Bright yellow letters on the side of the truck say: "BP—The Green Alternative." A cyclist whizzes past, wearing a gas mask but no helmet. I walk toward The Strand for a luncheon meeting.

The stately old buildings are interspersed with glass and chrome high-rises. Next to a stiff-upper-lip Marks & Spencer department store is a small shop selling sex magazines, skimpy underwear and "inflatable bonking sheep." French Connection, a trendy clothing store that promotes itself as FCUK, is located across the street. An advertisement in the window says: "French Connection—Much Fancy…Don't Yours FCUK?"

My Gwich'in companions are waiting at the restaurant Simpson's in The Strand. When I walk in from the rain, I see Norma Kassi; David Krukto, the elected member of the Northwest Territories Legislature from the Mackenzie Delta; Alan Hayton, a young man from Arctic Village; and Athan Manuel, the Arctic campaign director for U.S. PIRG (Public Interest Research Group). Simpson's is not your ordinary greasy spoon. Sepia-toned paintings hang from gloomy wooden walls. An antique chess set in a glass case has a plaque explaining that Simpson's was a favorite haunt of Charles Dickens when he was writing *Oliver Twist* and *A Christmas Carol.*

"We're supposed to meet Clive Wilkes for lunch," Norma says to a white-bloused, dark-skirted woman. "He's from Woof-Woof."

"I beg your pardon?

"Oh, sorry," says Norma, laughing. "In North America, we say 'Woof-Woof' instead of WWF."

"Is that so?" she says stiffly, consulting a list. "Mr. Wilkes hasn't arrived yet." She looks up and stares at me as though I shop at FCUK. "Your companions need jackets and ties to eat in the downstairs dining room. Please go upstairs to the lounge. I'll send your host up when he arrives."

"Did you come here on the subway?" asks Norma, as we sink into soft leather couches upstairs. "I can't believe how grouchy people are here."

"Norma shook up everyone on the tube," says Athan. "She asked them why nobody smiles around here. She told them that Gwich'in elders would have something to say if people acted that way in Old Crow."

Before long Clive Wilkes strides in, says hello, and waves a newspaper at us. "The cat will have jumped in with the pigeons when Sir John opened this morning's *Financial Times,*" he says.

"Sir John?" asks David.

"Sir John Browne," answers Clive, "is the CEO of British Petroleum. WWF is no doubt unpopular with BP this morning."

"This is your ad?" I ask, picking up the *Financial Times.*

"Yes. BP put some not-so-subtle pressure on us *not* to go public, but in the end we *are* a conservation group."

"I don't know much about the business world," I say. "Will this have much of an impact?"

"There was a poll conducted recently on public trust," says Clive. "More than 80 percent of the public trusted WWF to tell the truth. Do you know what BP's rating was? Less than 20 percent. When we take out an ad like this, the big financial institutions take notice. They don't like it when investors start asking questions."

"Will the ad will have an impact on the Shareholder's Resolution on Thursday?" asks Norma.

"Two-tenths of one percent of BP's shareholders control 85 percent of the company's stock. Big institutions like Barclay's Bank are certain to vote against the resolution, but BP will hear that they are concerned about the public reaction."

"We expect a 'Yes' vote of between three and five percent," says Athan. "Anything more than that would be a coup."

"How much did the ad cost?" asks David.

"Thirty-four thousand pounds," says Clive matter-of-factly, as if this is spare change.

Randy Snodgrass and Francis Grant-Suttie, WWF campaigners from Washington, D.C., and New York, join us, shaking raindrops from their overcoats. Clive signals, and a dark-suited headwaiter discreetly ushers us into the dining room. My table setting has two knives, three forks, and two spoons. A young waiter offers me a basket of dinner rolls.

"Simpson's offers classic British fare," says Clive. "Unless any of you are vegetarians, I'd recommend the roast beef and Yorkshire pudding."

"We've confirmed our meeting with British Petroleum this afternoon," says Francis. "We're due at Britannic House at two o'clock."

"Who will be there?" asks Norma.

"There is a chance that Sir John Browne himself may show up," says Clive. "In any case, there will be mucky-mucks who report directly to him."

"What should we talk about?"

"Be direct. Tell them how your people would be affected by oil development."

"If they ever came to our villages they would already know," says Norma flatly. "The caribou are everything to us." She starts talking about growing up in Old Crow flats, waiting for the caribou to come. I've heard Norma speak dozens of times, but even so, I'm struck by the power of her words. The Woof-Woofers listen in rapture.

A waiter carries a steaming haunch of roast to our table. He brandishes a razor-sharp carving knife. I'm the only one who watches his performance; everyone else is hypnotized by Norma. A plate appears in front of me: deep-fried halibut fingers floating on what looks like bright green mashed potatoes. Nine rectangular french fries are stacked like logs next to the fish.

"That's exactly what Sir John needs to hear!" says Clive enthusiastically when Norma finishes. "Straight from the heart."

I poke the bright green stuff with my middle-sized fork and take a tentative bite. Mashed peas. It tastes like Gerber baby food. I switch to the halibut. Inside its golden jacket the fish is as mushy as the mushy peas. I pick up a greasy french fry and chew it idly.

"They are bound to tell you that the Inupiat from Kaktovik are in favor of drilling," I say. "Who is going to respond to that?"

"I'll tell them that the Inuvialuit in the Mackenzie Delta are my constituents," says David, "and they want the calving grounds protected."

"Don't forget to say that the Inupiat hunt mainly whales and seals," says Norma, "and they are *opposed* to offshore oil development that might harm marine mammals."

"Norma, why don't you start off the meeting," says Francis, "followed by David and Alan. We'll sit in the background at a safe distance from the wrath generated by the *Financial Times* ad."

We finish our meals and head out into the drizzle. Norma, David, and Alan carry their messages from the Gwich'in Nation to the BP Nation. Norma must have given them an earful because BP immediately canceled the meeting that I was scheduled to attend the next day, even though Raymond Chrétien, the Canadian Ambassador to the United States and a friend of a BP director, had set it up.

In the next few days, London shows off its true climatic nature. It rains on Tuesday during our press conference at Church House, a stately stone building in the shadow of Westminster Abbey. It pours during my gig at the High Commission. It's my seventy-fifth slideshow since Wendy, Malkolm, and I hit the road in September. I've been counting. I'm glad when the last slide drops and my official duties are over.

It is still drizzling on Thursday morning when we emerge from our hotel to go to the demonstration outside the shareholder's meeting. Since I don't own any BP shares, I won't be allowed inside, but Malkolm has been looking forward to the demonstration for weeks. Wendy sewed a caribou calf costume for him before we left Vancouver. Yesterday the two of them walked to the Greenpeace offices, and Malkolm painted a placard.

We walk to King's Cross to wait for a bus. Two old women climb down from a red double-decker and shake out their umbrellas. They stare at Malkolm's placard. It says, "BP—Don't Drill for Oil in My Nursery!" They stride toward us purposefully.

"Where is your nursery, young man?" asks one briskly.

"It's not my nursery," explains Malkolm. "It's the nursery of the Porcupine caribou herd in the Arctic National Wildlife Refuge."

"Cor, I wondered," she exclaims. "I didn't think there was any oil in Islington!"

Malkolm puts on his costume when we arrive at the meeting place. He has perky calf ears, a short tail, and light-brown fake fur from Fabric Land in North Vancouver. He looks just like a caribou calf, except for his neon red cheeks. I check out the concrete plaza between the Thames River and the Royal Festival Hall. Greenpeace activists told us yesterday that the grounds surrounding the Festival Hall are private property and warned us that we would likely be "moved off" by security staff. The coast seems clear though, so we walk toward the front of the hall. Malkolm waves his placard proudly.

Wendy and Malkolm stop to inspect a huge bronze bust of Nelson Mandela that celebrates his long walk to freedom. The plaque says, "The struggle is my life." I snap a photo of Malkolm under the bust as three policemen round the corner and march toward us.

"Our demonstration could be ending prematurely," says Wendy.

"Why don't you keep going?" I suggest. "I'll take a picture of the caribou calf with a London bobby."

I set up my tripod and throw my rain jacket over the lens. A dozen pigeons peck around the calf's hooves. They burst skyward as the law surrounds the calf. I snap a couple of photos. Then I join them.

"We're trying to stop British Petroleum from drilling for oil in the Arctic Refuge," Malkolm says in a serious voice. "If the caribou are forced away from the coastal plain, the calf survival rate will drop."

"Blimey," says a bobby in a cockney accent, slapping the calf on the back. "You've convinced me. Go give 'em hell!"

Malkolm (Boothroyd) being interviewed by an NPR reporter, London

We walk around the corner to the big glass entrance doors. Malkolm walks up and down waving his placard. Soon, eight Greenpeace polar bears shuffle through the mist toward us. The bears have big black noses and sad, droopy eyes. Wilderness Society activists unfurl a big banner with a photograph of the calving grounds and the words, "Hey BP! Let it Be!" Greenpeace volunteers with bright green-and-yellow "SaneBP" buttons on their lapels get ready to give out leaflets and CDs about fossil fuels and alternative energy sources.

After a few minutes, shareholders start to show up. Most are prosperous-looking, middle-aged men, but there are also octogenarians with canes and mufflers around their necks, a scattering of young men with ponytails, and older couples holding umbrellas and leaning into wind. Journalists appear out of nowhere and start to swarm. They are like wasps at a picnic, their antennae twitching toward the juiciest sound bites. Before long a steady stream of shareholders flows through the gauntlet of polar bears, environmentalists, reporters, photographers, and a stray caribou calf.

Norma arrives, and a crew from CNBC focuses a TV camera and sticks a microphone in her face. "The Arctic Refuge is a sacred place to my people," she says. "How would English people like it if Exxon decided to drill for oil in Westminster Abbey?" Norma hops from microphone to microphone; Malkolm is also a hot ticket item. Reuters, Associated Press, and CNBC line up to hear about the Arctic Refuge straight from a caribou calf's mouth.

The rain finally stops, but the wind feels as if it blew across the frozen steppes of Russia before slamming into southern England. The calf and the polar bears are the only ones dressed for the weather. I shiver in my light jacket and walk over to a polar bear.

"How are you doing in there?" I yell.

"It's bleeding hot and I can't see a thing. Other than that I'm fine."

"You come down from the Arctic often?"

"Too often, but we don't have any choice. Scientists say that the Arctic Ocean will be ice-free in the summer in less than fifty years if we don't slow down climate change. How the hell will our grandcubs hunt for seals if there is no ice? They'll starve to death."

I wish the bear luck and join Malkolm, who is talking to a reporter from National Public Radio. Just before noon, the last shareholder disappears inside. Wendy and I are nearly hypothermic so we head into the Festival Hall coffee shop to warm up. We sip steaming coffee and gradually stop shivering. Liese Schneider, a PIRG intern, joins us and drops her AGM entrance ticket on the table.

"Things are really dragging, but the shareholders are hanging in there, waiting for their free lunch," she says. "I cast my proxy vote for the resolution, but I can't stay for the debate. I have to go to Heathrow for my flight to Washington."

"Why don't you use Liese's ticket and sneak into the meeting?" Wendy suggests.

"Go for it," says Liese. "They might let you in."

"Brush your hair first," suggests the Greenpeace media specialist. "You look like you've been in the wilderness for a week."

I run my fingers through my hair and trot up a broad staircase, pretending that I'm a shareholder who had to slip out for an important phone call. The security staff eye me suspiciously, but when I wave my ticket they move aside magically. I push open the heavy wooden doors and slip into a vacant seat.

The auditorium is vast and shadowy. BP Amoco's board of directors, nineteen dark-suited men and one woman, sit on the stage below a giant video screen. The director's names are illuminated below them in hot white lights. The stage has something of a Las Vegas glitz about it, as if Wayne Newton is about to pop out from behind the curtains. Sir John Browne's monotone voice shatters that fantasy.

"We have recently acquired a 2.2 percent holding in PetroChina for 580 million pounds," says Sir John. "This is a unique opportunity to expand our operations . . ."

The word "PetroChina" flashes on the video screen. The screen does not say that BP's unique opportunity translates to a moral and financial backing of China's occupation of Tibet. Fifteen hundred shareholders in the hall sit in varying modes of attention. An older gentleman in a tweed jacket beside me has his chin on his chest and is snoring gently.

"We have also acquired Burma Castrol, which will give us a great name in the lubricants brand—"

The words "Funding," "Innovation," and "Creativity" flash on the big screen.

"—the acquisition of ARCO for seven billion pounds..."

Seven *billion* pounds! I stare down at the stage, where the directors sit as still as lampposts, although not as useful. Bald pates gleam softly in the dim light. The man next to me snorts and twitches. His feet slide farther out in the aisle. I focus on Sir John who, ever since I set foot in the calving grounds, has been a symbol for everything that I despise about the oil industry. When I came to London, I was sure it would be hate at first sight. As he prattles away on the stage, I examine him closely. He's about my age. He's about my size. He wears reading glasses, like I do. I'm surprised to realize that I don't hate him. I just wish that I could drag him out of London and spend a week alone with him in the calving grounds. Then I'd drop him off in Old Crow to spend some quality time with the elders.

"Two billion people across the world use our services," says Browne as "Environmental Responsibility" lights up above his head. "We must realize our impact on economies, communities, and the natural environment. We pledge to decrease our emissions of greenhouse gases by 10 percent from 1990 levels by the year 2010 . . ."

Having just told us that BP will spew out greenhouse gases at current unacceptable levels for the next decade, Sir John sits down. Peter Sutherland, BP's co-chairman, stands up and says that Resolution 12 is next on the agenda. I read the text of the shareholder's resolution:

> RESOLVED that shareholders request the Board of Directors to implement the following policies for BP Amoco:

1. Cancel all plans for oil exploration and development on the coastal plain of the Arctic National Wildlife Refuge and in the Arctic Ocean.

2. Stop the expenditure of any funds by the company or its subsidiary or associate companies targeted to achieve these objectives, including investments for the development of the Northstar project.

3. Make capital freed up by the cancellation of Northstar available to BP Solarex to up-scale its solar manufacturing capacity.

"It is our responsibility to deliver long-term shareholder value," says Sutherland, "and so I must tell you that the Shareholder Resolution is opposed by the board."

Sutherland tells us that 25 minutes has been allotted for the debate. The board is in favor of free speech, in limited doses. He introduces the proponents of the resolution, Matthew Spence of Greenpeace and Simon Billeness of Trillium Asset Management.

Spence and Billeness are not dressed like polar bears. They look like merchant bankers. They talk about Northstar, a controversial offshore drilling project in the Arctic Ocean, about climate change, about financial and social bottom lines. They say Sir John is at the helm of the giant BP supertanker (single hull) steaming directly toward Bligh Reef. In a note of optimism, they say that it isn't too late to change course.

"This meeting is much more than a debating society," retorts Peter Sutherland, not bothering to hide the scorn in his voice. "We face broader moral issues. If they were right, then we as a board would have to respond. But we reject the basis on which this shareholder resolution is founded."

Sutherland uses up five of our 25 minutes telling us that Greenpeace and Trillium are using scare tactics. He says that 13 billion barrels of oil have been safely taken out of Alaska. He insists that oil development does not harm caribou or polar bears. He reads a letter from the mayor of the North Slope Borough and says that BP Amoco has the blessing of Arctic native peoples. The board believes in democracy, he tells us, and they wouldn't dream of interfering in what is a U.S. decision. He doesn't say that God is a major BP shareholder, but it is implicit.

"Now we'll take comments from the floor," he says. I get up and walk past my snoring neighbor. Sutherland points to a microphone in the lower level.

"My name is Alan Hayton," says a familiar soft voice. Alan is wearing dark blue pants and a beaded caribou-skin jacket. "I am Gwich'in from Arctic Village in Alaska. I am here to tell you that BP Amoco does not represent my people. The Gwich'in do not want oil exploration or development in the calving grounds of the Porcupine caribou herd . . ."

Alan speaks in a quiet voice that reminds me of the meeting I went to in the Old Crow youth center. If Sutherland or Browne visited a Gwich'in village, their opinions would be listened to and considered. Alan doesn't receive the same respect.

"You have already heard me read a letter from the mayor of the North Slope Borough," says Peter Sutherland shortly. "We are confident that *he* represents the views of the local people. I'll take the next speaker." He points to me.

"My name is Ken Madsen." My voice vibrates with anger. "Mr. Sutherland has said so many misleading things that I'm not sure where to begin, but I'll do my best. You pretend that you have the blessing of the local people, but the first time you bothered to even meet with the Gwich'in was two days ago. And that was because they came all the way to London."

I outline my Arctic experiences: six months of wilderness travel in the Arctic National Wildlife Refuge and the range of the Porcupine caribou herd, several years of working and traveling with Gwich'in and Inuvialuit people. I pause for a moment and stare down at the board. I wish I could freeze this moment. How often do you have the chance to lecture the dark-suited men (and one woman) who control a multinational fossil-fuel corporation that is more powerful than many governments? They probably wish they could call in the security guards to toss me into the Thames River. But they can't. They have to listen. I know that my words will have little impact on the Shareholder's Resolution; most of the votes have already been cast. I don't care at the moment. I'm enjoying myself.

I point out that scientific evidence does not support BP's claims that oil development has no impact on caribou, especially in the vulnerable calving grounds. I say that a scientist with the Canadian Wildlife Service is in London if they want more information. I tell them that the caribou are of utmost importance to native people, but that the Arctic Refuge is known for many other wildlife and wilderness values. I talk about polar bears, musk oxen, and migratory birds.

"It is ludicrous to say that 13 billion barrels of oil have been *safely* taken out of Alaska. Have you conveniently forgotten the *Exxon Valdez* oil spill? Have you forgotten the greenhouse gases and other air pollution that spews out from the oilfields? Have you forgotten the hundreds of oil and chemical spills that happen every year? Have you forgotten that BP was fined $22 million for illegally disposing of hazardous waste near Prudhoe Bay?"

There is a surprisingly loud burst of applause from the shareholders as I walk back to my seat. None of the directors clap.

I kick myself for forgetting something. Sutherland said that BP supports democracy, and that the United States should be left to make its own decision about the Arctic Refuge. What he didn't mention, however, is that BP is a major funder of "Arctic Power," a lobby group whose sole mandate is to open the Arctic Refuge to industrial oil development. BP's vice president for Alaskan operations is on the board of Arctic Power.

"I really intend to bring this issue to a close," says Peter Sutherland after a couple more speakers. "Thank you very much for the debate, however incomplete it has been." He turns and points an accusing finger toward Matthew Spence and Simon Billeness. "I really must ask you in the future to be accurate and not to deliberately mislead our shareholders and the public."

Sir John Browne, the star of the show, takes over to wrap things up. He's the good cop. He wants us to leave with sugar-sweet feelings about British Petroleum. I should have brought a syringe of insulin.

"I started my employment with BP in the Arctic," says Sir John. "I don't think my colleagues and I would allow anything bad to happen to the totality of the area. We are a company that prides itself on our environmental record. We say what we are going to do. And we do what we are going to say. Solar is an important business, but only one-thousandth of one percent of the world's energy supply comes from the sun. That is going to grow, but it isn't going to grow just by saying that it is going to grow..."

Our 25 minutes of democracy has been used up and we have no chance to rebut Sir John. One-thousandth of one percent of the world's energy supply comes from the sun? Where does he think fossil fuels came from? Santa Claus? I suppose we should be comforted knowing that BP will do what it is going to say.

As Browne is talking, a graphic materializes on the video screen, the preliminary numbers on the Shareholder Resolution vote: 1,491 million votes for, 9,541 million votes against. I make a quick mental calculation—more than 13 percent of the shares have been cast *for* the resolution. We've lost the vote by 8,000 million votes, but it's a moral victory. The next issue of the London *Times* will report that the vote "was an unprecedented demonstration of support of green issues" and that "city analysts were stunned by the size of the 'Yes' vote."

The meeting breaks up. The shareholders and I throng toward the exits and our belated lunches. Half a dozen people congratulate me on my rant and shake my hand as I fight through the crowd. Like the real shareholders, I'm ready for a boxed lunch and a well-deserved glass of BP's wine.

Epilogue

During an "average" year, the peak of calving for the Porcupine caribou herd occurs at the beginning of June, and almost all of the calves are born before June 5. In the year 2000, the caribou are well to the south of the coastal plain when they should be in the calving grounds, giving birth. Using womb-control unknown in a human maternity ward, the pregnant cows delay the onset of labor as they struggle northward. They aren't able to hold on long enough.

The caribou are strung out along their migratory route when they start to give birth. They drop their calves wherever they happen to be: in snowy spruce forests, along windswept ridges, near frozen lakes. Normally after calving, the new mothers have a few weeks in the calving grounds to regain their strength: time to graze on nutritious sedges and moss, time to rest, time to nurse their calves. That year they stagger to their feet, drawn by an inbred urge too strong to ignore. They grunt to their calves and struggle toward the coastal plain. Gwich'in elders have never seen calves born south of the Porcupine River before. They watch and shake their heads sadly as cows with calves swim across the river, which is running high with snowmelt and thick with ice.

I, too, am drawn back to the Arctic in early June, less than two months after picking up a glass of wine in the Royal Festival Hall and drinking a lonely toast to the future of the Porcupine caribou herd. I know that heavy snowfall to the south has delayed the migration. I believe that the unusual snowpack is due to climate change. I understand that intellectually, but it is an emotional shock to see the coastal plain empty of caribou.

Each day when I crawl out of my tent, I look southward toward the Brooks Range, expecting to see caribou trotting toward the calving grounds. I have a long wait. I wait through the normal time of calving. I wait through the post-calving resting period. When I finally see caribou descend from the mountains, it is nearly the end of June. Very few of the cows are shadowed by calves.

Some of the calves were killed by predators. Others drowned in turbulent, flooding rivers. Some calves simply couldn't keep up and were abandoned. By the time the caribou finally reach the coastal plain, 15,000 caribou calves have died, nearly 10,000 more than biologists expect during an "average" year.

Under normal circumstances, a caribou herd will shake off the impact of a season with high calf mortality. After all, caribou are survivors. Bad years will be balanced by better years to come. Unfortunately, the caribou are not living through "normal circumstances." They face an uncertain future of climate change compounded by the threat of oil development in their calving grounds.

Whose responsibility is it to speak for the wild creatures? Do I expect Sir John Browne or Peter Sutherland to voluntarily announce that BP will leave the coastal plain of the Arctic Refuge for the caribou, polar bears, musk oxen, and tundra swans? That they will make *real* progress in boosting solar power and reducing greenhouse gases? Not bleeding likely. Not unless people kick them in the only place where they have nerve endings and pain receptors.

In their Gucci wallets.

UNDER THE ARCTIC SUN

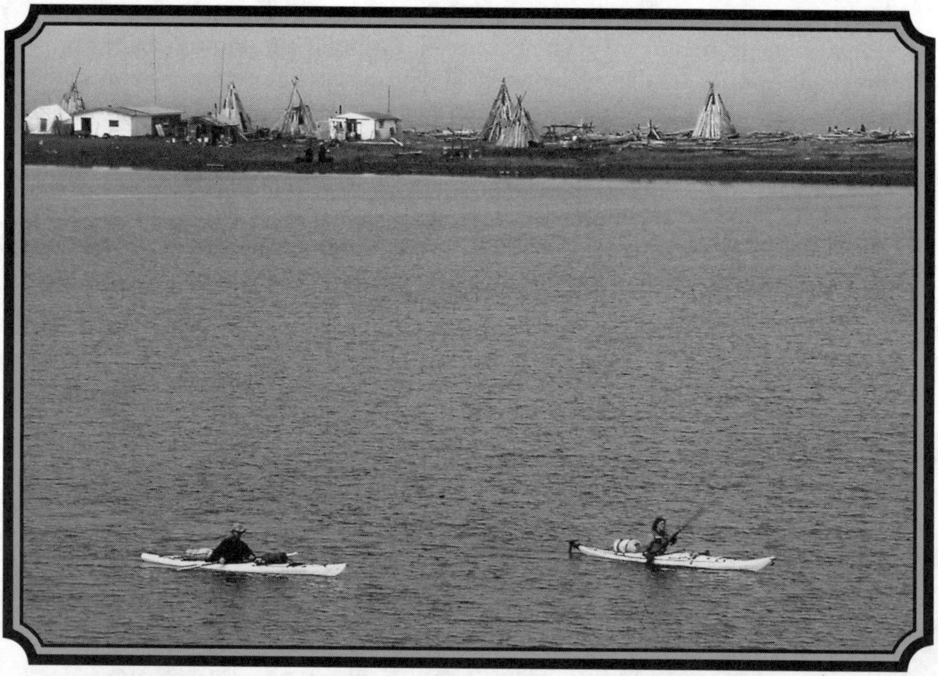

Our sea kayaks rise and fall in the swells. It is two in the morning, and the sun is a smoky-maroon sphere just brushing the horizon. I'm dripping like a seal. Blood oozes from my scalp and drips down my cheek. My hair is caked with sand and hangs in kelplike strands. Several gallons of saltwater slosh around inside my kayak.

"Are you OK, Ken?" asks Paul, concern in his voice.

"I'm fine." Surprisingly, I'm telling the truth.

There are a million worse places to be than floating on the Arctic Ocean. I could be inching along in a Los Angeles traffic jam, inhaling exhaust. I could be in line at a WalMart, waiting to buy a plastic trinket that I don't need. I could be at a tropical resort somewhere, Club Med-icated with a bellyful of Singapore slings, frantically looking for fun.

Paul Mason, Sharon MacCoubrey, and I just launched into a furious-looking sea. I helped Paul and Sharon, steadying their boats and shoving them into the surf at the critical moment. When it was my turn, I positioned my kayak on the beach while I went over the launching sequence in my head: wait for a lull in the biggest waves, dig my knuckles in the sand and push my kayak into the surf, keep the bow pointed directly into the waves, paddle like hell. Unfortunately, my overloaded kayak obstinately refused to budge from its perch on the beach. I sat helplessly as a wave came foaming up the beach at an oblique angle and spun me broadside. The backwash sucked me out to sea where the next breaker pitched me upside down. Arctic sea water burns like liquid ice, but my head was digging a furrow in the sand, and I didn't feel a thing. Raw fear overpowers the other senses every time.

I wrenched my paddle to the surface to try an Eskimo roll. A politically correct paddler would call it an Inuvialuit roll (or an Inupiat roll on the Alaska side of the border). However, "Eskimo roll" is ethnologically correct, since nowadays Arctic natives don't go to sea with anything less than an 18-foot aluminum runabout with a 4-cycle Evinrude 50. I've rolled whitewater kayaks thousands of times, but never a sea kayak. I swept my paddle and flipped my hips hopefully. The overloaded kayak wallowed upright slowly, reluctantly. Relieved to find myself upright, I plowed through the surf like a U-boat and joined Paul and Sharon out beyond the breakers.

Ten days ago, Paul and Sharon flew in to Nunalik Spit, hitching a ride on the Twin Otter that picked up my Firth River companions. We paddled across to Herschel Island, relaxed for a few days, then paddled eastward along the coast. We didn't get far before a windstorm pinned us down.

For days, we listened to the incessant flapping of our tents and chewed windblown sand in our soup and granola. Out on the tundra, poppies lashed back and forth like a Labrador's tail. Tundra swans didn't bother flapping in the gale. They rocketed overhead, wings angled to catch the wind. A couple of hours ago, at midnight, the wind suddenly died. We loaded our kayaks in a hurry. Who cares if it is the middle of the night when the sun is shining?

The ocean looks varnished in the bloody light, except for the five-foot swells that distort the sun's reflection. Each swell lifts my stern and corkscrews me forward. Then the bow rises, and I rock backward. Wave after wave. Endless waves. I get used to the motion and paddle hard when my stern starts to rise. I surf forward, slide off the back of the wave, and do it again. After a while I look back. Paul and Sharon are a hundred yards behind. I stop paddling and let them catch up. Sharon's face looks like a halibut's white underside.

"I shouldn't have cooked curry for dinner," says Paul as he slides in next to me. "Sharon is seasick."

"I've never heard of anyone getting seasick in a kayak."

He shrugs. Sharon leans over and curry-colored vomit spews into the Beaufort Sea. She must be instinctively keeping her balance as she throws up; her paddle is flopping uselessly in the water. I look at the waves crashing on the beach. Landing in big waves is more difficult and dangerous than launching. I don't want to chance it.

"It's about six miles to Roland Bay," says Paul, studying a marine chart on his deck.

"Can you keep paddling for a bit?" I ask Sharon.

"Do I have any choice?"

"No, not really."

"Let's do it, then," she says grimly.

The swells roll inexorably. Up, down, corkscrew to the right. I try to slow my pace so I don't get too far ahead, but I feel energetic, and it is hard to paddle slowly. The sun blazes up into the clear sky, changing from red to orange to yellow. The ocean is thick with eiders, scoters, loons, and long-tailed ducks. A beluga surfaces in the distance. Every time I look at Sharon's blanched face, I feel guilty to be feeling good. Up, down, corkscrew. She pukes again.

We limp along the coast, Sharon paddling doggedly between bouts of seasickness. After a while, I slip in beside Paul to check the chart. It's hard to distinguish the entrance to Roland Bay. It looks obvious on the chart, but from our vantage point out at sea, the coast all looks the same. Permafrost mud banks stretch eastward as far as I can see. Surf pounds on the shore.

"Is it much farther?" asks Sharon miserably.

"We must be just about there!" says Paul brightly. Then he leans over and whispers, "Do you think we've passed the entrance?"

"Could be."

"Maybe we can land at Stokes Point."

In the distance, three white telecommunication bubbles rise up, like giant golf balls teed up above the tundra. DEW line (Distant Early Warning) stations, like chunks of the Berlin Wall, are souvenirs of Soviet-American nuclear madness. What better place to hold a cold war than the Arctic? DEW line sites were billion-dollar presents to the Joint Chiefs of

Staff, designed to give them a few seconds' warning if the Soviets fired missiles across the North Pole. Peaceniks worried that a hungover radar technician would mistake Santa Claus and his reindeer for a Soviet missile, sound the alarm, and trigger a nuclear war.

"Are we at Roland Bay yet?" Sharon asks. She shivers and slumps forward.

"I think we must have missed it," I answer as brightly as I can, "but it isn't far to Stokes Point."

It doesn't *look* far, but distances are deceiving in the Arctic. We paddle for at least two hours before we are adjacent to the huge bubbles. I inspect the deserted-looking DEW line station from a half-mile out to sea. There is no sheltered beach. Waves pound furiously against the shore in an unbroken line. Cold War radar technology is not going to help us land safely.

"I wonder who named it Stokes Point," I say. "I don't see anything that looks like a point."

"Maybe we should keep going to Phillips Bay," says Paul. "Do you want to look at the map, Sharon?"

She shakes her head, too nauseated to care. I raft up with Paul and look at the map. Phillips Bay is 15 miles away, at least as far as we've come in six hours of paddling. Paul looks at me. I look at Sharon. Her face is puckered, like a jack-o-lantern withering on the compost pile after Halloween.

We point toward Phillips Bay, which shimmers like a fairytale castle in the distorted mirage light. I feel like a hamster on a rodent wheel, paddling endlessly but never getting any closer. I don't know where Sharon finds the strength, but she keeps going. I don't know where she finds the vomit, but she keeps throwing up. Periodically Paul and I yell some inane remark about our progress, but Sharon ignores us. After our recent navigational blunders, our credibility is as illusory as a mirage. Finally, 13 hours after setting out, we approach a decaying cabin. Paul races ahead to set up a tent. I stay with Sharon for a final half-hour of bladder-bursting kayaking (the last time I paddle without a pee-bottle). Finally we grind to a halt in the shallows. Sharon staggers across a swampy mudflat to the tent. I drag our boats up the beach. Sharon doesn't emerge for 24 hours.

The next day when I get up, Paul is squatting beside a greasy-looking pond with a water filter. The water is thick with algae, mosquito larvae, and other unidentified wriggling creatures. I thread my way through a maze of wetlands to stretch my legs. The swamps are quacking with green-winged teals, northern shovelers, and pintails. The air is buzzing with mosquitoes enjoying the windless day. I find fresh grizzly tracks a hundred yards from camp. The tracks about-face suddenly and lope out toward the tundra. I remember an important appointment with a mug of coffee and return to camp.

I light the stove and watch a pair of parasitic jaegers guarding a dead fish on the beach. Half a dozen glaucous gulls float out in the bay, watching with a proprietary interest. A gull lifts its wings to take off. Instantly the jaegers attack, like fighter jets hurled from the deck of an aircraft carrier.

The gull refolds it wings as if was only stretching. The jaegers swoop back to the beach. It's a stalemate. The gulls can't get off the water, but the jaegers don't have time to eat. Paul joins me, carrying three bottles of cloudy water.

"Might be best to boil this," says Paul.

Paul and I are finished eating by the time Sharon finally crawls out of the tent. She clumps across the mudflats and sits down on a silty log, her face veiled in mosquito netting.

"How does your stomach feel about cold oatmeal?" asks Paul.

"Sounds fine," she replies. "I'm starving."

Mosquitoes jive around Sharon's face as she spoons congealed porridge under her head-net. I pour lukewarm motor-oil coffee into her mug and add a handful of milk powder. I see why they call it "instant." It instantly forms rubbery lumps.

Sharon slides forward onto the muddy ground, leans back against the log and picks up her book, *Under the Tuscan Sun*, by Frances Mayes.

> "Listen to this," says Sharon: "In the delicious stupor that sets in after the last pear is halved, the last crust scoops up the last crumbles of Gorgonzola, and the last drop empties into the glass, you can ruminate, if you are inclined that way, on your participation in the great collective unconscious."

"I'm in a delicious stupor," I say, "my fingers scooping the last lumps of undissolved milk powder."

"Maybe you should call your next book *Under the Arctic Sun*," suggests Sharon.

"I'm too busy ruminating about the great collective unconscious."

"This book reminds me of my brother," says Sharon. "He works hard and then takes his family for two-week holidays at luxury golf resorts. The swimming pools have imported sand at the bottom. He'd never understand why I like this kind of trip in a million years."

"Are you telling me he wouldn't love throwing up all night from a kayak? Or filtering swamp water for coffee? Or sitting in the mud sharing lumpy oatmeal with a trillion mosquitoes?"

"Right," she laughs. "He's weird."

The next morning it is still windless, and fog squats over the Beaufort Sea. We load our kayaks and I duct-tape a compass to the deck. We push off into the bay. A bearded seal surfaces with a huge splash just behind Sharon's kayak. She zips forward with a spurt of adrenaline. The seas are calm until we paddle through the barrier reefs that protect Phillips Bay. Then we begin to rise and fall with the swells. I wonder about Sharon's stomach.

"How are you feeling?" I yell.

"I'm OK," she shouts. "I popped a Gravol. My mother insisted that I bring some for the bush plane flight. Thank goodness for mothers."

The fog thickens as we edge along the reef. The ocean and sky are the color of tinfoil. I steer a course by watching the gyrating compass needle and listening to the surf pounding on shore. Sharon, Paul, and I huddle together, like eider chicks under the predatory shadow of a jaeger. A loon squawks in the mist, confirming that there is a bigger world out there, beyond the tight, sheet-metal horizon. A beluga surfaces a few feet away and peers at my kayak with a big eye. She dives under Sharon's boat, shadowed by a gray calf. We feel our way blindly along the coast until the sun finally vaporizes the fog.

"How did we get so far out," I say. "We must be a mile from shore."

"Hey," yells Paul. "Look! A whale spout!"

It is a V-shaped bowhead spout, the twin vapor jets formed by the whale's double blowholes. The spout looks like a peace sign hovering over the ocean, although life is not yet completely peaceful for bowheads. Commercial bowhead whaling was banned in 1946, but they are still hunted by the Inupiat in Alaska, and to a lesser extent by the Inuvialuit in Canada.

During pre-whaling days, an estimated 50,000 bowheads migrated through Arctic waters, each whale swathed in a two-foot thick "wetsuit" of blubber that protected it from the frigid water and allowed it to smash through ice to make breathing holes. Whalers did not look at the bowhead's blubber as a fascinating Arctic adaptation; they saw hundreds of barrels of oil. It's the same penetrating vision that allows foresters to look at an old-growth forest and see board-feet, and oil company executives to look at the tundra and see crude oil flowing south in a pipeline.

The price of whale oil dropped in the mid-1800s, when new petroleum products from John D. Rockefeller's Pennsylvania crude hit the market. That alone didn't save the whales, since there was still a market for baleen from the bowheads' massive heads. The baleen was manufactured into essential products like corset stays, skirt hoops, fishing rods, umbrella ribs, buggy whips, and portable sheep pens. Like their close cousin the right whale, bowheads were hunted to the brink of extinction. Their population is now estimated at 7,000, and though they are still listed as an endangered species, Arctic native people are allowed to kill whales for subsistence.

We watch the silvery cloud of whale breath float down to the surface. We paddle toward a friendly-looking beach. Paul surfs into shore first, hits the eject button, and manages to grab his kayak before the next wave swamps it. He waits on shore like a soccer goalie, grabs our boats, and hauls us up the beach.

The driftwood is thicker now that we are approaching the Mackenzie Delta. The beach is littered with logs, as if giant children have been playing pick-up-sticks. I carry my gear to a sheltered patch of sand. I'm securing my tent to a log when I hear a yell.

Paul points out to sea. I expect to see a pod of belugas, or a bowhead, but it's a bull caribou swimming just outside the line of breaking waves. I immediately think of the photo opportunity—a body-surfing caribou. I run toward my kayak, trip on a piece of driftwood, and sprawl on my belly. I pick myself up, sprint to the kayak, and kneel in the sand to get out my camera.

"A grizzly chased it into the ocean," says Paul in a surprisingly calm voice.

I hesitate for a moment. Then prudence wins and I grab my bear spray.

"There's the bear!" says Paul. "No, wait a minute. It's a wolf."

The wolf is light gray, shaggy, and long-legged. Its eyes are driftwood-brown, unblinking, hypnotizing. My boots grow roots into the sand while the wolf stares at us. Finally it turns its head and looks at the caribou in the waves. Then it circles around our camp to join the rest of its pack. The wolves are gone before I remember that I'm supposed to be a photographer.

I snap my camera to the tripod and hop over the logs to the beach. The caribou staggers onto shore, leaving a red swath in the foam. Its right hind leg trails uselessly, the tendons severed by slashing wolf fangs. It is no wonder the gray wolf looked relaxed; it knew the bull would be easy prey.

I hike along the coast after dinner. Lapland longspurs inspect me from tussock-tops and flutter into the air, singing lustily. After 60 days in the Arctic, their song is as familiar as the buzz of mosquitoes. On the edge of a permafrost bank that is melting and slumping toward the ocean, a white cross leans drunkenly. The words on the cross are succinct: "Gustav Wiik, 1906". Nothing else: no date of birth, no country of origin, no words of comfort.

I sit on a tussock and try to imagine Gustav Wiik's life. I picture a blond Norwegian boy, perhaps the son of a fisherman who grew up in a village on the edge of the Baltic Sea. The wooden ships that sailed past his cottage made him dream about palm trees and far-flung continents. One day he sailed westward in a tramp steamer, but it dumped him in San Francisco instead of Tahiti. Down on his luck, he steamed north on a whaling ship, hoping to make a fortune in bowhead baleen. He had almost saved enough money to return home to Scandinavia, but one day a thrashing bowhead tail crushed the small whaleboat he was rowing and he drowned. Or, maybe he picked up syphilis during his last drunken shore leave, paralysis creeping up his limbs and dementia clouding his brain.

I stand up and peer over the edge of the bank. A wooden coffin is perched in a hillside of oozing black muck. At the rate the warming world is melting the permafrost, it won't be long until Gustav Wiik is floating on the sea again.

The wind begins to blow in the night—the start of another two-day storm that pins us in camp. We wait impatiently for the next lull, and when it comes we launch again at midnight. Since the sun now arcs below the horizon briefly each night, it is dusky when we surf in and land at Shingle Point, a long eastward-pointing finger of sand lined with makeshift summer homes. The cabins, hammered together from driftwood and chunks of plywood, are summer homes for the Inuvialuit from the Mackenzie Delta. When we get up in the morning and walk down the beach, we meet mainly old people and children. The people in the middle are in Inuvik, making a living. The dollars feed and clothe their families but put them squarely in the no-man's land between their traditional ways and a flooding tide of globalization and cultural assimilation. The elders like it better out at Shingle Point.

We meet an old man named Jacob Archie who carves moose antlers and tosses nets into the sea to catch char and herring. Everyone calls his wife Grandma. She feeds us tea and fresh doughnuts, and Jacob gives us dried fish. Sharon makes friends with a herd of kids and lets them paddle around in our kayaks. It's a sign of the times—a woman originally from Ontario teaching Eskimo kids to paddle a plastic kayak.

It's a long way to Fort McPherson, and we can only afford to linger for a day at Shingle Point. We push off into the protected waters behind the spit and wave goodbye to the kids. Two days later we paddle into Shallow Bay, which is aptly named. The Mackenzie, the biggest river in the Arctic, carries a heavy load of silt, which settles onto the Arctic seabed. We detour far out from the shore but still have to squirm out of our kayaks and drag them across mudflats. Late in the day we reach the delta, a labyrinth of lakes, sluggish channels, and tangled willow flats. After three weeks of endless sunshine, the Mackenzie welcomes us with cold drizzle.

The delta is like an alligator-free Everglades swamp. The channels are lined with slick, glutinous muck, and the mosquito holiday we've enjoyed on the windy coast ends abruptly. I slip into the rhythm of paddling against the current, and we laboriously wind through endless brushy channels. The mind-numbing monotony is palatable only for those who are easily amused. Sharon whiles away the upriver miles softly singing snatches of old songs that are stuck in her head. She only knows one verse of each song, which she sings over and over. One day she transfers "Amazing Grace" to my brain when I innocently paddle near her. I try to overpower it with "Puff, the Magic Dragon," "Surfing USA," and "Early Morning Rain," but nothing works.

While we kayak upstream, the endless wilderness soap opera keeps playing on the big screen. A breeze ruffles the willows lining the shore, making the silvery undersides of their leaves glow like apple blossoms. An Arctic tern chases a bald eagle across the river, screeching, fluttering, and darting at the eagle's broad back. A black feather drifts into the willows. A mother lynx bounds up a steep cutbank, but her four kits slither and slide, mewing in dismay. She calls encouragement, waiting until they all scramble to the top. The family melts into the shadows. We stop for lunch and a wood frog hops into a blanket of horsetails. Wood frogs, the only amphibians able to survive in the Arctic, freeze solid in the winter, thaw in the spring, and hop happily away. A kestrel takes our place as soon as we finish lunch. It hovers over the horsetails, drops out of the sky, and flaps off with a frog skewered in its talons.

One evening, the north wind moans through the willows, and horizontal rain sweeps up the Mackenzie. We can't find a sheltered camp, so we keep paddling. Eventually we round a corner and see a cabin in the distance.

Jacob Archie had told us that "Police Cabin" was a communal shelter for delta travelers. We drag our kayaks up the bank and haul our food and sleeping bags inside.

"It's tempting to light a fire," I say, swinging open the door of an old oil drum that someone converted into a wood stove. "It's colder inside than out."

"There is a small pile of wood outside," says Paul, "but it's probably an emergency supply."

We decide to leave the wood for someone who really needs it. We put on our jackets, mitts, and wool tuques instead. Paul lights our little stove and heats water for macaroni and cheese. Sharon and I read the Inuvialuit graffiti that covers the cabin walls.

"Listen to this one," says Sharon, 'Roses are red, violets are blue, sugar is sweet, and so's my skidoo'."

"How about this?" I say. "Ronald, John, Dean & Dave, September 16, 1997—Billy and Casper never showed up (too much money)'."

"Do you think the gas for the boat trip cost too much, so Billy and Casper stayed home?" asks Paul.

"Maybe they had so much money they stayed in Inuvik to party," says Sharon. "Here is one from February 4, 1992, 'No Caribou, Skidoo trouble, No smokes'."

"'February 6'," reads Paul, "'Jack and Nestor went to Shingle to pick up gas and never came back. Might have to look for them. Bad weather. No more sugar on top of all that'."

"Here's their last entry," continues Sharon. "'February 7, Boys made it back. Going home now'."

"Listen to this," I say. "'February 21, 1998: Jimmy, Chris and Jonathon—eating Klik at 9:25 pm, playing cards at 9:50 pm'."

"What's Klik?" asks Sharon.

"I think it's like SPAM."

"Well," she says, "I don't know about Klik, but a game of cards sounds good. We've dragged a deck along this whole trip without using it once."

We eat dinner and then put water on for tea. We sit in our sleeping bags in the corner of the cabin to stay warm. Paul shuffles the cards and deals out a hand of hearts. An outboard motor whines in the distance. The whine becomes a roar then splutters to silence. Footsteps squelch in the mud and the door opens. Two men and a woman walk in. If they are surprised to find three white people shivering on the floor of Police Cabin, they don't say anything. We introduce ourselves and find out that the woman is Jacob Archie's daughter. It's a small world in the delta.

"It's cold in here," she says. "Why didn't you light a fire?"

The men walk out into the rain and return with armloads of wood. Before long a fire crackles in the wood stove and the cabin warms up.

"Help yourself to some tea and fruitcake," says Sharon.

Northern native people like strong black tea, but in the gloom of the cabin, Sharon mistakenly tosses a chamomile teabag into the pot. After stirring in brown sugar and powdered milk, it looks like swamp water. Our guests drink it politely and eat a token slice of stale cake. Before long, they tramp back into the stormy night and roar toward the coast.

"Maybe my tea scared them away," says Sharon.

Four days later we paddle into Aklavik, a small village on the western edge of the delta. Aklavik is not New York or Chicago, but it is bustling enough after 70 days in the wilderness. Paul and Sharon are heading home from here, catching the Mackenzie River barge back to Inuvik and the north end of the Dempster Highway. I'll be sorry to see them go. Unlike many couples, they don't bicker. They treated each other with respect, even under the duress of long paddling days, drinking water alive with wriggling creatures, mucky campsites, and sandy spaghetti.

The barge isn't due until late evening, so we walk up toward the Northern Store. We only make it a hundred yards before we run into Calvin Elanik, who we met three weeks ago at Herschel Island. Calvin had been on the island to visit his father, a park warden at the territorial park. We chatted with him a couple of times, and one day he dropped off two fat Arctic char at our camp. As soon as he sees us wandering into Aklavik, he appoints himself as our tour guide.

"What we're really wondering," says Paul, "is whether there is any place in town for a shower."

Calvin looks at our greasy hair, silty faces, and grimy fingernails. Then he heroically offers us his parents' shower. We walk across town and meet his mother, who is baking cookies. Paul and I sit in the living room while Sharon showers. Country Music TV wails from a large screen that dominates the room. Rugged men in cowboy hats and big boots sing songs in Southern accents, while sultry women slink in the background. Calvin's mother passes around a plate of steaming chocolate chip cookies, and Calvin tells us about his recent boat trip to Kaktovik to visit a girlfriend.

"I've heard that people in Kaktovik favor oil development in the calving grounds," I say. "Did you talk to them about that?"

"Not everyone feels that way, but the leaders do. Those people have been bought by the oil companies. They're just interested in dollars."

On the television, a woman in a low-cut white dress walks across the desert, singing a song about young lust. A darkly handsome young man drives up in a white convertible, leans out, and listens. Soon they roar off together, their long hair whipping in the wind as they weave through the saguaro cactus.

"You should see what they eat in Kaktovik!" says Calvin, ignoring the TV. "They mix whale blubber with meat and blood. Then they put it behind the wood stove and let it ferment for a week. I like *muktuk*, you know, whale blubber, but I couldn't eat that stuff."

I take my turn in the shower and then wash my clothes in the sink. The water turns black, and after ten rinses it is still dark brown. I put on my only clean clothes: red long underwear, green shorts, and a purple fleece shirt. We thank Calvin and his mother for their hospitality and walk down to the Northern Store. Teenage girls giggle, point at me, and whisper about red "tights" and ballet dancers.

The Northern Store displays a surprising array of pre-packaged foods: Aunt Jemima, Hamburger Helper, Doritos, and Klik. There is a small produce section with a few tired-looking fruits and vegetables. A woman in front of me hands the teller a cabbage. She returns it to the shelf in disgust when the teller rings in $8.50. I shell out $1.43 for an apple, $1.57 for a plum, and $3.49 for a quart of outdated orange juice. The Inuvialuit and Gwich'in hunt caribou for more than purely cultural reasons.

I head down to the river while Paul and Sharon wander around town. I haul my kayak up to a flat spot, dig out my tent, and start to put it up. A gnarled old man with a face like teak shuffles toward me, moving at the pace of a glacier. By the time the old man reaches me, the tent is up and my sleeping bag is flopped over a fence to air out. I say hello. He mumbles something I don't understand.

"Excuse me?" I say, leaning closer. "What did you say?"

"Lookin' for my canoe," he mumbles. "Probably take all night."

He inches toward the river. It is hard to imagine him paddling a canoe. If he lived south of the sixtieth parallel, someone would have slapped him into a nursing home. He'd be stretched out on a bed waiting for his meds, mumbling and staring into space. I hope I'm as spunky if I ever reach his age. I sit down in the dirt and pick up *Under the Tuscan Sun*, which Sharon has kindly loaned to me. I finished my other books weeks ago, and the Northern Store's literary offerings run to Harlequin Romances and comic books.

> We take the waiter's suggestion for tonight's Morellino....Praise Allah! What a wine. The dinner is superb, every bite, and the service attentive. Everyone in the small restaurant has noticed the young couple at the table in the middle from the moment they were seated. They look like twins. Both have that curly, magnificent black hair and hers has jasmine flowers caught in its ripples....They're dressed out of Milan or Rome boutiques, he in a somewhat rumpled tan linen suit and she in a yellow puckered silk sundress that was melted onto her.

An old white man walks by, pushing a wheelbarrow. He looks at my shorts and long underwear without blinking. "You from Toronto or somewhere?"

"No. I live in Whitehorse."

"Got to go check my nets." He pushes his wheelbarrow toward a line of small boats pulled up on the bank.

I take a bite of my $1.57 plum. Its skin is wrinkled and its flesh is as tough as a turnip. The mosquitoes start to harass me. I put on a head-net and return to Tuscany.

Our salads look as if someone picked them from a field this afternoon, and perhaps they did.... We will have to forego dolci but with coffee they bring a plate of little pastries anyway, which we manage to eat.... The lustrous girl now is holding out her hand, admiring a square emerald surrounded by diamonds I can see from here.... Spontaneously we all lift our glasses in a toast and the waiter, sensing the moment, rushes in to refill. The girl shakes back her long hair and little white flowers fall on the floor.

"You want a whitefish or an inconnu?" The old fisher asks, back from his nets. The fish are two to three feet long and covered in tough-looking scales. They hang out over the edge of the wheelbarrow, dripping slime.

"My pot is too small for those fish," I answer, "but thanks for the offer."

We hear a foghorn blast, and the Mackenzie River barge chugs upstream. Paul and Sharon return, followed by the whole town: old women in long dresses, teenagers in leather jackets with cigarettes dangling from their lips, kids on bicycles. I help Paul and Sharon drag their kayaks onto the deck, then retreat to the shore to wave goodbye. The kids ride their bicycles along the shoreline path, following the barge until it steams out of sight behind an island.

I unzip the tent, slide into my sleeping bag, and doze off. Then the tent shakes and voices intrude on a half-remembered dream.

"You think anyone in there?"

"You look and see."

"No, you."

"Boo," I yell. There is silence, then three small, grubby faces poke under the fly. It's two in the morning, but the six-year-olds are still out on the town.

"What choo doin' in there?" asks one.

"I sleep in here."

"Really?" he says.

"Don't you know anything?" says another. "He's a tourist. Where you goin'?"

"Up to Fort McPherson. I have to meet a couple of friends next week."

"What's this thing?" the first kid asks, picking up the cable release for my camera.

"I use that for taking pictures."

"Can you take a picture of us?" asks the third kid, sticking out his tongue.

"Come back in the morning and I will," I say. "Now shoo. Get out of here."

Their words fade into the Aklavik dusk, "Do you think he's *really* a tourist?"

They aren't back in time for me to take their picture before I leave in the morning.

Worlds Apart

It's two in the morning, and I'm feverish with the flu. It feels as if I've been circling aimlessly through the maze of interstates, parkways, tollways, and turnpikes that surround the Newark Airport for hours. The manager of our hotel in North Plainfield told me that the airport was 20 minutes away. "You can't miss it," he said. He forgot to say that there were no highway signs and that city planners had concealed it in the center of a maze.

Finally I make a lucky turn and see a small green Newark Airport sign. I follow a curving highway hopefully. A big jet roars over my head, coming in for a landing. I follow it to the airport. I accelerate up the ramp toward the parking garage but the van's roof rack smashes into the dangling rubber balls that warn about the low ceiling. I back up, turn the wheel, and steer toward the arrivals entrance. I pull into a No Parking zone guarded by a pair of traffic cops with their arms folded across their chests. I'm an hour late.

The cops frown and shake their heads as I approach, but I plead that I'm late to pick up someone from a tiny Arctic village who might freak out if she can't find me. They stare at me as if I'm from Pluto. Then they look at my license plates and see that I'm from the Yukon which, as far as they know, could be on another planet. They look at each other and roll their eyes. Finally the good cop shrugs and tells me I have 15 minutes. Kathie Nukon is just coming out of the gate as I run in. We find her bags on the carousel, lug them to the van, and thank the cops.

"How are you feeling, Kathie?" I ask as we rattle away from the airport.

"Oh, tired. But I'm OK."

Kathie Nukon talks in the same soft voice I last heard in the Youth Center in Old Crow. I have to lean over to hear her words above the engine clamor. Kathie is pale, and she has dark pouches under her deep brown eyes. She has been traveling for three days, including a missed connection in Vancouver and an eight-hour blizzard delay in Chicago.

"How are things back in Old Crow?"

"Oh, fine," Kathie answers, "but people are worried about the calving grounds. I heard you've been down here all year. That must be hard."

I follow the road signs toward I-78. The city lights stream past in a fuzzy yellow haze. Sirens wail behind me, and I pull over to the right lane. A police car rockets past, then a huge yellow fire truck, its lights winking and flashing like an overexcited video game. I follow the lights into a cloud of acrid chemical smoke from a four-alarm fire. A highway sign informs me that we're heading for Paramus and Hackensack. I've never heard of either place. I glance at the map on my lap nervously. I don't want to admit to Kathie that I'm lost. I know she is worried about traveling in big cities, and I'm supposed to know what I'm doing. I veer to the right onto a nameless freeway. My high-beams light up the smoke like the walls of a tunnel.

"It's a bit of a change from home," I say with forced cheerfulness.

"Yes," she says. "it is. Those city lights in front of us are really bright."

I suddenly realize that we're headed straight for New York City. The Big Apple's magnetic field is sucking us in, like light into a black hole. Exits peel off, like the sections of an orange, until the only section left is the one heading into the Holland Tunnel, which speeds you under the Hudson River into Manhattan. I veer frantically across six lanes toward the U-turn lane. I wheel around, merge onto the New Jersey Turnpike, and rumble back toward the Newark Airport. We left the airport an hour ago, and we're back where we started from. It isn't until 3:45 that we crest a hill and see the yellow lights of North Plainfield glowing below us.

"Oh, no!" says Kathie. "We're back in New York City again!"

"I hope not," I say, "but I guess it looks about the same when you've just come from Old Crow."

The next day we drive west into Pennsylvania. Our first show is at Slippery Rock University, way over near the Ohio border. It is the end of January, and winter is snapping at the heels of the Northeast for the first time this year. Great billowing clouds of snow trail the giant trucks that zoom past us in the fast lane.

"It's warm down here," says Kathie. "It was minus forty when I left Old Crow."

"Depends on your point of reference," says Wendy. "Everyone down here is complaining about the cold."

"I'm glad it's snowy. At least it looks a little like home. I've been wondering, though, what should I say to these people tonight?"

"Just tell them what it is like up in Old Crow," I suggest. "Tell them what caribou mean to the Gwich'in. You'll do fine."

"I hope so," she says nervously. "It's been a long time since I spoke to strangers."

Kathie is so soft spoken it is hard to believe she was once a politician. Back in the early 1980s, she was elected to the Yukon Legislature, a Member of the Legislative Assembly from the riding (administrative jurisdiction) of Old Crow, population 200. She left her friends and family behind and headed for the bright lights of Whitehorse, the capital of the Yukon Territory. Whitehorse is smaller than Walla Walla, Washington; Moose Jaw, Saskatchewan; and Florence, South Carolina. Still, with a population of nearly 20,000, it is by far the Yukon's biggest apple. To Kathie it was a big, indifferent, intimidating city. Then her life was shattered when her husband drowned in a boating accident, leaving her a single parent with three small children. She filled the void with alcohol, and her life went into a tailspin.

We check into a Super 8 Motel in Grove City and walk across the highway to a King's Family Restaurant. A Certifying Council must rigorously inspect restaurants before handing out the prestigious "Family Restaurant" label. When you see it you know what's coming: food so bland that even the pickiest kid will eat it. It's two-for-one night at King's, and we get two tasteless meals for the price of one. Wendy and I order water. We don't drink wine when we're traveling with Gwich'in speakers, in deference to the massive social problems that alcoholism has inflicted on native communities. Kathie doesn't order alcohol, either. She went to an addictions treatment center a decade ago and stopped drinking.

One hundred and fifty people crowd into a lecture hall for our presentation at Slippery Rock U. After I finish my slideshow talk, Kathie gets up to speak. Even with a microphone, her voice is as soft as snow floating to the ground. When we're done, half a dozen people crowd around Kathie. A young woman comes up to me and asks a question about photography. She drifts away, then plucks up her courage and returns to say what's really on her mind.

"Do you mind if I ask you something personal?" she says.

"Fire away."

"How do you manage to do what you do?" she says hesitantly. "I mean, everything I do is so irrelevant. You obviously follow your dreams, but I don't even know where to start."

I don't know what to say. I look at her. She looks like any of the other students milling around. They are wearing torn jeans and sweatshirts and tennis shoes. They're scruffy and idealistic, and they're living in a world that doesn't fit quite right, like their clothes. They remind me of me.

Malkolm and Kathie Nukon, Newark, New Jersey

"I guess you start by choosing something that needs fixing, something you care about," I say. "You don't need any particular talents, except maybe stubbornness. Just look at Kathie. She misses her family, she worries about traveling on her own, and she's scared stiff about public speaking. You know what she says? 'If I can do it, anybody can.'"

She walks over to talk to Kathie, and I pull apart the sound system. In the morning we drive to Penn State University, which has a population twice that of the entire Yukon. For another two weeks we bounce across Pennsylvania and eventually end up back in New Jersey. Our last slideshow is at an elementary school in Newark. We check in to a Holiday Inn in Bloomfield and drive through quiet residential streets to eat spaghetti with the people who are organizing the show.

"This is an inner-city school we're talking about," says Dawn, who teaches at the school. "Most of these kids have never seen a forest. Most have never even been to the beach."

"They've never seen a forest?" asks Kathie in disbelief.

"You'll see when we get to the school," says Dawn. "Many of my students have been abused, both physically and emotionally, and some are malnourished. The kids are looking forward to meeting you, though. One of them wants to know if you've ever seen a caribou."

Kathie laughs.

"A reporter from the *Newark Star-Ledger* will be there at 10," says Inga, who did the publicity legwork for our presentation. "Our neighbor Jay will drive you down to the school."

"Wouldn't it be easier for us to meet you there?" I say.

"With the bicycles and kayak on top of your van?" asks Inga, surprised at our naivete. "The thieves in Newark would take that as an invitation."

"We could lock the bikes up at the hotel. The kayak should be OK. What would someone do with a whitewater kayak in Newark?"

"They'd steal it because it's there," says Inga dryly. "Then they'd strip the rest of your van. They'd consider it a challenge."

We load up Jay's hatchback in the morning and drive southeast through a prosperous sea of suburbia. Jay tells us that Martha Stewart grew up nearby. The prosperity drains out of the neighborhoods as we leave Bloomfield and West Orange and drive into Newark. We turn off a main highway onto a street with seedy-looking bars and pawnshops. Another turn and the road is flanked by brick fences topped with razor wire. A few men walk down the sidewalk, their hands in their pockets and their eyes down. Jay stops in front of the Broadway Elementary School. The "Projects," blocky, pollution-stained, high-rise tenements, rear up across the street. This is where most of Dawn's students live. Many of the windows are smashed and boarded-over. They leer over the school like pirates with eye patches.

Armed security guards greet us at the front door. They check off our names on a list and tell us to sign in. We lug the gear down a hallway decorated with whales and daisies. An official-looking notice tells us that January is Persuasive Writing Month. While I set up the projectors the *Newark Star-Ledger* reporter introduces herself and a bored-looking photographer. She asks me what caribou look like, if they are vegetarians, and whether they are dangerous.

The students file into the auditorium at 10:30. I expect to see swaggering young hellions with switchblades outlined in their back pockets, but these kids look surprisingly docile. The teachers nip at their heels like sheep dogs, and the kids sit down. The principal walks to the front of the crowd. She's wearing a white blouse and a long dark skirt.

"Good morning, boys and girls," she calls out expectantly.

"Good morning, Mrs. Moustakas," shout 100 voices in unison.

"Children," she says firmly. "You have a special treat this morning. I want to introduce Mr. Madsen and Mrs. Nukon. They have come all the way from Alaska to talk to you. They *need* you to be on your best behavior."

"Yes, Mrs. Moustakas."

I begin the slideshow, but the kids quickly wilt as I talk, like houseplants that haven't been watered in weeks. I try to keep their interest by showing as many animal photos as possible: polar bears, musk oxen, Arctic foxes, bowhead whales, and grizzly bears. Since Malkolm is the same age as the students, I pass the microphone to him. He talks about the animals he saw during a sea kayak trip we took between Demarcation Bay and Kaktovik. Then he reads a letter he has written asking President Clinton to designate the Arctic Refuge as a National Monument. A caribou photo flashes on the screen.

"That looks like one of Santa's reindeer," yells a boy from the front row.

"That's right," I say. "Caribou are almost the same as reindeer. Now I'd like to introduce Kathie Nukon."

"Hello," says Kathie. "I'm a Vuntut Gwich'in from the Yukon, in Canada. Do you know where Canada is?"

"Yes, Mrs. Moustakas," they answer in a ragged chorus. Kathie is wearing a black tracksuit with bull caribou embroidered down the side of the legs. She looks nothing like Mrs. Moustakas, but the kids are trained like tamed sea lions barking for fish. "Mrs. Moustakas" pops out whenever they hear a cue.

"I live in a small village called Old Crow," says Kathie, "The caribou are very important for our people, especially for the elders and our children. We eat a lot of caribou. In the morning, we might have fried caribou and pancakes. Doesn't that sound delicious?"

"No! Gross!" the kids shout. They probably don't understand the connection between meat and live animals. Maybe they are imagining tiny fried reindeers, antlers and all, on their plates.

"Sometimes we have caribou three times a day," continues Kathie. "We might have caribou sandwiches for lunch and boiled caribou for dinner. We put meat over a pole to dry it, or smoke it to keep it for later."

I hear a faint "pop" and a flash illuminates Kathie's face. The *Star-Ledger* photographer is sprawled out on the floor, snapping photos of the exotic Arctic native. The reporter is perched on the edge of a child's chair, scribbling notes.

"Up in Old Crow we have a school like this one, only it's smaller, maybe 100 kids," says Kathie. "The students in the school wrote letters to tell other children how important the calving grounds are. I'm going to read one now."

"To all the children of the world: My name is Kelly Ollett I am a student at Chief Zzeh Gittlit School in Old Crow. I have lived in Old Crow all my life, long enough to know how important the caribou is to our people . . ."

The kids in the room are silent as Kathie reads in her soft voice. Many small heads are pillowed on their desks. Sleep is more urgent than a wilderness controversy 5,000 miles away.

"If oil drilling happens in the Arctic Refuge, we will no longer get any caribou coming through Old Crow," reads Kathie. "Which is why we need your help to stop the oil drilling. Write letters, tell people about this, because with your help we could stop oil drilling from happening in the calving grounds of the caribou."

"I want to thank you for listening," she says, putting down Kelly Ollett's letter. "It has been a pleasure to talk with you."

Mrs. Moustakas thanks us on behalf of the school. She glares at the kids, and they remember to clap dutifully. Then they file slowly back to their classrooms. We carry our gear down the hall, which is lined with paintings of lily pads and bridges. Big letters cut out of red and orange construction paper spell out "Our Impressions of Monet." None of the paintings look remotely like Newark. I don't think that Monet's impressionist swirls could capture the sharp-edged razor wire and the projects. Maybe Picasso or Salvador Dali will be February's painter of the month.

We hop in Jay's hatchback and leave the graffiti, garbage, and gang warfare behind. We walk into our rooms at the Holiday Inn and shut out the outside world. In a few days, Kathie will be back in Old Crow. The kids at Broadway Elementary School will still be walking back and forth from the projects, which are on a different planet than the one with caribou and musk oxen.

Gordon in L.A.

Hey," says Clayton. "Guess what happens when an Eskimo sits on the ice too long?"

In most circles, it is no longer politically correct to say "Eskimo." It's OK for Clayton, though, because he *is* one. I have been introducing him as an "Inuvialuit," at least until he told me that the singular form is "Inuvialuk." *Eskimo* would be a hell of a lot easier. After a succession of Gwich'in speakers, Clayton is the first Inuvialuk to come down from the Arctic to join our traveling slideshow-circus.

The Inuvialuit live in and around the Mackenzie Delta and Canada's Western Arctic. Their brothers, sisters, cousins, and friends in Alaska are called "Inupiat." You couldn't tell them apart if you looked at them, but there is one big difference. The Inuvialuit in Canada want the calving grounds of the Porcupine caribou herd protected. The leaders of the Inupiat favor oil development, even though 95 percent of their traditional territory on Alaska's North Slope is already open for business. The Arctic Refuge is the last stand for wilderness in the American Arctic.

Clayton is living proof that not all "Eskimos" have been bought (or, more accurately, "rented") by Big Oil. When the last drop of oil trickles out of the Trans-Alaska Pipeline, the oil barons will be gone, taking their rent money with them. They will leave things behind, however, as they did in Pennsylvania and west Texas when the oil dried up: social problems, old drill rigs, rusting pipelines, pollution, and disrupted wildlife populations.

"I don't know what happens to an Eskimo sitting on the ice," I say.

"He gets Polaroids." Clayton stares out the window at the cloudburst drenching the freeway. "I thought it never rained in California."

"That's Chamber of Commerce propaganda to lure unsuspecting Eskimos down to Disneyland."

Clayton points past the flapping wipers toward the GMC pickup in front of us that is spraying our windshield with greasy freeway slop. "Do you know what GMC stands for?"

"No. What?" I pump the brakes nervously as the reflected glare of brake lights ahead on the freeway turns the wet pavement to blood-red. I check the rearview mirror to make sure that the cars behind me are slowing down, too. The rush hour is freezing traffic like an Arctic cold front.

"GMC—Got a Mechanic Coming?" says Clayton. "What about Ford? You know what that stands for?"

"No idea."

"Fix Or Repair Daily. Hey, look at that."

A ray of light from the setting sun slants under the smog, and rain bathes downtown L.A. in an unearthly smoky glow. The skyscrapers look unreal, like a mirage, but that isn't where Clayton is pointing. A huge black billboard looms over eight lanes of stalled traffic. Crimson letters spell out a spiritual message for our times: "Want to keep using my name in vain? I'll make the rush hour longer—God".

"I can't believe that people live here willingly," says Clayton.

"Are you telling me that the rush hour in the Mackenzie Delta isn't like this?"

He snorts and stares out the window. There are no roads to Clayton's home in Aklavik, a tiny village tucked in the watery maze of river channels and islands near the northern border of the Yukon and Northwest Territories. Clayton looks gaunt and tired, worn out by our frantic speaking schedule. The highway glare paints deep shadows below his high cheekbones that make him look faintly Mexican. Every Hispanic Californian we've met has rushed to his side like a long-lost brother and chattered to him in Spanish, although Clayton's ancestors did not come from Europe. They trekked across the land bridge from Asia during the last ice age.

"Have you ever been to Gordon?" he asks.

"You mean the abandoned trading post on the edge of Demarcation Bay?"

"That's right."

"Yeah, I've been there. What made you think about Gordon?"

"What's my name?"

"Is this another joke?"

"No."

"Your name is Clayton Gordon."

"Right. Gordon is named after my great-grandfather. I've never been there, but my grandparents and my father went through it when they migrated from Kaktovik to Aklavik. I always say they migrated, like the caribou."

We lapse into silence as we inch along the sodden freeway. I hadn't made the connection between Clayton and Gordon, a spot on maps in the extreme northeastern corner of Alaska. It's about as far away from the L.A. freeway as you can get.

Clayton, Wendy, Malkolm, and I have been tripping around Southern California for the past two weeks. We put on slideshows at UC San Diego, UCLA, and the Anaheim Sierra Club. We went to a Native healing center, where a shaman burned sweetgrass and gave us bundles of sage to keep away bad spirits. We lunched at a Kiwanis Club, where the members pledged allegiance to the flag before eating their salads, fined each other $10 for not wearing Kiwanis pins, and burst into song without provocation:

Take me down to Kiwanis
Take me down to the gang
Let's all be happy and let's all sing
We don't care—let the telephone ring
Come on—let's forget all our troubles
Loosen our ties and have fun
And we'll sing, sing, sing, and be gay
Whether cloud or sun!

Our final event was a luncheon at Kim Campbell's residence. Back in 1993, she was Prime Minister of Canada—for a grand total of 133 days. The Canadian electorate, who were in a surly mood after putting up with Campbell's predecessor Brian Mulroney for two terms, tossed Kim Campbell and her Conservative Party out of office in the worst election defeat in history. Campbell slipped out of the country soon after and became Canadian Consul General in Tinsel Town.

"Turn off at the next exit," Wendy called from the back seat, staring at the map on her lap. "Now Malkolm, I'm not sure how an eight-year-old should address a former Prime Minister."

"How about, 'Hi, Kim, how's it going?'" suggested Clayton.

"Sounds good to me," said Malkolm.

"Wait and see what everyone else is calling her," said Wendy, who is the manners police in our family. "The main thing is to be courteous."

"Speaking of courtesy," said Clayton with a grin, "what about the bizarre outfit Ken's wearing?"

"Speak for yourself," I retorted. "This suit is totally chic."

I was wearing a blue blazer, a burgundy shirt, and a navy blue tie with tiny bull caribou rutting under the midnight sun. Clayton had on running shoes, black pants, and a frayed white shirt with a black clip-on tie. Malkolm, in a white shirt with thin pinstripes, red tie, and shiny black oxfords, looked better than we did. His outfit cost $11 in a San Diego thrift shop.

Clayton Gordon, Ken Madsen, Malkolm, Pam Johnson, and Chance the dog at the residence of the Canadian Consul General, Los Angeles

I turned into a circular driveway in Beverly Hills and parked by the front door. We climbed out, and Malkolm pushed the doorbell. Pam Johnson, the Consulate's Director of Cultural Affairs opened the door, ushered us inside, and bustled upstairs to find Kim Campbell. Clayton stared at an ornate, black-and-red Haida mask on the wall and said "Hello." When it didn't reply, he wandered to the back door and looked out.

"Hey," he said, "the gardener is better dressed than we are."

After a couple of minutes, a blonde wearing a shapeless black tunic with a Nehru collar and big brass buttons walked down the staircase. “Hello,” she said cheerfully. “I’m Kim Campbell.”

“Hello, Kim Campbell,” replied Malkolm in a formal voice, reaching out to shake her hand. “I’m Malkolm.”

“I think my sister Jill was at law school the same time as you,” said Wendy.

“What year was she in?” asked Kim.

While they chatted about small-world stuff, Clayton and I unloaded the van, and Malkolm disappeared into the garden. Clayton walked in with the speakers. I walked in with the projectors. Malkolm ran in with mud splattered over his white shirt. Wendy took him to a bathroom to dab at the stain with a wet towel. Clayton and I lugged everything into a large parlor, where a pair of waiters with bow ties and a deferential manner were smoothing white tablecloths and arranging silver cutlery. Clayton set up the screen in front of a marble fireplace. I was on my knees searching for an electrical socket when a large black poodle romped into the room, followed by young man wearing baggy gray sweatpants and a white T-shirt.

“Calm down, Chance!” he said to the poodle.

He stood and surveyed the room with a frown. I wondered who he was. He wasn’t well dressed enough to be a waiter.

“I *have* to practice the piano,” said the man. “Kim and I are entertaining this evening.”

I stood up and dusted my pants. Then I introduced Clayton and myself.

“I’m Hershey,” he said, “and this is Chance. Chance! Calm down. How long will you be in here? I really *must* practice this Schubert. *Sit,* Chance!”

I might have paid more attention to Hershey had I read any recent Canadian newspapers. Hershey, an accomplished concert pianist, had become better known as Kim Campbell’s “Boy Toy.” The media had had a field day lampooning Campbell and her much younger partner. Hershey sat down and flawlessly banged out Schubert on a grand piano. Clayton and I plugged in the last wires and walked outside through the French doors.

“If that dog ever went to Aklavik,” said Clayton, who comes from a land where dogs are more often work animals than pets, “the other dogs would eat it in about five minutes.”

A few minutes later the music stopped, and Hershey walked outside, looking distracted, “Did Chance come out here? Chance! Chance, come to Daddy!”

Chance charged out from the parlor, barked at Clayton and me, and bounced over to Hershey. He lifted his fuzzy muzzle and licked Hershey’s face enthusiastically.

“If that’s the daddy,” whispered Clayton, “then I’d hate to see the mommy.”

“The guests are beginning to arrive,” called Kim Campbell from the hall. “Come and meet everyone. We’ll have lunch shortly.”

The Consulate had done a good job of organizing our event. The 30-odd guests included mission staff, journalists, and VIPs (although we didn't see Robert Redford or Julia Roberts). I got into the lunch line between Wendy and Clayton. We shuffled through a dining room and loaded our plates from a buffet table.

"What's that stuff?" asked Clayton doubtfully, looking at Wendy's plate.

"This is tortellini with pesto sauce," she said, "and here's some spinach lasagna. The salad is full of yuppie greens. This is kale, this is radicchio, and I think the spiky green stuff is arugula."

"Eskimos can't survive on salad," said Clayton ruefully. "I'm going to starve if I don't get home to Aklavik soon and eat some caribou meat."

Kim Campbell introduced us with a few surprisingly succinct and thoughtful sentences, especially considering she used to be a politician. I showed the slides. Clayton talked about Eskimos, caribou, and life in the Mackenzie Delta. Then we packed up in a hurry, hoping to beat the rush hour, and left Kim Campbell and Hershey to their next engagement.

The rain beats down on the freeway, the traffic in front of us plugged like a toilet. The headlights on the other side of the freeway look like a blowup photo of the Milky Way galaxy.

"Somebody must have used His name in vain," says Clayton.

"What?" asks Wendy, leaning forward from the back seat.

"That billboard we just saw. Looks like God already made the rush hour longer."

When we finally get to our cheap Anaheim hotel, we change out of our scruffy dress clothes into our scruffier street clothes and meet at Ricky's Restaurant, home of Ricky's Famous Apple Pancake ($7.95 plus tax). We sit on red plastic seats and stare at plastic menus. Wendy and I, still full of tortellini and salad, order tea. Malkolm asks for a glass of juice.

"I'll have coffee and your famous apple pancake," says Clayton to the server.

"This is the first time you've ever ordered anything besides steak," I say.

"This is in honor of you vegetarians," he replies. "Salads are fine for California, but you'd never survive a winter in the Arctic."

The server slides the famous apple pancake in front of Clayton with a flourish. It sprawls across the plate like a bulging, doughy pizza. Clayton stares at it thoughtfully, then slices it into four pieces. He shovels them onto side plates and passes them around the table.

"Thanks Clayton," I say. "This reminds me of traveling along the Arctic coast. Everyone we met out on the land offered us food."

"That's part of our culture," he says. "In the old days, starvation was never far away. We had to depend on each other."

I prod my chunk of famous apple pancake with a knife. The spongy blob quivers, as if it's alive. I cut off a small chunk and fork it into my mouth. It tastes like uncooked bread dough laced with cinnamon and sugar.

"It's weird how choked up I get when I speak to these audiences about the caribou," Clayton says. "We talk about politics and protecting wildlife habitat, but it's more than that. None of my family would even be around today if it wasn't for the caribou."

Clayton stares out the window. The clouds have drifted toward the Sierra Nevada, and a few stars shine insipidly though the yellow glow of smog and light pollution. He doesn't even pretend to eat his famous pancake.

"My father was born in Kaktovik. When a famine hit the village, my grandparents decided to leave. My grandfather only had four dogs, so he traded a rifle for a fifth. Then he loaded up his sled and migrated to Aklavik with my grandmother, my dad, and his younger brothers and sisters. They were somewhere near Gordon when a blizzard hit and pinned them down."

It's tough to imagine the ferocity of a midwinter Arctic storm when your backside is sliding around on Ricky's slick plastic seats. I remember summer storms in the Arctic Refuge that were bad enough. My tent, which is supposed to be durable enough for the south col of Mt. Everest, had flattened like one of Ricky's pancakes during the rage of a mid-July storm near Gordon.

"They couldn't move anywhere because of the blizzard, and then they ran out of food," Clayton says. "After three days with no food, my father took the sled and went into the storm by himself. He was the oldest of the kids, about 20 years old. He was gone for three days while the rest of the family waited, stranded in the blizzard.

"They had just about given up hope when my grandfather saw a dot coming across the snow. At first they were afraid that it was a polar bear, but when it got closer they saw that it was the sled. It was piled high with caribou meat and skins, but there was no sign of my father. My grandparents started to cry, thinking he had died in the storm and the dogs had returned without him.

"Then the pile of meat and fur started wriggling," Clayton continues. "My grandfather rushed over and ripped it all off the sled. Out popped my father! He had buried himself to keep from freezing and told the dogs to head back to camp."

Clayton's grandparents and family waited out the storm and eventually reached Aklavik safely. After a few years, Clayton was born. Now he has three sons of his own.

"It was my boys who convinced me to come down here for this slide tour," says Clayton with a grin. "I wasn't sure whether I should leave home, but they know the story about how the caribou saved our family. They told me to go get 'em.

"And so, here I am."

Gordon, Alaska

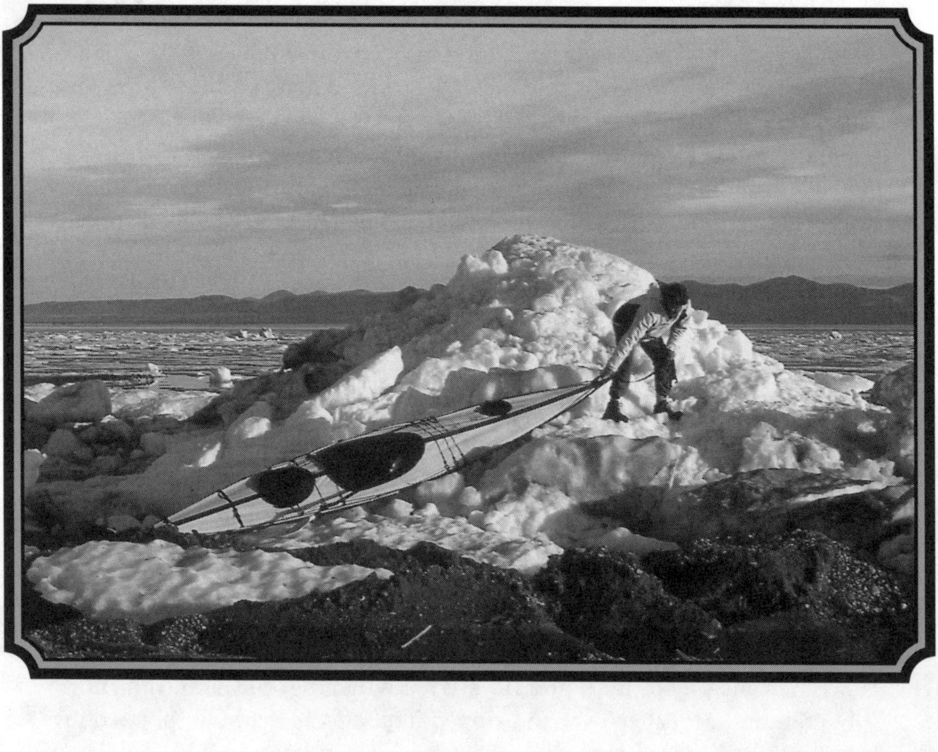

My kayak and I are alone together in a wilderness of sea ice, 100 yards from shore. I slither forward and jerk the sling attached to my kayak. The overloaded boat follows reluctantly, like a black Lab that wants to sniff at every tree where another dog has been. I hear what sounds like thunder, but the overcast that sprawls over the Arctic coast looks nothing like the towering cumulonimbus clouds that usually spawn thunderstorms. Besides, lightning doesn't happen on the Arctic coast—unless the climate is changing even faster than I thought. Probably it's the rumble of a jumbo jet speeding to Tokyo.

Then I hear a long, deep-throated growl of honest-to-god thunder. Damn. I'm in a bad spot. Federal Emergency Management Agency lightning-safety rule number one is *Get into a building or car.* I'd look pretty silly sitting in my kayak, even if there are only bearded seals to see me. Rule number two is *Avoid tall structures such as towers, tall trees, fences, telephone poles, or power lines.* I am the only tall structure in this flat prairie of ice, but I can't avoid myself. Final rule: *Stay away from rivers, lakes, or other bodies of water.* This frozen ocean surely qualifies as something to stay away from.

The thunder rumbles again. Rules are made to be broken, but not when it comes to being skewered by lightning. I jump over an open channel and drag the kayak toward shore. I haul my kayak off the ice, and I hunker down ten yards away from a permafrost mud bank that is taller than I am. The thunder sounds close, although I can't see any flashes. Can lightning dance from cloud to cloud, or does it have to strike the earth? I can't remember that detail from grade ten science. A chilling rain begins to fall, as if the lightning has ruptured the lining of the clouds. I put on my rain jacket and hunker down, shivering, until the thunder rumbles and rolls away to the east.

Forty-eight hours later, rain still drips steadily, an unusually long rainfall for this part of the world. If Glen Davis were here he'd be grumbling about how much it rains in the Arctic desert. I started this "paddling" trip after a three-week wilderness journey with Glen. We rafted down the Kongakut River and hiked across the coastal plain to Demarcation Bay. We set up camp beside the Turner River on a gravel bar that doubles as an airstrip. When Don Ross flew in to pick up Glen, he brought in my folding sea kayak and the food I had pre-packed for a solo trip to Herschel Island.

"Not much open water out there yet," said Don. "I wasn't sure whether you would really want this kayak."

"Maybe it'll be melted along the shore," I said hopefully. "Maybe the snowmelt flowing down the rivers will clear out the ice."

"Well, maybe," he said, shrugging and passing the kayak down to me.

Unfortunately, Don doesn't know how pigheaded I can be when I am fixated on an idea. It would have saved me a lot of trouble had he bluntly pointed out that it is ludicrous to try sea kayaking in a frozen ocean. Kayaking to Herschel Island had *sounded* good during the winter when Wendy, Malkolm, and I had made plans in our warm, ice-free living room. They would drive up the Dempster Highway to Inuvik with a double folding kayak and lots of food. They would load it onto a charter airplane bound for Herschel Island. We'd meet on July 2 and paddle together happily under the midnight sun.

That fairy tale ending is looking less and less likely. I've been slipping and sliding on the ice for four days although, to be fair, I have paddled some of the way. Once I even managed to kayak along a skinny lead of open water for several miles before it ended in another frozen quagmire. Now it is June 28, and I'm only a quarter of the way to Herschel Island. My last hope is that the Clarence River has flushed the ice out toward the North Pole.

The mouth of the Clarence looks like a large lake with albino sand shores. I steady my kayak on an ice floe, wriggle into the cockpit, and seal-launch into the water. Fifteen minutes later, the ice closes in again. I paddle to shore, beach the kayak, and walk along the edge of the tundra to check out the ice conditions to the east. It's hopeless. An endless series of pressure ridges are jammed against the shore. They look like giant Hawaiian waves, fast frozen in the Arctic deep freeze.

The only way to keep going would be overland. If I unloaded my kayak and divided everything into manageable Sherpa loads, I would need to take three trips to backpack everything along the coast. Including the return trips to pick up the next load, 20 miles of progress would take 100 miles of walking.

I sit on a log to decide what to do. The log is an antique, bleached by the sun and sand-blasted by blizzards. Captain John Franklin might have sat on this log in 1826, when he looked across the tundra and named the Clarence River for the British Lord High Admiral. Three cheers for the Lord High Admiral, and let's all get promoted if we ever get back to London. Franklin had barely survived his first Arctic trip six years earlier. He became famous in England as "the man who ate his shoes," after his horrific expedition had been battered by starvation, accidents, murder, and cannibalism.

The Admiralty took careful note of Franklin's first failure and sent him out again, this time to explore westward from the Mackenzie Delta. Not long before he reached the Clarence River, he met a group of 200 Eskimos, the ancestors of people like Clayton Gordon and Calvin Elanik. The Eskimos decided to massacre the British and steal their goods, but Franklin got wind of the plan and managed to escape. As the Eskimos watched the British Navy struggling westward, battling the waves and ice, they asked each other why men would use boats rather than dogs and sleds.

There are no Eskimos at Clarence Lagoon to tell me I'm crazy to be kayaking on a frozen ocean. My only company is a yellow-billed loon floating in Clarence Lagoon. It stares at me with its bright red eye, submerges suddenly, and pops up with a wriggling fish. That is the only advice the loon is prepared to give. It's enough. I know that if I keep groveling toward Herschel Island, I'll be a week late for my rendezvous with Wendy and Malkolm.

Explorers in Franklin's era did not have rescue beacons or satellite phones. When Franklin ran into trouble during his third (and final) Arctic trip, it was years before the British Admiralty realized something was wrong and sent out rescue ships. All they found were a few tattered journal pages, buttons, and bones. Like Franklin, I'm not carrying a beacon or phone. That's where the similarity ends. If I don't show up at Herschel Island on schedule, a rescue plane will come looking. That's the last thing I want. Besides, it would prove that I'm not only stubborn, but stupid.

Retreating to Demarcation Bay feels like failure, but if I hustle back to the Turner River gravel bar/airstrip, I can try to flag down a passing bush plane. By my calculations, Wendy will be leaving for Inuvik in two days. I'll have to be fast and lucky to get word to her before she starts driving. She would not be pleased to drive 800 useless, dusty miles. I've already been traveling for eight hours today, but I decide to go as far as I can before camping. I wave goodbye to the loon and walk back to my kayak.

I paddle across the open water, get out, and drag the kayak across the now-familiar ice floes. It is still drizzling, and rainwater is lying on the sea ice in a slippery film. I shift into cruise control and keep going. After several hours I start to wonder if I might be able to make it all the way without stopping. I find my one lead of open water and paddle past the Alaska-Yukon border. Yesterday I crossed illegally into Canada. Today I'm crossing illegally back into the United States. A double negative is a positive. Sometime in the middle of the night the rain finally stops, and a wedge of clear sky appears on the northern horizon.

About noon the next day I reach an impassable jumble of ice blocks. I decide to take a shortcut directly across the tundra toward Demarcation Bay. I unload my kayak and look gloomily at my huge mound of gear. Along with three weeks of food, my clothes, and camping gear, I have two cameras, five lenses, a tripod, and 50 rolls of film. I'm glad Glen isn't here to tease me about traveling light. It is going to take three trips to hump all the stuff. I start with the kayak. I grab the sling attached to the grab loop and drag it through the tussocks. I haul it past an Arctic fox den, past a pond with nesting tundra swans, and over a headland. Demarcation Bay shimmers in the brightening light a mile away. When my hands cramp on the towline, I abandon the boat on the tundra. My fingers look like eagle talons. I massage them back to life as I walk back to the ocean for more gear.

I load up a heavy pack and retrace my route. I pass the forlorn kayak and trudge toward the bay. As I near the water I see a snowy owl perched on the slumping remains of a log cabin: downtown Gordon, Alaska. Gordon doesn't have much to offer a weary tourist: no endless strip mall of cheap motels and fast-food joints, no tourist information center, no casino run by the local natives. City center is a meandering creek, the windswept tundra, and the drooping cabin. The population of Gordon is seven: the owl and six caribou hanging around on Main Street. The town isn't big enough for the caribou and me. They clear out when I stagger into town. The owl waits a little longer, until it sees me rummage in my pack for my camera. Then it spreads its pale wings and flies jerkily toward the Brooks Range.

I dump my backpack beside the bay and hike back to retrieve the rest of my gear. When the job is done, I'm lightheaded from lack of sleep. I sprawl on a log and munch crackers, cheese, and chocolate. A mirage hovers over the ocean to the north: shimmering, elongated lines of blue-and-white light. Mirages are common over the Arctic Ocean: The light bends as it arcs upward through sun-warmed layers of air. Arctic explorers were often confounded by mirages, charting new islands where no land existed.

The distorted image reminds me of Clayton Gordon and the Los Angeles skyline that we'd seen through a smog-lens. Back in California, Clayton had asked me if I'd ever been to Gordon. Now I'm in here again, thinking about an Eskimo in L.A. and how quickly his culture has had to adapt. Before the coming of Europeans, Eskimos survived by enduring. They sat hunched over a seal's breathing hole, as still as a snowdrift. They survived endless winters that would drive me mad. They bent in the storm-swept polar night like tough willows, whipping back to reach for the light when the sun returned in the spring.

The decaying log cabin is the only sign that Tom Gordon, Clayton's great-grandfather, once built a trading post here. Gordon was not an Eskimo. He was from Scotland. Why would a man pack up his kilts, travel halfway across the world, and build a trading post in such a lonely corner of the Arctic? Scotland has its share of windswept moors, but they are like the French Riviera compared to the shores of Demarcation Bay.

I take a last look at Gordon then launch wearily into the bay, fixed on reaching the Turner River before I collapse. It's only eight miles away. Before long though, ice hems me in again. I slither out of my kayak and start hauling across the slippery ice that is riddled with holes, like a huge slice of Swiss cheese. The holes, some big enough to swallow a recreational vehicle, are hidden under six inches of dirty brown melt-water from the peat banks that are oozing from the recent rain. I inch forward, tapping my paddle like a blind man's cane. For the first time I'm happy that I'm towing such a hog of an overloaded kayak. I keep a death grip on the sling and use it to haul myself out whenever I slide into an ice-water pit.

I finally beach the boat at the mouth of the Turner River. Limp, soggy, and bruised after traveling nonstop for 36 hours, I set up my tent in a stupor, listening to seabirds loudly celebrating the coming of summer. Long-tailed ducks jabber ceaselessly. Red-throated loons wail like lost children. Sandhill cranes hoot from the tundra. A flock of surf-scoters rockets overhead and lands in the bay. The wind rushing over their wings makes them sound like a squadron of F-18 fighter jets.

I blow up my Therm-a-Rest and squirm into my sleeping bag, but I'm too wired to sleep. I listen to the birds and wonder how many days it'll be before a plane happens by. Forty-five minutes later I hear a drone. I poke my head out of the tent. A black Cessna 206 zooms toward the Brooks Range, turns, and swoops down to land. It's a small world in the Arctic, and I know who is flying the plane: Walt Audi, an old-time bush pilot from Kaktovik.

I had flown with Walt the previous summer when we were filming a TV documentary with the embarrassing title of "Champions of the Wild." Later in the summer, Wendy, Malkolm, and I hitched a ride with Walt to Prudhoe Bay after we had kayaked to Kaktovik. We had camped out in Walt's old Chevy van in Deadhorse while we waited for a flight to Fairbanks. The van smelled like diesel and old socks, but it was better than spending $300 for a room in the Prudhoe Bay Hotel.

"Hey Walt," I yell as Walt clambers down from the cockpit. "Am I glad to see you!"

"Hi Ken," Walt says nonchalantly, as though we run into each other on deserted gravel bars every day.

I must look as wild as the Mad Trapper of Rat River. I haven't shaved in a month, washed for a week or slept in nearly two days. This is the North, however, and Walt has seen wackier things than me since he arrived in Kaktovik back in 1964. He looks at me without blinking. He doesn't ask what I'm doing or why I'm there. Walt knows that it's best to let "bushed" people tell their stories in their own sweet time. I blabber my story right away.

"Do you want a ride back to Kaktovik?" he asks.

"I guess that's my only option."

"Let's go."

I pluck the tent pegs out of the tundra while Walt dismantles the kayak. We chuck it all in a heap in the back of the plane. An hour later we land in Kaktovik, transfer my gear to the back of a pickup, and drive to Walt's hotel, the "Waldo Arms." I say hello to Walt's wife, Merlyn, then head to the pay phone, which is tucked behind the pool table and the bathrooms. I dial home.

"Hi Wendy," I say when she answers. "Guess where I am!"

"Ken? Is that you? Are you in Fairbanks? Did you have an accident?"

"No, I'm fine, except I'm not going to be at Herschel Island on schedule." I tell her the sordid details of my trip.

"I *was* surprised that you didn't come back with Glen," she says.

"I thought you'd be pissed off. At least I caught you before you headed up the Dempster Highway."

"I'm not pissed off. It's the kind of thing I expect from you. The food is all packed, and we're ready to go. What are you going to do now?"

"I guess I'll have to fly back to Fairbanks, but the next flight doesn't leave until the day after tomorrow. Then I'll take the bus to Whitehorse, but that only goes three times a week. I may have to wait for a couple of days. Do you still want to go up to Herschel Island?"

"Of course I still want to go to Herschel! We'll wait until you get here, and then we can drive up the Dempster Highway together."

"Right. I'll call you when I get to Fairbanks."

We whisper a couple of sweet nothings, and I hang up. I walk around the corner and sink into a soft couch. I stare blankly at a large-screen TV tuned to a news broadcast from Anchorage. I'm spaced out from sleeplessness and the abrupt transition from the windswept shores of Demarcation Bay to the overheated sitting room in the Waldo Arms. I'm happy that everything at home is fine. On the other hand, I'm bummed out about my new and depressing travel itinerary to Herschel Island.

I flip idly through a book somebody left on Walt's coffee table: *Fifty Years Below Zero* by Charles D. Brower. I stop turning pages when the name Tom Gordon leaps off the page into my bloodshot eyes. I read that Gordon had abandoned Scotland in the waning days of the nineteenth century and sailed to North America. He worked his way westward to the Pacific and drifted up the coast to Alaska, where he teamed up with Charles Brower to hunt bowhead whales.

Gordon and Brower journeyed to the Arctic with dollar signs in their eyes, anxious to exploit the North's natural wealth and siphon it into southern bank accounts. Globalization is not a new phenomenon: The health of communities, local subsistence economies, and the environment are only important if they affect the corporate bottom line. The whalers were not much different than the oil barons who would come north a century later.

One day, Gordon and Brower went to an impromptu party to celebrate the bowheads they'd killed that summer:

> Amid general jubilation over the fine season we'd had, the inland people began trading what furs they had for whiskey. In the light of what happened, I've never begrudged them the good time they had on that bad whiskey.
>
> For the ships stayed just long enough to give the Eskimos a germ of some sort, probably a kind of flu....
>
> "They're a strong, healthy bunch," said Mac. "I doubt if it's hit them hard."
>
> But when we had a chance to go out there and see how they were making out we found whole families down with the sickness. Too sick to

> move, nevertheless they were being urged by their "devil-doctors" to pack up and leave for home. The coast, it seemed, wasn't good for them....
>
> It was pitiful to see all those fine men and women grown so weak that only their devil-doctor's ranting coupled with their own will power enabled them to crawl about trying to load up their oomiaks for the interminable voyage up the rivers and home. We had to stand there helpless on the littered beach and watch them go, the whole 50 boatloads.
>
> Two or three of our own sick died late from pneumonia, but when the rest recovered rapidly we thought maybe we'd been too pessimistic about those inland natives. They had seemed a husky lot. And, as Tom [Gordon] put it, "Maybe their damned devil-doctors knew what they were doing, after all. They kept telling them they'd soon be well, didn't they? Y'know Charlie, some of these devil-doctors do funny things!"
>
> ...Not long after this, an Eskimo from the village who had been far inland and so hadn't heard of any sickness, burst into the station to tell of a lot of dead people scattered along the banks of a river where he'd been hunting.
>
> We left for Berniak at once. Following the homeward course of the strickened people we came upon the first evidence of disaster not ten miles away—a woman with a young baby. She had died on the bank of the lagoon. The child had lived a while longer. His body lay quite a way off.
>
> The farther we went, the greater the tragedy. It was clear that from the day they set out for home in their oomiaks they had been dying all along the coast and up the rivers. From the postures of the bodies, we could almost visualize it happening—the stronger members dragging the weaker on to the banks to die, then paddling a little farther until it came their turn to be abandoned....
>
> It is my opinion that of those two hundred or more husky inland Eskimos who so light-heartedly danced with us at Utkiavie, not one was left alive.

Tom Gordon hunted whales with Brower for several years, overwintering in the Arctic. The whalers traded food, metal tools, weapons, and alcohol to the Inupiat. In return they received wild meat, furs, and warm skin clothing. The Inupiat abandoned their bone and stone implements for sharper-edged metal knives and axes. They put down their spears and learned to shoot rifles. Gordon sailed south just before the bowhead whaling industry collapsed in 1910. Bowhead whales were almost extinct, and the Arctic's first economic "boom" was over. The inevitable bust followed. The Inupiat picked up the threads of their seminomadic culture, traveling along the coast in search of the wild animals that had sustained them since the last ice age.

Gordon found work with a trading company in San Francisco. They loaded him up with trade goods and shipped him north on the "Bonanza."

He established a trading post in Kaktovik and another on the shores of Demarcation Bay. He married an Inupiat woman and fathered children, including Clayton's grandfather. He traded pots, pans, rifles, bullets, and processed food for furs and wild meat. When the price of furs dropped in the late 1930s, the Inupiat could no longer afford the manufactured goods that they now depended upon. The trading posts closed, one after another. Tom Gordon died in 1938.

The whales the Inupiat had hunted were nearly gone. All of the musk oxen in Alaska had been killed. Walruses were scarce—and so were the manufactured goods that the Inupiat had learned to depend upon. People went hungry. Some starved. Families packed up and migrated toward Canada, including Clayton's grandparents.

The Inupiat were largely forgotten by the "real world" until the Arctic coast became strategically important during the Cold War. The Air Force bulldozed out a runway in Kaktovik in 1947. A Distant Early Warning (DEW) line station was built in Kaktovik in the mid-1950s. DEW line stations were strung across the North American Arctic like Christmas lights, ready to light up at the first blip on the radar screen.

In 1958, an anthropologist named Norman Chance traveled to Kaktovik to study the Inupiat. He interviewed the superintendent in charge of the Kaktovik DEW line station.

> "I'd like to get a better understanding of the kind of work villagers do at the site and what your experience with them has been." Norma began:
>
> "I see. Well, they do lots of things, maintenance, mostly; although some of the men run heavy equipment and repair machinery—both here and at the smaller stations. It's a six-day work week beginning at 7:30 in the morning. All permanently employed Eskimos work on rotation. They spend six weeks here at the main site and then six weeks at a smaller one down the coast. Right now, we badly need eight more Eskimos and will probably have to go to Barrow to get them."
>
> "Sounds like there's a quota."
>
> "No, not exactly. But hiring local people keeps the labor costs down. Since there is no union and the Eskimos live here, they don't have to be paid as much…."
>
> "But why are local people paid less if they do the same work?"
>
> "Do you know what Eskimos get in Canada for working on the DEW Line? Two hundred a month. We give them three times that amount. By comparison, the people here are making out really well. Sometimes I think we do too much for the Eskimos. Eventually, they become unappreciative."
>
> "What about women?"

"Women? No women have ever been hired at any DEW Line site, Native or otherwise. Strictly a man's world up here. Got enough problems as it is."

"Do any involve local people?"

"Sure. The worst one is that some Eskimos just up and quit whenever they feel like it....I know they look at the world differently than we do, but if they want to work here they are going to have to learn to be responsible."

"Perhaps they have responsibilities at home."

"Could be. But that's no excuse for just taking off....Like I said, sometimes they are unappreciative. Even take advantage of us...."

"I expect they see it differently. It is, after all, their land."

"Not really. Of course, they can use any land that is not needed by the military. But they don't control it."

"Who does?"

"The Air Force."

"What about alcohol use here at the site?"

"To my knowledge, there is no problem either here or in the village. Very little hard liquor is brought in although beer flows fairly freely. All the men at the site have a quota of a six-pack a week. Occasionally, Eskimos will take advantage of this opportunity, but they can't do much damage on six cans of beer...."

"How well do the people work together—those in the village and Whites from outside?"

"Quite well, really. Life is hard up here, especially in winter. The Eskimos often know more about the weather than we do—what to expect, how to take care of themselves in a snowstorm, that kind of thing. You have to respect them for that....They are also good workers, too, especially when they think what they are doing is important. It's just that they always want time off to hunt. That's the big problem."

"I guess they are trying to keep their options open. Hunting has got to be their major form of security—that and sharing."

"That may be, but I don't think the emphasis on sharing will last much longer. A doctor at the Barrow hospital told me recently Eskimos making high wages over there are plagued by relatives looking for handouts. An uncle or cousin will come around and expect to receive food, clothing, even money and other things from any family that is bringing in the bucks. Some are even sponging off their relatives right here at Barter Island."

Norman Chance returned to Kaktovik several times over next few years. Toward the end of his last trip he visited with an Inupiat elder, Vincent Nageak. The two of them walked along the edge of the village to an embankment overlooking the Beaufort Sea, a favorite lookout for Inupiat women when their men were out hunting seals.

"Do you miss the old days, Vincent?"

As usual, he answered by telling a story.

"Ten years ago, Apik and I went on a trip to hunt caribou. A day's ride from here, a big storm came up. We knew it was going to be a bad one, and I pointed my lead dog toward an old abandoned house nearby. Just then, Apik saw a caribou. We stopped, and he killed it, but then it was too late to get to the house. The snow came down so thick, we couldn't see anything. We had to make a snow house in the bank. We had meat, a small stove, and tea, that's all.

"It was all right for a day or two, but the storm was so bad we could only get a little way toward home before the wind came up and we had to stop again. Pretty soon we ran out of fuel. We jumped up and down and ran around in our little house to keep warm. We think we never get back to our home. But we went on. Next day we made it. Apik, he never liked to hunt after that. He works in Barrow now. But I don't think that old way is so bad. Anyway, people around here, they don't hunt so much any more. The young ones, they hardly know how."

Social and industrial change accelerated in the Arctic after Norman Chance's last visit. In 1968, oil was discovered at Prudhoe Bay. In 1973, Vice President Spiro Agnew broke a tie vote in the U.S. Senate that allowed the passage of the Trans-Alaska Pipeline Authorization Act. Oil flowed south. Money flowed north.

Many Inupiat now work in the oilfields, and the average income in Kaktovik is $46,250. The average income in the nearest Gwich'in settlement, Arctic Village, is $9,661. The Gwich'in say that a bust is coming after the oil boom—and what will happen then, if the caribou are gone?

The current Inupiat subsistence hunt focuses on marine mammals: mainly seals and endangered bowhead whales. They are dead set against offshore oil drilling, which they believe might force whales away from Barter Island. Yet the Inupiat leaders are in favor of oil drilling in the Arctic Refuge, which would affect caribou hunting for both the Gwich'in and the Inuvialuit of the Mackenzie Delta.

The sitting room in the Waldo Arms is warm and stuffy. My eyelids begin to droop. The phone rings, and Merlyn answers it. I can't help overhearing her half of the conversation.

"You're kidding! When? You know, I don't feel safe walking around this town anymore." She talks for a couple of minutes, then hangs up and calls to me. "There was just another fight in town. A man shot at his brother with a shotgun. He missed with the gun, and then went after him with a knife."

"Is there much violence in Kaktovik?" I ask.

"Yes, and it is all alcohol-related, even though this is supposed to be a dry town."

Every town in the North—white, Inupiat, Gwich'in, or Inuvialuit—deals daily with social problems: alcohol and drug abuse, domestic violence, alienated youth. The communities that handle it most effectively are those that maintain their cultural identity, their connection with the land. For the Inupiat that means a healthy Arctic marine environment. For the Gwich'in and Inuvialuit, it means a healthy caribou herd. For white folks? Who knows? When I'm driving on a L.A. freeway, it is hard to believe we have any connection with the land, although I sure like knowing there is wilderness to get lost in out there somewhere.

"You know," yells Walt from the dining room, "I could probably fly you past the worst of the ice if you want."

"Don't you need a permit to fly across the Canadian border?"

"Oh probably," he says with a grin, "but this is an emergency, right? I found you stranded on the beach."

"Sounds good to me," I say. "I'll call Wendy and tell her my travel plans have changed again."

The next morning, Walt and I reload the plane and take off for our clandestine flight. Demarcation Bay is still plugged with ice. Gordon, Alaska, is almost invisible from the air. In a few years it will sink completely back into the tundra, and the boom years of the whalers and traders will be nothing but a few lines in dusty books. The oilfield installations will take longer to crumble once the oil stops flowing south.

Walt dips down lower as we zoom across the border, flying just above the ice to avoid enemy radar. A pair of musk oxen gallops along the beach beside Clarence Lagoon. Walt lands on the sand spit at the mouth of the Firth River, tosses my gear out of the plane, and hurriedly takes off. I look cheerfully at the open water that stretches toward Herschel Island. My good cheer doesn't last long. Half an hour later I see a pair of rafts rowing toward me from the mouth of the Firth. It is the Superintendent of Ivvavik National Park along with the warden responsible for law enforcement (whose main concerns are illegal flights and poaching). They were finishing their annual inspection trip down the Firth when they saw Walt's black plane fly in from Alaska. And fly back to Alaska. They know that no one has a permit to land today. They are spitting mad, expecting to find a poacher lurking. They find me, hastily stretching my kayak's skin over its frame.

But that's another story.

A Clash of Cultures

The flight of stone steps is as wide as a football field. They march up toward the great front doors of the U.S. Supreme Court in Washington, D.C. Above the doors, two marble statues stare coldly over my head toward the U.S. Capitol. The statues' job is to guard the words chiseled between them: "Equal Justice Under Law." I jaywalk across the street toward the United Methodist Building, an unassuming gray structure sandwiched between the Supreme Court and the Senate office buildings. I dodge a car and hop onto the sidewalk, scattering a dozen starlings scratching under a pine tree. A tiny plaque says it's the "Tree of Peace."

The Tree of Peace was planted by the chiefs and clan mothers of the Six Nations/Iroquois. It was a seedling when the Gwich'in Nation came together in 1988 to talk about the threat of oil development to the Porcupine caribou herd. The tree is now 50 feet tall, and the Gwich'in are still struggling to protect the calving grounds. The Arctic Refuge is more at risk today than ever before. This morning the Gwich'in are holding a press conference in the Methodist Building.

I go inside and find an empty seat next to Stanley Njootli, a friend from Old Crow. Ten serious-faced native leaders are sitting on folding chairs at the front of the room, their faces bathed in the harsh glare of television floodlights. Two banners are taped to the wall above their heads. On the first, a bull caribou stands silhouetted against the blood-red background of a setting sun. One of its antlers is curled into a human fist. The second banner is the teal blue "Proud to be Gwich'in" flag that I saw fluttering above Caroline Kay's camp up on the Rat River.

Dune Lankard stands up to welcome us. Dune is an Eyak tribal member from Alaska's Copper River Delta. Like the Gwich'in, the culture and subsistence lifestyle of his people has been soaked in crude-oil politics. The homeland of the Eyak people is in Prince William Sound, which is still trying to recover from the *Exxon Valdez* oil spill. Dune tells us that he is honored to be standing here in solidarity with the Gwich'in. Then he introduces Sarah James.

Sarah walks slowly up to the bank of microphones. She is holding a caribou skin drum and a drumstick. She looks just the same as when Matthew, Glen, and I visited her tiny cabin up in Arctic Village. She hasn't learned to put on a different face for different occasions. She doesn't know how to be anyone but Sarah James.

"This is a drum dance," says Sarah. "It's called the caribou skin hut dance. We welcome you into our skin hut. We welcome you into our spirit."

We all stand up. Sarah pounds on the drum and sings in the Gwich'in language. The drum beats are thick and regular. If we were in a real skin hut up in the boreal forest, the walls would expand and contract with the rhythm, like a beating heart. Stanley Njootli knows the song. He sways with the beat and sings along. When Sarah finishes, he takes a deep breath. We all sit down.

"Back in 1988, our elders told us that that the oil companies were threatening the sacred calving grounds," says Sarah. "At that time no one knew about us. The Gwich'in were the last indigenous culture to be contacted by the Columbus culture. We are caribou people. We had food on the table. We had our own language. We thought we were safe."

While Sarah is speaking, a zip-lock plastic bag circulates through the room, passing from hand to hand. The bag is full of dried caribou meat and "bone-grease," marrow from caribou bones. I pass the bag to Stanley.

Jonathon Solomon, the U.S. chair of the Gwich'in Steering Committee from Fort Yukon, Alaska, shuffles up to the microphones when Sarah finishes. He says that he started fighting for the land decades ago when Alaskan politicians concocted a plan to construct the Ramparts Dam, a project that would have flooded Gwich'in villages in the Yukon flats. He tells us that the future of the caribou and the future of the Gwich'in are the same.

Bull caribou, coastal plain, Arctic National Wildlife Refuge

"I used to be a big macho man," says Jonathon. "Then I came down to Washington, D.C., to lobby. There was so much drinking in the offices back then, I became an alcoholic. Now I've stopped drinking, but deep down I'm still an alcoholic. It's like being a developer. There is nothing in between. You drink or you don't drink. They develop or they don't develop. There's no in between."

One by one the aboriginal leaders come forward to talk. They come from tiny villages in Alaska and from the National Congress of American Indians. They come from Hawaii, the Southwest deserts, and the Great Plains. The last to stand up is Russell Means of AIM, the American Indian Movement. He is a veteran from the standoff at Wounded Knee.

"My people were here 120 years ago when the Europeans killed 60 million buffalo," he says, staring grim-faced at the mostly white faces in front of him. His face could be a statue cast from bronze.

"We are now less than one half of one percent of the people, and still you won't leave us alone. I come from a people out of sight, out of mind. We talk about people in Africa whose culture is being taken away. What about our own people? The Gwich'in are the last of the last. The last of the indigenous people."

He speaks slowly and deliberately, each word like a throbbing drum beat. The words bounce around the room, and when they finally come to rest they still hang heavily in the air.

"The last of the last. And you're going to eradicate them. You come to Pine Ridge—you'll see what's going to happen to them. Pine Ridge is the poorest county in America."

He turns and walks back to his chair. Dune Lankard returns to the microphone and asks for questions.

"I was just over at the Senate building watching Kenneth Lay take the Fifth Amendment about Enron," says a reporter sitting in front of Stanley. "I want to know, has Dick Cheney approached the Gwich'in people? Has there been consultation at any time?"

"Dick Cheney hasn't consulted with us," answers Sarah James. "We had Gale Norton though; she came to Arctic Village."

Glen Davis, Matthew Lien, and I happened to be in Arctic Village last June when Gale Norton, the U.S. Secretary of the Interior, was in town. We saw her plane on the gravel runway when we arrived on the scheduled flight from Fairbanks. A hot wind swept out of the boreal forest, and gravel was flying around the airfield. We had been hoping that our pilot, Dirk Nickish, would fly us directly to the coastal plain, but thick gray clouds squatted over the Brooks Range. There would be no further travel today.

We carried our gear into a dusty shack next to a derelict old Airstream trailer. A crudely painted sign on the shiny metal side of the trailer said "Snacks." Glen wandered over hopefully, but the snack shop had been long abandoned and was full of spider webs and ground-squirrel droppings. I dug out the stove to make soup, but Matthew stuck his head into the shack before the stove was lit.

"Ken! Grab your camera! Gale Norton is out here. I gave her my 'Special Envoy' card and asked if I could have my picture taken with her."

Matthew is a musical superstar in Taiwan. He is more popular than the Backstreet Boys and Bryan Adams. His CDs are platinum. He gets mobbed by crowds and has a line of bed sheets named after him. The Yukon Government, hoping to use his fame to generate tourism interest in the Yukon, designated him as Special Envoy and printed him business cards complete with the official Yukon crest. I grabbed my camera case and tripod.

A dozen people milled around the plane, looking brisk and important, a little slice of Washington, D.C., channeled to the Arctic. I wondered if the one behind the mirror glasses was a Secret Service agent. Either that or Cam Toohey, who was recently plucked from his job as executive director of Arctic Power to be Gale Norton's new special assistant for Alaska. Arctic Power's sole mandate is to lobby for oil development in the Arctic Refuge. Arctic Power is funded to the tune of millions of dollars by the oil industry and the Alaska legislature.

"Over here, Ken!" yelled Matthew.

Matthew and Gale Norton were posing beside the nose cone of her airplane. She was dressed in the casual African safari look: khaki shirt and pants, a braided leather belt, and a black fleece vest. She wore a name tag made by the kids of Arctic Village: "Gale N", surrounded by gaily colored flowers. The wind blowing down from the mountains whipped their hair around their faces. Matthew leaned toward her in an oddly intimate manner, and I snapped their picture. She headed for the plane, and a man came over and introduced himself. He turned out to be an Arctic Refuge biologist with whom I had corresponded. He grimaced when I complimented him on the company he was keeping.

"Have you heard where the caribou are now?" I asked him.

"The migration is late again this year," he answered. "Last I heard, they were still in Canada. If they knew what this crowd has planned for them, they'd stay there." We shook hands and wished each other luck. He turned and headed for the plane.

Matthew, Glen, and I returned to our hut for a frugal meal of soup, bread, and cheese. Then we walked along the airstrip toward town. The wind had the freshness of glaciers, and the year's first lupines swayed and shuddered. We poked our heads into the community hall which had been spruced up for the important visitor. Handmade posters covered the walls. They featured drawings of caribou with headlines such as: "Our Arctic Way of Life Has Endured for 20,000 Years; Must We Now Die for 6 Months of Oil?" and "The Buffalo Died—Let the Caribou Live!"

We walked up the hill and knocked on the door of Sarah James' cabin. She opened the door, smiled, and invited us in. She gave us juice and cookies. We had to move "Proud to be Gwich'in" T-shirts to find places to sit.

"We won't stay long," I said. "You must be tired after the meeting with Gale Norton."

"How did it go?" asked Matthew.

"It was a good meeting," said Sarah. "We fed them good. Evon Peter, the chief, told her that we need to protect what we have, which includes the caribou. I was especially proud of our young people. They all stood up and told her why we need to protect the calving grounds. Boy, we had a lot of good speakers. I think we touched her heart."

"That's great!" says Matthew.

"Everybody did good," says Sarah. "I just hope she is a good listener."

"I'm afraid that Sarah will be disappointed," said Glen as we walked back toward the airport.

"When I told Gale Norton that the coastal plain was the most beautiful place I'd ever seen," said Matthew, "she looked like she'd swallowed a lemon."

"You sure she didn't swallow a lemming?" asked Glen.

Sarah James was out on the land when we flew back through Arctic Village after our three-week trip in the Refuge. I didn't hear what had happened after Gale Norton's visit, although I did read an article in the *Washington Post* that described her testimony to the Senate Energy Committee. The newspaper reported that Secretary Norton gave false information and ignored key U.S. Fish and Wildlife Service data about potential environmental impacts of drilling in the Refuge. Her testimony relied heavily on information from an oil-industry consultant's report that acknowledged BP Exploration for its "encouragement, funding, and useful comments."

"If Congress is going to have a serious discussion on the future of the Arctic Refuge," said a Fish and Wildlife employee, who requested anonymity, "it ought to have the whole story, not a slanted story. We tried to present all the facts, but she only passed along the ones she liked. And to pass along facts that are false, well, that's obviously inappropriate."

The next time I saw Sarah James was in Washington, D.C.

The reporter in front of us leaned forward and started scribbling in a notebook.

"We hosted her very well, and she seemed to listen very well. But then she went away and said that we were naive. She said we only think about ourselves. She said we didn't think about the poor American kids that need oil. Our kids, our Gwich'in kids, came together just after her visit. We dedicated a solar panel to create energy for them. That's for their future.

"When we first heard that the oil companies wanted to drill for oil in the calving grounds, we asked our elders, 'What are we going to do?' The elders gave us a good direction, to do this in a good way, to teach the world a good way. We dance the caribou dance. We tell the caribou stories. When the caribou come, our hearts beat fast, we get excited. Everybody says '*Vutzai, vutzai!*' ['Caribou!'] The Gwich'in are caribou people, and the coastal plain is vital to our caribou. We call their calving grounds '*the place where life begins.*' We cannot allow it to be ruined by oil drilling."

After the press conference I walk outside. In the Capitol and the Senate office buildings, people are preparing to debate the energy legislation and the future of the Arctic Refuge. The February sun shines weakly, and a political wind whips around Capitol Hill. I don't believe that Sarah James is naive to try to protect the future of the Gwich'in and the caribou, but then again, what do I know?

RETURN TO OLD CROW

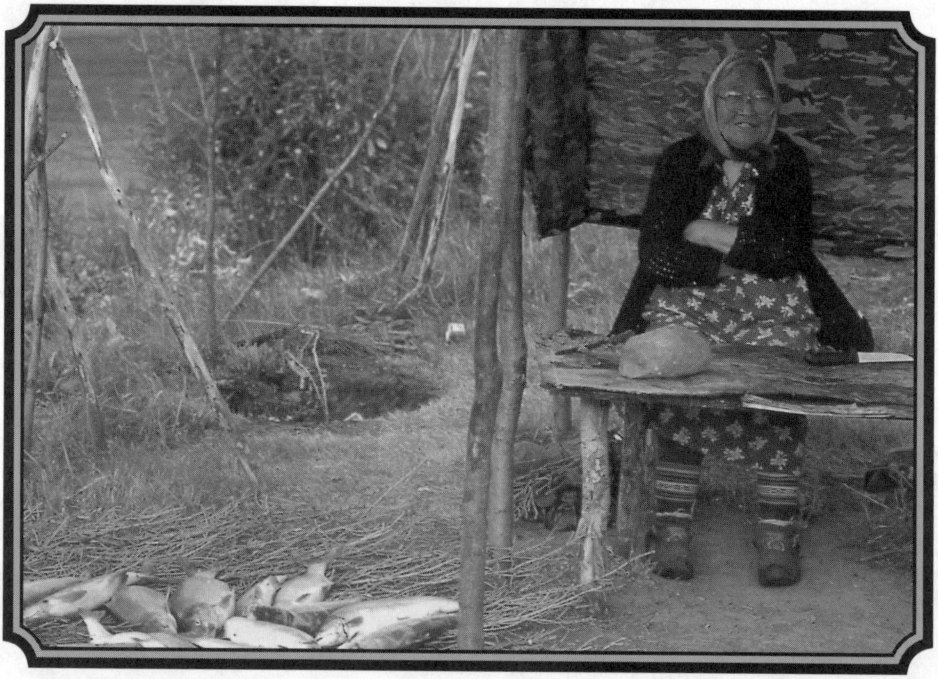

My solo canoe refuses to go in a straight line. It has high ends and no keel and is designed to turn quickly in whitewater. It also turns quickly in the wind that is screaming up the Peel River. It acts like a politician, yawing to the left or right, depending on the angle of the breeze. A gust catches the bow and spins it toward the east bank of the river. I paddle like hell, broad-sweep strokes that are supposed to turn the canoe. All they do is increase my speed, and I sail off as if I'm in the America's Cup.

"Come back," yells Rachel. "You're heading for the Mackenzie."

"Laugh it up. It's just about your turn to paddle this damned thing."

Rachel Shephard was my student 20 years ago when I was an instructor at Outward Bound. Every morning we ran several miles before breakfast and jumped into an icy river. We hiked over alpine passes. We kayaked down swift rivers. We climbed to the top of a granite peak and bivouacked on a ledge. While snow swirled around our sleeping bags, I read quotes from Oliver Wendell Holmes and J.R.R. Tolkien. Our orange climbing helmets had stickers with the school motto inscribed below a stylized compass: "To Serve, to Strive and Not to Yield." A few years later Rachel became an Outward Bound instructor in Ontario. She mailed me a T-shirt that described my values more precisely: "Awkward Bound—To Swerve, to Hide and Not to be Found." Rachel still teaches outdoor pursuits and, during the winter, migrates south to Chile and Antarctica to manage logistics for an adventure company.

I met up with Rachel and another friend named Devon McDiarmid after paddling up to Fort McPherson from Aklavik. Devon is strong and enthusiastic and guides ski trips to the South Pole in his spare time. It's a good thing he is fit, as the next stretch of the trip is an upriver slog. Our first challenge, though, is to find the Rat River. We paddle down the Peel and turn left at the Husky Channel. According to the book *Paddling in the Yukon—A Guide to the Rivers*, the Rat flows into the Husky Channel about a kilometer down. I should know, I wrote the damned thing. It's a good thing we know not to believe everything we read. The river has changed channels since the book was published, and its mouth is now 10 miles farther downstream.

Hauling canoes up rivers is not a glamour sport like rock-climbing, parasailing, or kayaking. We won't even be able to claim a "first ascent" if we make it to the top of the Rat. For thousands of years, aboriginal travelers have known that Rat Pass is the easiest route from the Mackenzie Delta to the Yukon interior. They guided the merry traders of the Hudson's Bay Company up the Rat and were paid with trinkets, alcohol, and disease. The river was also part of a roundabout route to Dawson City during the Klondike gold rush. A hundred "stampeders" who didn't make it over the pass before freeze-up in 1898 spent a desperate, scurvy-ridden winter at an encampment on the Rat that became known as Destruction City. Not many people have trudged up the Rat in the past few decades—mainly weirdoes such as us, people bored with floating downhill, and looking for a little hardship to temper their characters.

When we eventually get to the mouth of the Rat, we find a pair of young Gwich'in men gutting char. We pull into an eddy beside their riverboat. They wave bloody knives at us and walk down the bank.

"Where you going?" asks a man wearing a red-splotched jean jacket and an Oakland Raiders T-shirt. "Heading down to Inuvik?"

"No," answers Rachel. "We're going up the Rat to Summit Lake."

"Oh?" he says. "Some Germans tried that last week, but they didn't get too far."

"What happened?"

"I don't think they liked the rapids. They gave up after a couple of days and hitched a ride on a riverboat back to McPherson. I heard they chartered a plane and flew up to Summit Lake instead. Smart, eh?"

"We aren't that smart," says Devon.

"We'll see," says the man.

The Rat River winds sinuously through the thick Mackenzie Delta willow jungle, but it doesn't flow sluggishly like the lazy channels I kayaked up from the Arctic Ocean. It still surges with gravitational energy from its headlong rush down from the snowfields in the Richardson Mountains. I can't make any headway against the current in the solo canoe, so I toss Rachel my bow rope, and she ties it to their stern. They jerk me upstream, like a giant trout. Occasionally we catch a glimpse of the alpine surrounding Rat Pass. It floats high above us and looks a long way off.

A cold breeze tumbles out of the mountains on our second day out. We struggle against the wind and the current. I'm cold and tired. I can tell it is time to start looking for a campsite because Rachel and Devon have stopped teasing me. We paddle around a corner and see a Gwich'in camp. A stovepipe pokes out of a white canvas wall tent, and blue smoke dribbles over the scraggly spruce forest. A pair of ravens swoops above the river like kites, and a flag flutters in the wind. The flag is teal blue with a bull caribou silhouetted under the midnight sun and the words "Proud to Be Gwich'in." We pull into shore, drag our canoes up the beach, and tie them to a stout willow. Two women, mother and daughter, sit on low wooden benches, cleaning fish. The older woman is wearing a purple dress, scarf, and mukluks. She is surrounded by red strips of fish, draped over thin wooden poles to dry in the sun. A knife flashes in her wrinkled hands.

"My name is Caroline Kay," she says, scraping blood and guts into a pail and plucking the next fat Arctic char from a pile of fish on the ground. "There's hot soup and bannock in the tent. Go warm up. Have some tea and something to eat."

The wall tent is warm and humid and smells of wood smoke and forest. We duck to avoid the stovepipe, lift the flap, and go inside. The floor is hard-packed dirt. The beds in the corner are made of spruce boughs and caribou skins—no Therm-a-Rests or Gore-Tex sleeping bags here. A radio sits on a wooden table made from logs and a weathered plank. It hisses with CBC radio voices from Toronto talking about modern spirituality and John Lennon. I pour a mug of tea and feel the warmth seep into my fingers. Then I spoon homemade blueberry jam on steaming crusty bannock and devour it in a couple of bites.

When we go back outside, two men have appeared and are standing around the fish-cleaning station where the two women are working. Caroline introduces them: her son and grandson. The men smile but don't say anything. The older man picks up an ax and walks over to a pile of wood. The grandson, who is in his late teens, plugs in earphones, turns on a Walkman and starts strumming an air guitar.

"We heard on the radio-phone that you were coming," says Caroline. "But those men at the mouth of the Rat didn't think you'd get here until tomorrow."

"Thanks for the soup and bannock," says Devon. "That was great."

"Those Germans liked the bannock, too," says Caroline. "They ate lots! Then they went up the river a little way and gave up. When they came back they asked for more, eh?"

"They didn't talk normal," says her daughter. "It was hard to understand them."

"We asked them, did you see any bears?" laughs Caroline. "They said, 'No, thank you!' They thought I asked if they wanted any beers! We had a bear in camp two weeks ago. Black bear, eh?"

"Would you mind if we camped here tonight?" asks Rachel.

"It's a free country," she says, looking surprised at the question, as though private property is not a bush concept.

In the morning I get up early, but Caroline's son is up before me. He paddles a wobbly little canoe across the river to check his nets. He kneels in the canoe, pulls the net over the gunnels, and works the canoe down the eddy, disentangling wriggling fish and dropping them into the bottom of the boat. I return to our tents, and by the time we've had breakfast and packed up, Caroline and her daughter are cleaning fish again.

"We caught 14 fish today!" says Caroline as we walk up to say goodbye. Then she points at the drying fish, suspended like laundry on a clothesline. "You have to watch that fish. Those birds—those whiskey jacks—they try to get at it. That's why we put a net over it."

"How long will you stay out here?" I ask.

"I come for as long as I can every summer," she says. "I've lived in the bush all my life. Now I'm 84 years old, and in winter I go to McPherson. We eat bush food all winter, though—caribou meat and dried fish."

"She'd stay here all winter if we let her," says her daughter dryly.

"I lost my husband two years ago," says Caroline, "but things are still good in the bush. Where are you going?"

"We're heading up the Rat to Summit Lake, then down the Porcupine to Old Crow."

"You'd better take some fish for your trip," she says. "Take a char, and I'll give you some dried fish for later."

"We don't want to take your winter's supply of fish," says Rachel.

"We always share food in the bush," says Caroline. "My mother taught all us kids to speak nicely and help each other out."

Before we walk down to the canoes I tell her about my trip, about the caribou herds and musk oxen and bowhead whales. I tell her about our plans for publicizing the need to protect the calving grounds, although Washington, D.C., seems very far away. Before I'm finished, Caroline starts to laugh. She laughs so hard she puts down her knife and wipes her eyes with the sleeve of her dress.

"You're working for *me*!" she says, still spluttering. "You're working for me! Now we like you! Now we like you! We need the caribou. It is always good to welcome travelers, but now we like you!"

"It was very nice to meet you," says Rachel.

"It was nice to meet such friendly people, too," says Caroline, still giggling softly.

"She likes you because you are working for the caribou," says her daughter with a shy smile.

We kneel in the canoes, push off from the squelchy mud banks, and head upriver. When we round the first corner, the river kicks up its heels and gallops toward us. We paddle as hard as we can, and the Gwich'in flag slips out of sight behind the willows. The current doesn't let up. Before long our arms give out, and we pull in to a gravel bar.

"The picnic is over," says Devon, looking upriver.

I untie the solo canoe from its big cousin and walk up the beach, towing the boat behind me. "Tracking" a canoe upstream can be precise and elegant. The trick is to angle the bow slightly out into the current using the bow and stern ropes. As you stroll along the shore, the current pushes the boat just far enough out so it doesn't bump in the shallows. The canoe follows your lead obediently, like a well-trained dog. It doesn't work that way on the Rat. The gravel bar disappears into a jungle of willows, and before long we are wading up to our chests in the river, manhandling the boats past logjams and fallen snags that vibrate in the current like jackhammers.

"This must be where the Germans turned back," says Rachel grimly.

"Watch out," says Devon. "There's a wasp's nest here."

Devon ducks his head underneath a gray, papery nest the size of a small pineapple. A dozen wasps circle menacingly. I'm allergic to wasp stings, so I paddle to the opposite shore, hop out, and start wading upstream. We grovel upstream at a wood frog's pace. We stop to camp before the August sun sets behind the Richardson Mountains. We hang our sodden clothes on bushes and light a cooking fire. We drink mugs of hot chocolate and watch voles scurry back and forth between their holes. A wolverine appears in a clearing across the river. It sniffs the smoke from our fire suspiciously and lopes back into the bush. Rachel flops the char into a frying pan and sets it on the coals.

"That fish smells great," says Devon. "I can't believe how generous Caroline is."

"Imagine how differently people would treat her if she was traveling down south," says Rachel.

"They'd treat her fine as long as she brought lots of money," I say sarcastically.

"She was even willing to feed us before she liked us," laughs Devon.

"I'm glad she liked us, though," I add.

In the morning we slog westward toward the tumbled slopes, where the scraggly forest gives way to alpine meadows and talus. At river level, the willow jungles are punctuated by gravel bars where we can walk on dry land. When the bush closes in and it becomes impossible on one side of the river, we paddle as far upstream as we can and dart across the river, like salmon swimming from eddy to eddy. Much of the time we're up to our waists or chests in cold water. After lunch the we encounter a steepened streambed, and before long we're wrenching the canoes up rocky rapids. Great blasts of wind from the interior funnel through Rat Pass, kicking up a strong headwind. The willows bend and thrash and spray flies off the tops of the waves. Rachel steps around a corner out of the shelter of the willows, and a gust knocks her on her back.

"That gust was stronger than 50 knots," says Rachel casually, picking herself up.

"How do you know?" I ask.

"I don't get blown off my feet until at least 50 knots," she says, as though it's a fact I should have learned in elementary school. "We measured the winds in Antarctica."

Late in the day we are all tired, hoping to find a great campsite around the next corner. I wade through a willow-choked narrows and slosh out of the river onto a gravel bar. I hang on to the rope and trudge on, leaving sloppy footprints on the rocks. Suddenly, a chubby ball of jet-black fur explodes out of the bush a few yards in front of me and bolts upstream, mewing like an overgrown cat.

"What the heck was that?" asks Devon, who is submerged to his waist and peering through a thicket.

"A black bear cub," I answer.

"Did you see its mother?" asks Rachel.

"No."

I look around nervously. The bush looks as impenetrable as a Costa Rican rainforest. I imagine the glint of dark eyes in the shadows and pull the safety tab from my bear spray. We wait for a few minutes, then tiptoe to the end of the gravel bar, ferry across the current to the opposite shore, and paddle like hell. We decide to go a bit further before stopping to camp.

Around the next corner we see the steepest rapid yet. The Rat swirls and boils down a chute peppered with rocks. The boulders are round and slick with slimy green algae, like greased bowling balls. I clutch the canoe for balance and lurch forward, but the lace of one boot catches in the eyelet of the other, and I go flying like a cartoon character, slamming into a rock with my left knee. I swear and haul myself upright, dripping wet. Before I get to the top of the rapid my lace catches again, then I pirouette and hammer down on the same knee. I shuffle to the first clearing, haul up the canoe, and pull down my pants. I poke around the joint, which rapidly becomes the color and texture of an overripe avocado.

"Didn't your mother teach you to tuck in your laces so you don't trip on them?" asks Devon.

"No," I answer caustically, "she didn't."

I limp around gingerly while Devon collects driftwood for a fire and Rachel puts up our tent. They give me a wide berth, knowing I'm the type who prefers to nurse my grouchiness in solitude. I stump up and down the shore, hoping that if I keep moving my knee won't seize up like an overheated engine running dry of motor oil. My adrenaline finally runs out, and I grab my journal and sit on a log. For the first time since leaving the calving grounds, I wonder if I'll make it to Old Crow.

I scribble dark thoughts about abandoning the trip and floating back down the Rat like the Germans, asking Caroline for more bannock. I notice the date and calculate that I've been out for precisely 80 days. In Jules Verne's novel, Phinias Fogg made it *Around the World in Eighty Days*. He wouldn't have given up for a mere smashed knee. A furious flapping distracts me. A ptarmigan flutters madly over the river, a steely-gray gyrfalcon in deadly pursuit. Devon ducks. The ptarmigan barrels over his head and crashes into the willows. The falcon swoops up, like a kite at the end of its string.

The ptarmigan and falcon have more important things to worry about than I do.

In the morning my knee is sore but doesn't feel unstable. I pack up quickly, load the solo canoe, and hobble upriver. I know I'll be moving slowly, so I'm taking off before Rachel and Devon are ready. Just upstream, the walls of a limestone canyon loom above the forest. It looks like a major obstacle. I lean on the canoe for support and splash into the canyon. Fortunately, I'm able to paddle from side to side to avoid the sheer rock walls that plunge into the river. A nesting pair of peregrine falcons wheels around the lip of the gorge, shrieking at me to move faster. I pull the canoe through the final rapid and wave to Rachel and Devon, who are entering the canyon below me.

The Rat's gradient eases after the canyon, as if it was a test we needed to pass to qualify for the next grade. The rapids become less frequent and finally disappear. We are able to paddle more often. If we can't paddle, there are often gravel bars with firm footing. At the end of one long bar, we find a reddish mound of flesh and fur, topped with velvet antlers. Wolf tracks dance around the caribou carcass in an intricate pattern, the moisture from their claws and pads not yet dried from the gravel. Gray jays and ravens, the first scavengers at the scene, scream from the edge of the forest. We move upriver before a larger scavenger joins the party. Grizzlies, like vultures, are attracted to carcasses.

The river dwindles until it is no more than a creek, winding sedately through the wetlands under the Richardson Mountains. The miles slip behind us, and one day we realize that we'll make it to Summit Lake ahead of schedule. We plan a "rest day" so we can hike into the alpine. The clouds mass over the mountains, and it starts to rain. I set up the tarp for the first time since I left Caribou Pass in this summer of climate change.

It is still late summer down by the river, but the bearberry leaves are already flaming in the high country. The willows and dwarf birch leaves glow golden and orange, as if painted by an Impressionist giant. Four pure-white Dall sheep look warily down on us from the crest of the ridge. I see what looks like the curving sheep horn and stoop to pick it up. The "horn" turns out to be the hairless tail on a dead muskrat, a long way above the Rat River. The body of the muskrat has not been mutilated by predators or scavengers. It looks as if it is sleeping.

"How did it get up here?" asks Rachel. "It's like finding a salmon in an alpine meadow."

"Maybe it got lost," I say. "I feel like that some days."

"Maybe an eagle dropped it here," says Devon.

We leave the mysterious water rat and hike upward. Ground squirrels chatter shrilly, upset at being disturbed from their pre-winter face-stuffing. A dozen Canada geese wing southward in a ragged "V", honking madly. We sit in a clearing, and Rachel pulls out a bag of chocolate.

"I'm worried about this chocolate," she says. "It would be the *worst* if it went moldy."

"Maybe we better eat it," suggests Devon.

While we do our chocolate duty, a single goose cruises just overhead, honking forlornly. It flies over our camp, across the river, and behind the mountains to the south. The honking gradually gets fainter, and then strengthens, as if the goose cranked up its voice-box volume. The goose reappears and arrows over our heads to the north.

"It'll be back in a minute," says Devon, and he's right.

"It must be looking for its friends," Rachel and I say in unison.

"I said it first," says Rachel.

"No you didn't."

"Well, it was my idea first!"

"No way."

"Mine, mine, mine!" she says.

"You are *so* weird."

"Of course," she answers smugly. "That's why you invite me on trips, so you aren't the only weird one."

The next day we paddle through the Rat's serpentine upper channel, which is barely wide enough for a canoe. The stream drains a shallow lake at the headwaters. There is a dense line of aquatic plants across the outlet of the creek. Devon shoves the stern of my canoe, and I paddle as hard as I can. I plow through the plants, glide into the lake, and stare at a pair of bulging moose eyes at close range. She hisses like an angry goose and steps toward me. The hair between her shoulders stands up as if pulled by a static-electric force field.

"Shit," I whisper to Devon and Rachel. "There is an unhappy moose ten yards in front of me." I backpaddle, but the canoe squelches to a stop in the shallows. I mumble to the moose in as calm a voice as I can muster, "It's OK, Ms. Moose. Relax. I don't even eat meat."

She lowers her head as if she doesn't believe a word I'm saying and steps toward me again. Her front hooves are solid and lethal. Old-time Northerners respect moose as much as bears. I suddenly feel like an old-timer. The moose takes another step, which brings her out from behind the willows into view of Rachel and Devon. She turns and stares at them for a moment, then swings her head back toward me. Finally she swivels and splashes across the lake in great lumbering strides.

The next morning we portage our canoes across a vivid red-gold carpet of moss, kinnikinnik, and low-bush cranberries. It looks flat, but somewhere before we reach Summit Lake we pass over the crest of the Arctic-Pacific divide and start to go down. Two bull caribou trot past us, modeling their new fall coats: glossy chestnut flanks with bold white chest ruffs. The caribou disappear into the first snow flurry of the autumn. Three wolves, a mother and two pups, howl at us from across the lake as we paddle across to find a campsite.

In the morning a plane flies in from Inuvik, dropping off Wendy, Malkolm, my daughter Polly, and Peter Mather. Devon clambers into the plane and waves. The return flight will take him to Inuvik and the beginning of the Dempster Highway. The road leads south to anywhere. To Whitehorse, Calgary, New York, and Antarctica.

We explore the mountains surrounding Summit Lake for a day. In the evening, we pick low-bush cranberries for tomorrow's pancake breakfast. Blackflies rise up like mist, swarming up our pant cuffs and down our necks. Malkolm sits in one spot for an hour and fills a plastic bag full of deep-red berries. In the morning he has so many blackfly bites he looks like he has chicken pox. We squelch through the wetlands surrounding Summit Lake and carry our gear down to the willow-choked Little Bell River. The river doesn't look like much, but it leads to the Bell River, which leads to the Porcupine, which leads to the Old Crow airport, Whitehorse, Vancouver, Newark, London, and Washington, D.C.

The Little Bell is a toddler of a stream. It dashes through splashy rapids, staggers forward slowly in squiggly curves, and bounds off again. The Bell is an older and more sedate river, flowing slowly and purposefully through the boreal forest. We meet my other daughter Kirsten and her boyfriend, Colin, who have paddled down the Eagle River and are waiting at its confluence with the Bell. The next day we reach the Porcupine.

Flocks of sandhill cranes, geese, and swans fly overhead in long lines, and the forest quivers in anticipation of the oncoming winter. Beavers gnaw their winter's cache of willow and alder branches and submerge them in the mud near their dens. They slap their tails in warning when we paddle past. Gray jays flutter from branch to branch, and a hawk owl sits hunched on the top of a spindly spruce, ducking down as a kestrel divebombs it. An otter watches us float past, its whiskered face blending into the tangle of roots on the edge of the bank.

We see people, too. The Gwich'in are out on the land, motoring up the river in long wooden riverboats, setting salmon nets in eddies, and waiting for the caribou. We pull in at a camp where smoke wisps into the sky from an old wooden cabin. A raven croaks, and a boy and a girl Malkolm's age wave frantically. Spruce trees lean drunkenly from the permafrost forest behind the camp. Thunderheads glower above low alpine ridges, and dark lines of rain slant down in the distance.

The kids meet us at the beach and lead us up a trail. An old woman with long, dark-gray braids and a bright look in her eye sits in a wooden chair at the edge of a three-walled hut. The other side is open to the sky and the forest. There's a wood stove at the back, and drying caribou meat hangs from the rafters. Spruce boughs cover the floor. It smells like Christmas.

"I'm Lydia Thomas," says the woman, standing up to shake our hands.

She says something to the kids in Gwich'in. They dash toward the main cabin and return carrying enough mugs for all of us. Lydia pours us tea, and the boy carries around a platter of doughnuts like a waiter at a cocktail party. He makes sure we are all served before he takes one himself.

"These doughnuts are great," says Peter. "Are they homemade?"

"You won't find Indians in the bush eating store-bought doughnuts," laughs Lydia.

"How is the fishing?" asks Kirsten.

"Oh, not very good," she says. "We catch fish here every year, but I've never seen it like this before. Not many salmon coming up the river."

"What about the caribou?" I ask.

"A few have come down, but most are still up in the mountains. They'll start to move when the north wind begins to blow."

We finish our tea, thank Lydia, and head back to our canoes. Storm clouds chase each other across the sky. I think about salmon politics: overfishing out in the Pacific, drift nets, draggers, and habitat destruction.

Squabbles between British Columbia and Alaska about who "owns" the fish. Their cold calculations don't include Lydia Thomas and the other Gwich'in along the Yukon and Porcupine Rivers.

We look for the first good campsite. In the night, moose grunt their rutting songs, and the wind swirls through the alders, rustling the few remaining leaves that haven't drifted to the ground. The breeze moves from grove to grove, the sound approaching and receding, like the hiss of waves lapping on a gravel beach. I stare at my journal while Wendy reads a bedtime story about Bilbo Baggins and a bunch of dwarves struggling toward the Lonely Mountain.

"Look at that worm," says Malkolm.

A small green inchworm jackknifes slowly across the roof of the tent. It inches between the dead carcasses of black flies from Summit Lake and faded blood splotches of squashed mosquitoes from the coastal plain.

"It isn't very speedy," I say. "It's called an inchworm because it moves at an inch per hour."

"That's the cheetah of inchworms," says Malkolm. "I bet that's the fastest inchworm in the tent."

Wendy continues reading, and I stare back down at my journal. Tomorrow we'll round a corner and see wood smoke spiraling above the cabins in Old Crow. It will be my 100th day out. My "normal" life is rushing toward me at warp speed. The range of the Porcupine caribou herd is a world where money doesn't matter, and too many possessions bog you down. Freedom comes when you travel light. That will all change. Soon I'll be in Whitehorse, drinking a glass of wine, eating pizza, soaking in a steaming bath.

Then I'll get to work. I'll sort slides, write proposals, schmooze with funders, send emails into cyberspace, and spend hours with a telephone jammed in my ear. I don't have any choice. I now have a full-time job. I'm working for Caroline Kay.

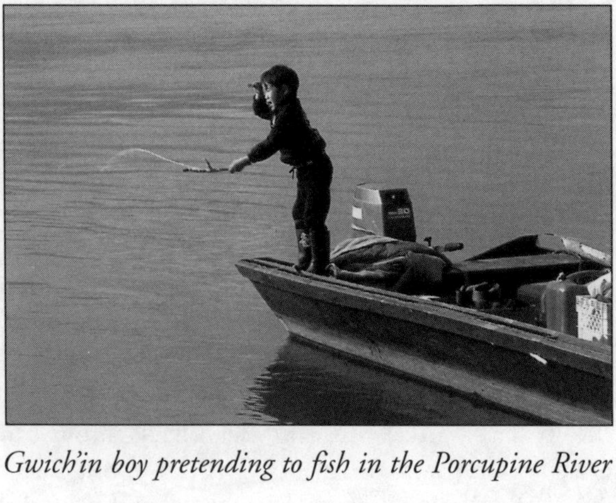

Gwich'in boy pretending to fish in the Porcupine River

Afterword: The Fight to Protect the Arctic Refuge

"Come in," I yell when I hear the knock on the back door. "Hey, Norma! How are you?"

"I'm fine," she says, coming inside and unlacing a pair of ski boots. "I have to go skiing after we talk. It's so warm out."

January is the coldest month of the year in Whitehorse. The mean temperature is minus 20 degrees Fahrenheit, and occasionally the thermometer plunges below minus 50. This year, however, the thin red mercury line has set up shop near the freezing point. It's another climate-change winter in the Yukon, and the weather is perfect for cross-country skiing. Not so perfect for maintaining the delicate balance of life in the North.

"Would you like some coffee or tea?"

"Sure."

"Which do you want?"

"Maybe tea. I have an upset stomach. I think it's stress thinking about my lobbying trip to Washington, D.C. I'm worried about the Senate energy vote."

Norma is wearing a sky-blue track suit. Her hair is pulled back in a ponytail and secured with a caribou skin clasp. She's wearing earrings that she and her son Yudii beaded and a necklace made from an old Canadian coin, the bull caribou quarter.

"Man, your house is colder than outside!" she says. "My feet are freezing. Can I borrow some slippers?"

"I'll get you some of Wendy's."

During the winter our house seldom warms up above 60 degrees. It's part of our effort to burn as little oil as we can. That way we don't feel so guilty when we charter planes to fly into the wilderness. The back door opens and Malkolm bursts in. He drops his jacket on the floor and kicks off his snow boots. He says "hi" to Norma and heads for the fridge. She grabs him for a hug as he walks by.

"Don't nibble my ear!" he laughs, wriggling away from her grasp. He pours a glass of grape juice, sits down at the table, and doodles a picture of a red-throated loon.

"When are you leaving for Washington?" Norma asks me.

"I'm going to Chicago on Tuesday. I have two weeks of slideshows in Indiana and Illinois, and then I fly to D.C. on February 10. Our presentation at the Canadian Embassy is the next day."

"What I want to do before I start lobbying," says Norma solemnly, "is to acknowledge all of the bad things that have happened in the past year for the calving grounds."

"George Bush got elected," says Malkolm.

"Then the House of Representatives passed the energy bill that included a provision to drill in the Refuge," I say.

"And September 11," says Norma. "That was horrible! Then the oil lobby made it worse, by wrapping themselves in the American flag and saying we have to drill for oil in the calving grounds for national security."

"We have to talk about energy efficiency and safer energy alternatives," I say. "Oil development in the Arctic Refuge won't make us more secure."

"Caribou are our security," says Norma.

"Norma," says Malkolm, "did you tell Yudii about what Gale Norton said about manatees?"

"What about manatees?"

"The Department of the Interior is going to allow special permits to ignore boat speed limits in critical manatee habitat," I say.

"That woman!" says Norma. "She told Congress that most years the caribou don't have their calves in the Arctic Refuge, then claimed she accidentally got her figures reversed."

"Can Yudii and I go back to Florida to picket?" asks Malkolm.

"Gale Norton is in Washington, not Florida," laughs Norma.

"OK," says Malkolm, "we can go to Washington, and then Florida."

"Not this year," I say. "Manatees are important, but right now we're concentrating on the Arctic Refuge."

"Let's get past all the bad stuff," says Norma. "*Something* good must have happened this year."

"Well, so far the Senate seems to be holding firm despite pressure from the oil lobby...." The shrill ring of the telephone interrupts me. I pick it up. "Hello?"

"Mr. Madsen? I'm calling from the Goldman Foundation. Is Norma Kassi there?"

"She is. Just a second." I hand Norma the phone.

"Hello?" Norma listens for a moment then puts her hand over the mouthpiece. "She wants me to go somewhere private," she whispers. She walks into the hall and says, "OK, I'm alone now." She spins around, walks back to the kitchen table and sits down.

"Come on, Malkolm," I whisper. "Let's go downstairs and play a game of Ping-Pong."

"Why does Norma have to talk privately?"

"I hope it's about the Goldman Prize. It's the highest-profile conservation award in the world. I helped with Norma's nomination papers."

As we bat a ball back and forth we hear Norma's voice float down through the heat vents. "You're kidding! I can't believe it." We finish the game, throw some darts, and trot back upstairs. Norma is bouncing around the kitchen with a huge smile on her face. She hugs me, then Malkolm.

"Hey! No ear nibbling," he yells.

"Guess what!" says Norma. "We're getting the Goldman Prize! Sarah James, Jonathon Solomon, and I are going to share it!"

"That's fabulous!"

"I'm supposed to keep it confidential until the ceremony at the San Francisco Opera House in April. I won't even be able to tell Yudii. He'd never be able to keep it quiet."

"This will be great publicity for the calving grounds," I say. "And you'll be in good company. People like Ken Saro-Wiwa have won it."

"Who?" asks Malkolm.

"Ken Saro-Wiwa? He was the man who led the protest against Shell Oil in Nigeria. It was a conservation and a human rights struggle—just like the Arctic Refuge. The Niger Delta, where the Ogoni people live, was trashed. The fish and wildlife were wiped out. He was eventually killed by the Nigerian government."

"They won't kill me," says Norma, "but if we lose the caribou, it will be the death of our culture."

"I bet Oprah will want to interview you after you get the award," says Malkolm.

"You'll be a good strategist when you grow up," says Norma. "You know about Oprah even though you don't have a TV."

"Guess what?" says Malkolm.

"What?" asks Norma.

"I'm the only person in my class whose ear has been nibbled by the winner of the Goldman Prize!"

Norma laughs. Then she tells us that she is too excited to plan strategy any more. She puts on her ski boots and jacket, says goodbye, and walks outside. As the door closes I see her throw her arms in the air.

"Thank you, Creator!" she shouts. "*Mussi cho* for helping us!"

Three weeks later I fly from Chicago to Washington, D.C., and catch a cab from National Airport. Indiana and Illinois was a blur of 15 slideshows in 14 days. I've inhaled and exhaled the Arctic Refuge. My blood isn't oxygenated, its Arcticgenated. The cab driver has never heard of the Refuge. He tells me that the U.S. Olympic hockey team is going to kick Canada's butt but stares blankly at me when I ask about the energy bill. I close my eyes and lean back against the seat. I feel tired and spread thin, like a brittle rubber band, ready to snap the next time it is stretched.

The 1.5-million-acre coastal plain of the Arctic Refuge is the most fought-over chunk of wilderness in the world. The battle started back in the 1950s, after the National Park Service (NPS) conducted its first surveys. The NPS recommended that the region be preserved as a wildlife refuge and a secure land base for indigenous cultures. In the mid-'50s, the Conservation Foundation and New York Zoological Society sponsored a scientific expedition to the Arctic Refuge. The expedition was led by Dr. Olaus Murie and included George Schaller. As the word spread about the biological wonders of the northeastern corner of Alaska, support for the creation of an Arctic Preserve grew.

In 1960, the 8.9-million-acre Arctic National Wildlife Range was established by President Eisenhower. In 1980, the Alaska National Interest Lands Conservation Act expanded the "Range" to 19 million acres and renamed it the Arctic National Wildlife Refuge. Nearly 8 million acres of the original Range was designated Wilderness. In a last-minute compromise under Section 1002 of the act, the 1.5-million-acre coastal plain was left out of Wilderness designation, and the Department of the Interior was mandated to conduct biological and geological surveys. For years, the calving grounds were known as the "1002 Lands." Section 1003 of the act prohibited oil exploration, leasing, and development unless Congress approved otherwise.

In 1987, the Department of the Interior released its report on the calving grounds. The report concluded that oil development would have a major negative impact on caribou, musk oxen, aboriginal subsistence economies, water quality and quantity, recreation, and wilderness. Then it went ahead and recommended that Congress authorize full oil leasing on the coastal plain.

The Interior Secretary of the day, Donald Hodel, had once again proven that campaign contributions are mightier than morality or science, a proud tradition that still thrives in the Department of the Interior.

In 1988, Gwich'in elders realized their danger and called for a gathering in Arctic Village. It was the first time the nation had come together in a century. They passed a resolution calling for Wilderness designation of the coastal plain. Then they chose spokespeople like Norma Kassi, Sarah James, and Jonathon Solomon and gave them a mission: to leave their villages and tell the outside world about the Gwich'in way of life and their dependence on the caribou.

Despite the Gwich'in, despite the science, despite the outcry from conservation groups, despite the fact that the U.S. government had signed international treaties on the conservation of polar bears, migratory birds, and the Porcupine caribou herd, support for oil development on the coastal plain increased in Congress. By 1989, political climate change had heated up Capitol Hill and both houses of Congress were ready to pass drilling legislation. George Bush, Sr. had a pen in his hand, ready to sign. Then, on the quiet evening of March 24, 1989, the *Exxon Valdez* struck Bligh Reef, spilling its deadly cargo of crude Arctic oil. American voters suddenly remembered that the oil industry had promised "zero spillage" in Prince William Sound and that it was the same oil industry that wanted to drill in the Arctic Refuge. American politicians suddenly remembered that they cared about the environment. Drilling plans were put on the back burner where they were not forgotten but quietly allowed to simmer.

In 1995, the Republican-dominated Congress tried again, attaching an Arctic Refuge oil drilling "rider" to the annual budget bill. President

Clinton vetoed the bill, which cut off the flow of money from U.S. coffers and effectively shut down the government. Clinton said that the need to protect the Arctic Refuge was one of the main reasons for his veto.

In 2001, the oil lobby cranked up the heat under the drilling debate once more. The House of Representatives passed an energy bill calling for drilling on the coastal plain. The Democrats had a one-vote majority in the Senate, however, and the Refuge seemed safe. The horrendous acts of terror on September 11 changed that in a heartbeat. National security became the political mantra. Oil development proponents insisted that we needed the black crude under the calving grounds to save us from Osama Bin Laden and Saddam Hussein.

This is the political climate as my cab speeds past the White House. I rub my eyes. If I feel this discouraged to be coming back to the center of the known political universe, what is it like for Norma Kassi? And Sarah James, Jonathon Solomon, Chief Joe Linklater, Luci Beach, Sandra Newman, Stanley Njootli, Daryl Charlie, and all of the other Gwich'in who are fighting for their way of life?

The Gwich'in know that the coastal plain has existed since before white people started poking around up there. They know that woolly mammoths lived with the caribou during the last ice age. They know that their own ancestors have hunted the caribou for more than 12,000 years. Despite their long history in the range of the Porcupine caribou herd, they know that the U.S. Congress will not make its decision based

Tundra swan and cygnets, coastal plain, Arctic National Wildlife Refuge

on Gwich'in traditional knowledge. Backroom deals and political horse-trading, not ethics and morality, will decide their fate. Politicians in favor of opening the Arctic Refuge have already tried to "attach" drilling to legislation to help retired railway workers, a defense authorization bill—even an anti-cloning bill.

When I think about the coastal plain, I remember clear, sharp images. A caribou trotting across the golden tundra, anxious to reach the calving grounds. A red-throated loon settling down on its nest beside a pond that is still half covered with ice. Young ermines popping up from their holes to wrestle, standing rigid like sentries, then scurrying back into the safety of their burrows. None of the animals doubt that they are where they are supposed to be, doing what they are supposed to be doing.

The debate about the future of the caribou, the loon, and the ermine is not clear and sharp. The object of the exercise is not to have a well-reasoned dialogue that fully informs the American people, but to win at any cost. Keeping track of the media reports is like watching a video on fast-forward. Distorted images flicker and flash on the screen, but before you can respond they are gone. Day after day, drilling proponents pull out new recipes for oil development, as if they've just read *The Joy of Drilling*.

The Joy of Drilling:

Recipe 1—The "New" Oil Industry Is Clean and Safe (Baked Alaska)

Despite evidence to the contrary, oil companies tell us that they are kinder and gentler than they used to be. British Petroleum (which paid $22 million in criminal and civil fines for illegally disposing of hazardous wastes at its "model" Endicott oil field in 1999) says in its ads that BP stands for "Beyond Petroleum" and that it is the "Green Alternative." In early March 2002, a BP worker met with Senators Joseph Lieberman and Bob Graham. He said that working for BP is "like working for a drunk driver that is your boss and insists on driving you home." He claimed that maintenance backlogs and employee shortages were worsening the threat of serious oil spills at Prudhoe Bay.

Alaska's northern oil development sprawls across more than 1,000 square miles of Arctic tundra. There are thousands of miles of roads and pipelines and more than 55 contaminated sites. The oilfields emit more than 56,000 tons of smog and acid-rain-producing nitrogen oxides every year (more than the states of Vermont or Rhode Island). The oil and chemical spills go on, day after day, year after year—an average of more than one spill each day. Some are small, but many are huge. In the spring of 2001, there were three spills of more than 10,000 gallons in the "newer, safer" Arctic oilfields, including one of 92,000 gallons in the Kuparuk oilfield.

The Joy of Drilling:
Recipe 2–The 2,000-Acre Limitation (Scrambled Tundra)

When the House of Representatives passed its energy bill in the summer of 2001, it promised to use only 2,000 acres of the 1.5-million-acre coastal plain. Drilling proponents say that oil development would only cover the same surface area as Dulles Airport near Washington, D.C. On March 12, 2002, Senator Frank Murkowski of Alaska stood up on the Senate floor and held out a map of the Arctic National Wildlife Refuge. He pointed to a small rectangle on the coastal plain to show just how tiny the "footprint" of development would be.

Some newspapers have printed editorials saying that the "2,000-acre limitation" demonstrates that the oil industry can now be a good steward of the Arctic Refuge. We can have our oil and polar bears, too. However, the 2,000-acre limitation only applies to "surface acreage covered by production and support facilities." It doesn't include seismic or other exploration activities, which have forever altered the Arctic environment to the west. It doesn't include gravel mines or roads. Because it applies only to "surface acreage," the 2,000-acre limitation does not count pipelines that are elevated above the tundra—only to the vertical supports that actually touch the ground.

The Alpine oilfield to the west of Prudhoe Bay contains 37 miles of pipelines. If we apply the oil industry's "new math," that would equate to less than one-quarter of an acre. Paul Krugman of the *New York Times* recently calculated that his work "impact" is only a few square inches—the bottom of the legs on his desk and chair and the soles of his shoes. The rest of his office is pristine wilderness. Theoretically, British Petroleum or Exxon could blanket the Refuge with 296,000 miles of pipeline and still not exceed the 2,000-acre limitation.

The U.S. Geological Survey says that the oil under the coastal plain is not in a single large pool but is spread across the coastal plain in about 35 smaller deposits. Drill sites would be spread across a vast landscape and interconnected by a network of roads and pipelines. Wild creatures do not understand that the 2,000-acre limitation is good for them. As I discovered when I was in the calving grounds, caribou are affected by even a lone human at a distance. Biologists have shown that there is decreased caribou calving within a 2.5-mile radius of roads and pipelines. They also warn that oil development infrastructure would hamper the summer migration of the great aggregations of the Porcupine caribou herd.

Imagine the world's largest drift net. Imagine bunching it up and dropping it on the tundra, where it would cover 2,000 acres. Then take the net, spread it out, and fling it into the Pacific, where it would scoop up nearly everything in its path. That is a more realistic analogy for the 2,000-acre limitation than Senator Murkowski's tiny rectangle on a big map.

The Joy of Drilling:
Recipe 3—Oil Development for National Security (Terrorist Stew)

Few North Americans would dispute that national security is a top priority. Few would dispute that oil politics are mixed up with security issues in an impossible-to-unravel tangle. Many of our politicians are influenced by energy money. It is tough to tell who is setting our political agenda. Senator Frank Murkowski alone has received $378,835 in campaign contributions from oil and gas companies and electrical utilities since 1997. I wasn't surprised when, as soon as the dust settled at Ground Zero after September 11th, politicians said that we needed to drill for oil in the Arctic Refuge for national security.

The United States spends $200,000 per minute on foreign oil. It burns 26 percent of the oil that is consumed across the planet. The United States, however, has only 2 percent of the Earth's proven oil reserves (as opposed to 66 percent in the Persian Gulf). The United States could drill for oil off every coastline and in every National Park and Wildlife Refuge, and it still wouldn't come close to becoming energy independent. Even Sir John Browne, the CEO of British Petroleum, acknowledges that. "The only way to break free," he said recently, "is to use less—a lot less."

The quickest way to reduce our demand for foreign oil is not by drilling in the Arctic Refuge but by improving the fuel economy of new vehicles. If we increase fuel efficiency standards for passenger vehicles to 39 miles per gallon during the next decade, we would reduce our oil consumption by 51 billion barrels over the next 50 years. That's more than 15 times what we could pump from under the Arctic Refuge. Raising standards to 55 mpg by 2020 would save twice the oil that the United States imports from the Persian Gulf.

We can do even better than that. We can encourage the mass production of gas-electric hybrid vehicles and promote the production of renewable, nonpetroleum fuels such as ethanol, which can be made from crop wastes. And we can initiate a new "Manhattan Project" to research hydrogen-powered fuel cells. If we can put a man on the moon, we can ensure that nonpolluting vehicles become economically available as soon as possible.

Using less fossil fuel would reduce our dependence on foreign oil, slow our headlong rush into a future of climate change, and allow us to protect special places such as the coastal plain of the Arctic Refuge. Our political leaders may not have the courage to work to ensure a future that includes caribou, wilderness, polar bears, buff-breasted sandpipers, and Gwich'in. Politicians, though, *can* become courageous if their voters insist on it. Citizens' voices need to be very loud, however, to be heard over the insistent clamor of energy industry lobbyists.

Drilling for oil in the Arctic Refuge would do little or nothing to reduce America's dependence on foreign oil or to address future energy needs. And drilling does nothing to address short-term national security issues. Industry officials admit that, even if drilling were to be authorized today, oil wouldn't be available for 10 years. Many people believe that drilling in the Refuge would weaken America's national security by increasing our reliance on the Trans-Alaska Pipeline.

"A key vulnerability of drilling in the Arctic Refuge is the Trans-Alaska Pipeline," said James Woolsey in the days leading up to the Senate vote. Woolsey is the former director of the Central Intelligence Service. "It was shut down last fall by a drunk who shot one bullet…it has been sabotaged and incompetently bombed twice…and these people are children compared with the sophistication of people who attacked us on September 11."

"The bottom line is that we'll be dependent on the Middle East as long as we are dependent on oil," Woolsey added. "Drilling in ANWR is not a recipe for America's national security. The only answer is to use substantially less petroleum."

THE JOY OF DRILLING:

Recipe 4—Billions and Billions of Barrels of Oil (Deep-Fried Refuge)

In a speech on the Senate floor on February 15, 2002, Frank Murkowski said, "It is estimated by the geologists that the recovery of oil in this area is somewhere between 5.6 and 16 billion barrels."

Senator Murkowski has long been an advocate for oil development in the Arctic Refuge. He knows that Alaskans love their annual "Permanent Fund" check, which is currently in the range of $2,000 for every man, woman, and child who resides in Alaska. The Permanent Fund was established from state oil revenues. It isn't hard to understand why most Alaskan politicians are wedded to the oil industry in general, and to drilling in the Arctic Refuge in particular.

No one knows for sure how much oil lies under the calving grounds. The U.S. Geological Survey (USGS) says, however, that there is less than a one-in-twenty chance of finding Senator Murkowski's 16 billion barrels. And what *might* be in the ground is not the same as what is economically possible after the high costs of exploration and production in the Arctic. The USGS's mean estimate is that 3.2 billion barrels of oil are economically recoverable from under the coastal plain. That would fuel the United States for less than six months. That doesn't mean that the oil industry would be in and out of the calving grounds in six months. It would take 50 years to extract the oil: half a century of industrial impact on the coastal plain's fragile tundra ecosystem.

The Joy of Drilling:

Recipe 5—The Ugly Arctic (Frozen Icing)

"It is not beautiful," Gale Norton told a group of Arkansas Farm Bureau members. "There are no mountains like they show on the television commercials. It is a plain." In the days leading up to the Senate vote, Secretary Norton sent an industry-sponsored video to news anchors like Tom Brokaw of NBC. The video was prepared by Arctic Power, the lobby group whose sole mandate is to open the Arctic Refuge to drilling. It showed a barren landscape in the depths of winter. Representative Edward Markey is a senior member of the House Resources Committee, which oversees the Department of the Interior. Markey warned Norton that she was breaking the law by trying to influence Congress by using industry propaganda.

President Bush also likes the Ugly Arctic recipe. "I would urge you all to travel up there and take a look at it," he said. "You can make the determination as to how beautiful that country is."

Unfortunately, beauty is not the issue. I wish it were. There is nothing more beautiful, through the eyes of this beholder, than a land where the drama of life still unfolds as nature intended. If the fate of the Arctic Refuge depended on whether or not it was beautiful, I would sleep better at night than I do.

The Joy of Drilling:
Recipe 6—Jobs, Jobs, Jobs (Worker's Gumbo)

One day the Teamsters Union loudly insisted that we need to drill for oil for the jobs that will be created. *700,000 jobs* flickered for a few days on the newspaper headlines and on the lips of CNN announcers. The study that spawned the 700,000-job estimate was commissioned by the American Petroleum Institute and has been discredited numerous times, including twice by the Congressional Research Service. The Economic Policy Institute estimates that only 46,300 jobs would be produced, and most of those would be temporary. Despite the dubious foundation of her facts, Gale Norton was still insisting as late as March 2002 that 700,000 jobs would be created if we drilled in the Refuge.

The Tellus Institute, a nonprofit research and policy organization, does say we can create more than 700,000 new full-time jobs by 2010—not by drilling in the Arctic Refuge, but by investing in energy efficiency and cleaner alternative energy sources. This approach to job creation would allow us to jump off the fossil-fuel treadmill and work toward a future with hope for both wildlife and people.

The Joy of Drilling:
Recipe 7—The Price at the Pump (Petroleum Turnovers)

Some things in life are predictable. No matter how long the winter lasts, spring will eventually come. If you pull over at a "family restaurant" along the interstate, you'll be served plastic food. And whenever the price of gas goes up, the oil industry's political allies will scream that we must drill for oil in the Arctic Refuge.

The price of a barrel of oil, however, is determined by international supply and demand, not by what is produced in North America. North American Arctic crude is a drop in the barrel. Commodity traders wouldn't even blink if oil from under the Arctic Refuge started flowing down the Trans-Alaska Pipeline. They wouldn't put down their Styrofoam cups of coffee or look up from the stock market quotations. The price of oil went *up* after oil from Prudhoe Bay reached markets.

The Joy of Drilling:
Recipe 8—No Impact on Wildlife (Skewered Caribou)

The oil industry and its political partners insist that oil development can take place without risk to wildlife. They love to display photos of caribou beside pipelines and tell us that the Central Arctic herd has grown since the Prudhoe Bay oilfields were developed.

The oil companies don't mention that the population increase of the Central Arctic herd occurred when climate and forage conditions were favorable. Caribou herds all across the Arctic were also increasing. They don't mention that female caribou with newborn calves are extremely sensitive to human activity and oil development. They don't mention that caribou from the Central Arctic herd have withdrawn from the oilfield area and found acceptable calving habitat elsewhere. They don't mention that alternative calving habitat is not readily available for the Porcupine caribou herd, which is seven times bigger than the Central Arctic herd but uses a calving area one-fifth the size. They don't mention that pipelines and oilfield installations in the Arctic Refuge would likely restrict the age-old migratory patterns of the herd.

In the waning days of Bill Clinton's presidency, 13 Northern caribou biologists wrote a letter to him outlining their concerns. The letter ended:

> In summary, state-of-the-art technology has not prevented displacement of calving from even the newer oilfields on the North Slope, and no proven technology exists that would ensure unrestricted passage through an oilfield of the large midsummer aggregations of Porcupine Caribou. Considering the high degree of uncertainty regarding mitigation of oilfield impacts on caribou, ensuring the integrity of the calving grounds and early summer range of the Porcupine Caribou Herd is a compelling reason for applying the most precautionary management to the Arctic Refuge coastal plain. The Porcupine Herd is an international resource too important to put at risk.

The Arctic Refuge contains important habitat for 200 other animal species besides caribou. More than 180 bird species have been observed in the Refuge, and 135 species visit the coastal plain. Most are migrants. They come from every continent and through every state in the United States. Arctic terns migrate all the way from Antarctica, golden plovers from South America, tundra swans from Chesapeake Bay, and tiny bluethroats from Africa.

Oil development causes the direct displacement of birds from nesting and foraging habitat. Oil spills are fatally toxic to bird embryos. Oil-slicked feathers lose their flight and insulating properties. Birds with small or declining populations are most at risk, including red-throated and yellow-billed loons, king and common eiders, long-tailed ducks, buff-breasted sandpipers, and peregrine falcons. Because of the risks associated with oil development, the American Ornithologists' Union has recommended that Congress designate the Arctic Refuge as a Wilderness Area.

The coastal plain of the refuge is the most important onshore denning area for polar bears in the United States. The International Union for the Conservation of Nature lists petroleum exploration as a major threat to polar bears. The risks come from human harassment, ingestion of oil or other toxic substances, and indirect impacts on the food chain that supports all life in the Arctic. Even wintertime oil exploration puts polar bears at risk. Pregnant females have abandoned their maternity dens because of seismic oil activity.

It is easy for scientists to describe the risks that oil exploration and development pose for individual animal species such as caribou, bowhead whales, Arctic char, grizzly bears, musk oxen, and golden eagles. An ecosystem, however, is much greater than the sum of its parts. This complex web of life is one of the last naturally functioning ecosystems left on our planet.

The Gwich'in and conservation groups are not demanding that no oil development take place in Alaska. Ninety-five percent of Alaska's Arctic is already open for oil leasing and potential development. The Arctic National Wildlife Refuge is the last place, the last five percent, where Americans have the option of protecting a wild chunk of Arctic coastal plain that is untrammeled by human industry.

The Joy of Drilling:

Recipe 9—The Arctic Refuge Is an Alaskan Issue (Smoked Forked Tongue)

Politicians who favor oil development almost never say the words Arctic National Wildlife Refuge. Instead, they call the Refuge *ANWR*. That way, the embarrassing word *National* does not have to leave their lips (not to mention *Wildlife* and *Refuge*). They say that this should be an issue for Alaskans to decide.

If Arizona politicians wanted to dam the Grand Canyon to generate power (not an impossible scenario), would that be an issue for the people of Arizona to decide? If an electrical utility wanted to tap Yellowstone's Old Faithful for its geothermal energy, would the citizens of Wyoming have the final say? Thankfully, both the Grand Canyon and Yellowstone are *National* Parks, just as the Arctic Refuge is a

National Wildlife Refuge. This is an issue for all Americans to decide (although Canadians, particularly the Gwich'in, should also be consulted).

The Joy of Drilling:
Recipe 10—Safety on Our Highways (Hybrid Squash)

As the Senate began to debate its energy legislation, the White House warned Congress against passing a bill that would boost automobile fuel efficiency. More efficient cars on our highways, according to the White House, would mean more traffic deaths. Presumably they are telling us that those little hybrids would be squashed by the larger, heavier SUVs rampaging around on the interstates. Strangely enough, the White House is not suggesting that we phase out the heavy gas-guzzlers to make it safer for fuel-efficient vehicles. Maybe they think we should all drive tanks.

In any case, evidence suggests that both fuel economy *and* safety have more to do with engineering than with the weight of vehicles.

My cab turns down Independence Avenue toward the tiny apartment that will be home for a few days. Then I'll be off for another slide tour in New Hampshire, Massachusetts, Connecticut, and Rhode Island. I've never been to New England, although my mother has told me that my roots on the continent can be found there. On February 5, 1631, my great-great-great (lots of greats) grandfather Roger Williams jumped off the good ship *Lyon* in Boston. He became famous as a champion for religious freedom in Rhode Island. Three hundred and seventy-one years later, I'm going there to talk about the rights of caribou, loons, and the Gwich'in. Three hundred and seventy-one years seems an impossibly long time—until I compare it to the more than 10,000 years that Norma Kassi's ancestors have lived on the continent.

Euro-Americans like me are newcomers in the North American neighborhood. We have pushed back the frontier with our horses, bulldozers, chainsaws, dams, steel plows, pesticides, and seismic "thumper-trucks." Our rivers are not fit to drink. Our air is not fit to breathe. We've tamed wild nature and confined it in parks that are small islands in a sea of development. Now we want to build oil wells in the last pristine five percent of America's Arctic.

At one time there was a political will for making tough decisions to safeguard our environment. In the late '70s, America imposed a

55-miles-per-hour speed limit across the nation in an effort to reduce fossil-fuel use and pollution. Corporate Average Fuel Economy (CAFE) standards were put into place to increase automobile efficiency. In 1980, the Alaska National Interest Lands Conservation Act created 100 million acres of new protected areas in Alaska: designated national parks, monuments, and forests, wild and scenic rivers, conservation areas, and recreation areas. About one-third of Alaska was set aside in "conservation system units."

We have gone backward since those days of hope. We are running out of intact ecosystems to protect. Speed limits are going up and up. Last year was the worst year for automobile efficiency since CAFE standards were first set into place. We are burning more fossil fuels than ever before, and dark clouds of climate change loom heavily over the future horizon. If current trends continue, climatologists tell us, by the time Malkolm is my age the Arctic Ocean will be entirely ice-free during the summer. An iceless Arctic might be great for the big cruise lines and the next take of an *Endless Summer* surfing movie, but it would not be good for whales, seals, caribou, or polar bears.

I asked Malkolm this morning if he wanted to live in a world without polar bears. "No way!" he answered.

During the last ice age, caribou roamed as far south as the Gulf of Mexico. As the ice retreated they followed favorable habitats northward. If we don't do something about our greenhouse gas emissions, ecosystems and wildlife habitats will "shift" northward. In fact, they already have. The tree-line is creeping northward, and robins have flown to islands in the high Arctic. What will happen to caribou as the climate warms? Will they jump into the Arctic Ocean and swim north to some promised land?

My cab driver doesn't know it, but history is being made. Rightly or wrongly, the Arctic Refuge is now the conservation Battle of Waterloo, a battle people who care about the Earth can't afford to lose. The health of the natural systems above the ground are bound to the black crude below the permafrost. If the developers and pro-oil politicians have their way, it will send a message that nothing is sacred. The line in the sand has been drawn, a line beginning at the western border of the Arctic Refuge that stretches through the center of the Senate floor.

I don't need to ask my Gwich'in friends if they want to live in a world without caribou.

POSTSCRIPT

After several months of political dithering, the Senate finally got down to dealing with its energy legislation. On Tuesday, April 16, 2002, Alaska's Senators Frank Murkowski and Ted Stevens filed amendments that would open the entire coastal plain of the Arctic Refuge to oil development. Murkowski took a picture of Saddam Hussein with him to the Senate floor and jabbed his finger at it while he explained why we should drill for oil in the Refuge.

"It's hell in the wintertime," Senator Stevens said during his speech. He explained that people who call the Refuge a pristine wilderness are "liars."

As soon as the amendments were filed, 15 senators, led by John Kerry of Massachusetts and Joseph Lieberman of Connecticut, threatened to filibuster. A filibuster is an endless debate that ties up the Senate until hell freezes over (although if the Arctic Refuge in winter is hell, as Senator Stevens says, it is already frozen over). Filibusters are now routine in the Senate for any controversial legislation and require 60 votes to overturn.

It would be hard to imagine a more dangerous time for a decisive vote on the future of the Arctic Refuge. Detroit's recent fleets of gas-guzzlers have helped create an obsession on the supply side of America's energy debate. President Bush, who had made drilling in the Refuge a central derrick in his energy platform, was surfing the crest of a tsunami-size wave of positive ratings. The Middle East was becoming increasingly unstable, allowing the oil lobby to capitalize on its "national security" argument. Iraq had just cut off its oil exports, inflating Saddam Hussein's stature as the bogeyman of choice.

On April 18, the Senate voted: 54–46 *against* overturning the filibuster, and against paving the way for authorizing oil development in the Arctic Refuge. Considering the political climate, it was shocking that the Refuge received 14 more votes than its survival bottom-line of 40. Still, it was only a temporary victory. As Jonathon Solomon pointed out, developers, like alcoholics, are addicts. Once a developer, always a developer. They'll try again as soon as the political winds shift. The Refuge will not be safe until Congress passes Wilderness designation. No matter how cynical I am about the political process, however, the vote was a sign of hope. On that day, 54 U.S. senators voted to leave the oil in the ground.

Fittingly, the vote took place just four days before Norma Kassi, Sarah James, and Jonathon Solomon were awarded the Goldman Prize on Earth Day. The Gwich'in probably wished, when they finally got home, that they could stay in Arctic Village and Old Crow and Fort Yukon forever. That they could spend the rest of their lives eating caribou and breathing clean Arctic air. And never flying to Washington, D.C., ever again. They know, however, that it isn't over.

"How can we give up?" said Norma Kassi. "Drilling for oil in the Arctic Refuge would be like drilling in a hospital nursery. We will do everything in our power to protect the calving grounds because it means our life."

What You Can Do

Conservation Organizations

You can help protect America's last great Arctic wilderness and the wildlife and people who depend on it, by contacting any of these conservation organizations in the U.S. or Canada:

Alaska Coalition
www.alaskacoalition.org
Alaska Wilderness League
www.alaskawild.org
Audubon Society
www.audubon.org
Caribou Commons Project
www.cariboucommons.com
Defenders of Wildlife
www.defenders.org
Eyak Preservation Council
www.redzone.org
Gwich'in Steering Committee
www.alaska.net/~gwichin
National Wildlife Federation
www.nwf.org
Natural Resources Defense Council
www.nrdc.org
North Alaska Environmental Center
www.northern.org
Sierra Club:
www.sierraclub.org
Trustees for Alaska
www.trustees.org
Wilderness Society
www.wilderness.org
World Wildlife Fund
www.wwf.org

Ken Madsen

An award-winning writer and photographer, Ken Madsen is also well-known in paddling circles for his descents of difficult rivers, including Turnback Canyon on the Alsek River and a first descent of the Stikine River from its headwaters to the sea. He has traveled through many remote wilderness areas and feels a responsibility to speak out about their preservation. Ken has crisscrossed North America numerous times, presenting slideshows and promoting wilderness protection. He was instrumental in the successful campaign to establish the Tatshenshini-Alsek Wilderness Park, which is now a World Heritage Site.

Since 1998, Ken has worked full-time on the Caribou Commons Project, which started with a 1,000-mile, 100-day wilderness trip by foot, kayak, and canoe along the migratory route of the Porcupine caribou herd. Ken traveled from the coastal plain of the Arctic National Wildlife Refuge in northeastern Alaska to the Gwich'in village of Old Crow in Canada's Yukon Territory. In 2000, he was awarded the Northern Conservation Award by the Porcupine Caribou Management Board in recognition of his work to prevent oil development in the Arctic Refuge. Ken continues to advocate the preservation of the sensitive wildlife habitat in the Arctic and the aboriginal Gwich'in way of life that depends upon it. In the fall of 2002, Ken will be walking and cycling across America with his Gwich'in allies to draw attention to the need for permanent protection of the Arctic National Wildlife Refuge.